The Seventieth Week of Daniel

An Uncompromising Analysis of the End Times and the Rapture of the Church

Dale Bromell

WestBow Press books may be ordered through booksellers or by contacting:

WestBow Press
A Division of Thomas Nelson & Zondervan
1663 Liberty Drive
Bloomington, IN 47403
www.westbowpress.com
844-714-3454

ISBN: 979-8-3850-2955-6 (sc)
ISBN: 979-8-3850-2956-3 (e)

Library of Congress Control Number: 2024914526

Print information available on the last page.

WestBow Press rev. date: 7/29/2024

CONTENTS

ACKNOWLEDGEMENTS

It was the early 1990s and I had been away from my home in Oregon for nearly ten years. The Lord had taken my family and me on a spiritual journey to diverse locations: Livermore, California; Rapid City, South Dakota; Longbranch, Washington; and St. Charles, Missouri. During these stops along the way, God introduced me to some extraordinary people, and exposed me to wonderfully rich teachings. While living in the St. Louis area, a friend in the ministry invited my wife, Cheri, and me to accompany him to a home meeting. He did not indicate the nature of the meeting, but we had such respect for him and his ministry we agreed to attend. The topic of the home meeting was the End Times. The man who conducted the meeting presented an end times' message unlike any I had heard before. It was a message that, for the first time, made sense; one that agreed with my understanding of what the Bible had to say about the subject, however limited that understanding was at the time. His message inspired me to investigate scriptures pertaining to this topic, and for the next several years I was consumed with a study of the End Times.

Gary Wood, Sr., was the minister with the inspiring end times' message. Thank you, Gary, for the many years you spent studying this important biblical topic, and for faithfully presenting your Bible study to those who would listen. Your last days Bible study series, *Six Days to the Rapture*, was the foundation from which I launched my end times' study. I will be forever grateful for the opportunity I had to hear the message you taught, and for the guidance you provided during my studies.

Gene Bacon was the friend in the ministry who invited me to Gary's home meeting. Gene and his lovely wife, Terri, had graciously invited my wife and me to join their ministry. I feel especially blessed to have met you, Gene. Your dynamic prophetic ministry touched my life in a way that totally changed my focus in the ministry. I am appreciative of your counsel and friendship these many years. You spoke the word of the Lord that said "write the book" – this is the book.

I would like to thank precious people who have made an impact on my walk with the Lord. Thank you, Duane Langenberg and Judi Westberg, for showing me the love of Christ and for discipling me in the things of God. Thanks to the late Roy Hicks, Jr., whose godly example and preaching provided the firm foundation for my understanding of the principles of God. Thanks to the late Bishop Lorenzo Kelly for loving me and fathering me in the faith. I would not be the husband, father, and man of God I am today without his teaching, counsel, and encouragement. He made a tremendous impact on my life, and the life of my family.

I would like to thank those who have made significant contributions to the completion of this book. Kimberly Pherson, for creating illustrations and editing. Thank you, Kim, for taking an uncompromising approach and for not allowing me to settle for anything but the best. Jo Hinds, for encouraging me to continue with the project when I had become discouraged. My loving, precious, and beautiful wife, Cheri, for providing encouragement and support during the many years it took to complete this book. Thank you for patiently listening to my thoughts and ideas and for being the sounding board I needed. You were the first to know what I thought was an end times' Bible study would someday become an end times' book.

INTRODUCTION

The Church today could benefit greatly from a clear understanding of the events of the End Times[1] – the Seventieth Week of Daniel.[2] Because this period is a dominant and recurring subject of the Bible, and because the second coming of Jesus Christ appears to be near, it is essential Christians firmly grasp what the Bible says about this period. However, for many, this level of comprehension has been elusive. Some of the responsibility lies with the Church, which has consistently failed to teach even a basic level of knowledge about this critical subject. Instead, the Church has primarily concerned itself with a discussion of the timing of the Rapture,[3] offering a wealth of information related to this one topic, while ignoring other

---

[1] The phrase "End Times" does not appear in the King James Version of the Bible. It is a commonly used phrase referring to the second half of the Seventieth Week of Daniel. It is derived from "time of the end" and it appears five times in the book of Daniel. (Daniel 8:17, 11:35, 40, 12:4, 9) In a broader sense, the phrase "End Times" is often used to refer to the entire Seventieth Week of Daniel.

[2] The phrases "Seventieth Week of Daniel" does not appear in the King James Version of the Bible. It is a commonly used phrases referring to a concluding seven year period during which Jesus Christ's second coming will take place. The Seventieth Week of Daniel is derived from Daniel 9:24 where a seventy week period is mentioned. The seventieth week is the concluding one week of these seventy weeks and it is mentioned in Daniel 9:27.

[3] The word "Rapture" does not appear in the King James Version of the Bible. Rapture is derived from the text of the Latin Vulgate. The Greek word *harpazo* in 1 Thessalonians 4:17 is translated "rapture" in the Latin text and "caught up" in the King James translation. Every attempt is being made to use the most appropriate word or phrase that conveys the clear meaning of the original text. However, rapture is the word the vast majority of Christians associate with the catching away or gathering together (2 Thessalonians 2:1) of the saints at Jesus Christ's second coming. Since there is not a negative connotation associated with the word rapture, and since it does not add to or take away from the clear meaning of the original text, it will be used to describe the catching away or gathering together of the saints at His second coming.

equally important end times' events such as the signing of the Covenant, the Abomination of Desolation, the Great Tribulation, and the Day of the Lord. In addition, there is confusion because many end times' teachings contradict the Bible.

> Now we beseech you, brethren, by the coming of our Lord Jesus Christ, and by our gathering together unto him, That ye be not soon shaken in mind, or be troubled, neither by spirit, nor by word, nor by letter as from us, as that the day of Christ is at hand. Let no man deceive you by any means. (2 Thessalonians 2:1-3a)

The modern Church, just like its early counterpart, is confused about the End Times. Paul sent a letter to the church at Thessalonica to clear up any misunderstandings about the second coming of the Lord. Apparently, some were troubling them, teaching that the Rapture of the saints had already taken place. This confusion, both then and now, stems from erroneous teachings about the End Times. Paul told them not to be disturbed or frightened by false spirits, false words, or false letters. Similarly, the modern Church should not be troubled by false spirits and false teachers who are disrupting believers with false doctrines regarding the End Times.

Due to the confusion surrounding this topic some have suggested a study of the End Times should be omitted completely. They contend it is too controversial an issue – that there is already an excess of doctrine on which it cannot agree. Some say the subject has caused unnecessary division at a time when it needs to be united. Still others say the End Times are not meant to be understood, so why teach it at all? For all these reasons, and many more, Christians are avoiding an open discussion of this topic, and many congregations are choosing not to teach it altogether. However, the Church should not ignore this important topic. God would not have devoted so many scriptures to its elaboration if He had not meant for us to study and understand it. The End Times should be taught in the church. It is not inherently divisive, it is not confusing, and it can be understood.

The very name of the book of Revelation, the disclosing or revealing of divine truth, indicates God wants us to understand the End Times. Referring to that period, the Lord says, "but the wise shall understand" (Daniel 12:10). In Daniel 12:4, the Lord says, "But thou, O Daniel, shut up the words, and seal the book, even to the time of the end: many shall run to and fro, and knowledge shall be increased." As we approach the End Times the knowledge that will increase is spiritually discerned knowledge concerning the second coming of the Lord. We should expect this knowledge to be more prevalent today than at any time in church history because the time of the end, or the End Times, is very near. We can trust God to impart comprehension of End Times scriptures if we diligently study His word and ask the Holy Spirit to give us understanding.

As Christians, why should we be interested in a study of the End Times?

> Blessed is he that readeth, and they that hear the words of this prophecy, and keep those things which are written therein: for the time is at hand. (Revelation 1:3)

There are rich blessings associated with a study of the End Times—blessings believers cannot afford to miss. "The time is at hand."[4] The second coming of Jesus Christ is very near. If the apostle John said the return of the Lord was at hand two thousand years ago, how much more is the Lord's second coming very near today?

> And he shall send Jesus Christ, which before was preached unto you: Whom the heaven must receive until the times of restitution of all things, which God hath spoken by the mouth of all his holy prophets since the world began. (Acts 3:20- 21)

[4] The phrase "at hand" is contained in 2 Thessalonians 2:2 and Revelation 1:3. The phrase "at hand" has a different meaning in each of these verses. Paul warned the church in 2 Thessalonians 2:2 not to be deceived by those who say, "the day of Christ is at hand." "At hand" in this verse is translated from the word *enistemi,* which means present. Paul was warning the church not to believe reports that the day of Christ, the Rapture of the church, had already taken place. "At hand" in Revelation 1:3 is translated from the word *eggus* which means near. In contrast, the apostle John was saying the time or season of Christ's return is near, or ready to be revealed.

God the Father will send Jesus Christ a second time. That is what the Bible proclaims in hundreds of scriptures, and it is what nearly every Christian believes. We may not agree on the timing or the events of His second coming, but we agree He will come again.

Jesus Christ will remain in heaven until all the prophesied events concerning His return come to pass, and then He will come again. Much to our amazement, many of these prophesied events have been fulfilled in rapid-fire succession in recent history. Today, all of the prophesied events the Bible says must be fulfilled before the End Times can begin, have come to pass.[5] We cannot ignore a study of the End Times because the second coming of Jesus Christ is very near indeed. We are right on the edge of experiencing what the prophets have prophesied for thousands of years regarding the return of the Lord. What an exciting and significant time in which we are blessed to be living.

A study of the End Times is also appropriate and timely because of the tragic condition of the Church. The Church today is in real trouble. It has lost much of its peculiarity; it is going the way of the world. Many of its members want to be entertained—not reminded of the sacrifices associated with taking up the cross of Christ. The Lord said He wants us to be watchful and aware He is coming soon (Matthew 24:42, 25:13; Mark 13:33-37; 1 Thessalonians 5:6). He said He wants us to be looking for the signs of His second coming. Biblical prophecies point to significant events that will take place prior to the Lord's return (Matthew 24:3-14; Luke 21:25; Revelation 6:12-17). Many, however, do not believe there will be signs of His return; they are not watching, and are asleep spiritually. In addition, there will be a time of great distress prior to His return (Matthew 24:21). The Church urgently needs something that will shake it out of its

---

[5] Today, all of the prophesied events that must be fulfilled before the End Times can begin have come to pass. Some of the most notable of these prophecies were fulfilled within recent times. Ezekiel 37:22 and Isaiah 66:8 prophesy the formation of the nation of Israel, which took place on May 14, 1948. Jeremiah 31:7-14 and Ezekiel 37:21 prophecy the return of the Jews to the land of Israel. That return began with the formation of the nation of Israel and has continued to this day. Zechariah 12:6 prophesies the occupation of the city of Jerusalem by the Jews. Israel regained control of the city of Jerusalem during the Six Day War in 1967. However, and very importantly, all of the prophesied events that must take place before the Lord's second coming have not taken place, as we shall see in the following chapters.

spiritual slumber; something that will help bring back fire and vitality. If it were to adopt a biblical attitude of watchfulness and preparedness for the second coming of the Lord, and realize we will experience a time of great trials and testing prior to His return, then a very positive change could take place. Watching and preparing for the second coming of Jesus Christ, while being mindful of the consequences of negligence, could greatly contribute to a spiritual revival today.

In his book, *The Sign*, Robert Van Kampen stresses the importance of such a study.

> I have come to believe with ever-deepening conviction that God's holiness will not allow Him to disregard the moral and spiritual compromise that characterizes so many churches and individual Christians today, and that this compromise will grow still worse as the last days approach. God has in the past and will again deal severely with the natural line of Abraham (Israel), sometimes chastising them by means of ungodly nations—as He did with wicked "Assyria, the rod of [His] anger" (Isa. 10:5). How much more, then, will His holiness demand chastisement of unspiritual and disobedient Christians (part of the spiritual line of Abraham) who have so much more light through His completed Word and so much more capacity for righteousness by the power of His indwelling Spirit? The Bible is fearfully clear that all impurities in the church will be purged (1 Pet. 4:12, 13, 17, 18), in order that every believer might be presented to the divine Bridegroom "as a pure virgin" (2 Cor. 11:2), "blameless in the day of our Lord Jesus Christ" (1 Cor. 1:8).[6]

These are sobering words to contemplate. Spiritual compromise and disobedience are widespread. The Church must grasp the truth; Jesus Christ's second coming is very near and He is returning for a bride who is, "without spot, and blameless" (2 Peter 3:14).

---

[6] Robert Van Kampen, *The Sign* (Wheaton, IL, 2000) p. xxvii.

Marvin Rosenthal similarly warns of the perilous state of the Church in his book, *The Pre-Wrath Rapture of the Church.*

> At the present moment of history, the planet earth is in grave crises. This celestial ball is on a collision course with its Creator. Man has pushed the self-destruct button. Foundations of godliness have crumbled; things sacred have come unzipped. We have reached the day which the prophet had in mind when he wrote, 'Woe unto them who call evil good, and good evil.' (Isa. 5:20).
>
> The church, which was called to be a royal priesthood, a peculiar people, is, at the present time, neither royal nor peculiar. Rather, it has stooped in character to commonality with the world and in lifestyle to similarity with the unregenerate.
>
> Many pulpits, even among conservative evangelicals, are weak and vacillating. The fire has all but gone out. 'Thus saith the Lord' has become, instead of a thundering voice, an almost inaudible whisper. The pastor, by virtue of his calling, should be the voice heard in the land. More often, it is the scientist, educator, philosopher, sociologist, or politician.
>
> Many who name the name of Christ want the church to provide entertainment, not worship. They want the church to provide a hedged-in, antiseptic, country-club atmosphere, not a 'Go out into the highways and hedges, and compel them to come in' philosophy (Luke 14:23). Apart from some notable exceptions, at the present hour the church is splintered, polarized, carnal, materialistic, humanistic, and impotent. The world is burning, and the church is fiddling.
>
> If there is any hope for the present moment of history, any catalyst that can turn the tide, it is right thinking and

> correct theology concerning the events of the Seventieth Week of Daniel, including the emergence of the Antichrist, the Great Tribulation, the Rapture, the Day of the Lord, and Christ's physical return to the earth.[7]

During the last days the faith of many will be strong, and believers will be responsible for praying many souls into the kingdom. However, the Bible clearly states that many in the Church, like the world, will succumb to satanic deceptions. As the End Times approach it will be in a spiritual free fall.

> Now the Spirit speaketh expressly, that in the latter times some shall depart from the faith, giving heed to seducing spirits, and doctrines of devils; Speaking lies in hypocrisy; having their conscience seared with a hot iron. (1 Timothy 4:1-2)

These are "the latter times" and many are abandoning their faith and are falling prey to demonic deceptions. They are no longer able to perceive what is true and what is false. Among these doctrines of devils are outlandish theories—theories that contradict the Bible—regarding the Rapture of the Church and the events of the End Times. It is of great importance we are not seduced into believing these devilish doctrines.

> For the time will come when they will not endure sound doctrine; but after their own lusts shall they heap to themselves teachers, having itching ears; And they shall turn away their ears from the truth, and shall be turned unto fables. (2 Timothy 4:3-4)

The time has come when many no longer want to hear the truth of the gospel, but would rather study the wisdom of man. Today, Christians overwhelmingly believe there will be a secret Rapture—a Rapture that will whisk them away to heaven, sparing them from the trying events of the End Times. But there is not going to be a secret Rapture, and the Church

[7] Marvin J. Rosenthal, *The Pre-Wrath Rapture of the Church* (Nashville, 1990) pp. 295-296.

will enter the seventieth week of the book of Daniel and experience the Great Tribulation and the wrath of the Antichrist. The teaching of a secret Rapture is not sound doctrine. Sadly, many will not be prepared to meet the challenge of a time of trouble, "such as was not since the beginning of the world to this time, no, nor ever shall be" (Matthew 24:21b). Those who are looking for a secret Rapture and an escape from the trying events of the End Times may live to experience a great deal more than they ever expected.

> Then shall they deliver you up to be afflicted, and shall kill you: and ye shall be hated of all nations for my name's sake. And then shall many be offended, and shall betray one another, and shall hate one another. And many false prophets shall rise, and shall deceive many. And because iniquity shall abound, the love of many shall wax cold. (Matthew 24:9-12)

As the disciples of Jesus sat on the Mount of Olives, they asked the Lord to tell them, "What shall be the sign of thy coming, and of the end of the world" (Matthew 24:3b). Jesus answered them by saying many will be severely persecuted during the End Times and many will not have the endurance to stand up to the pressure, pain, and possible martyrdom that will come. Demonic deception will overcome many, and those who have been deceived will fall away from the faith. Is the Church prepared to endure persecution and martyrdom during the End Times?

> This know also, that in the last days perilous times shall come. For men shall be lovers of their own selves, covetous, boasters, proud, blasphemers, disobedient to parents, unthankful, unholy, Without natural affection, trucebreakers, false accusers, incontinent, fierce, despisers of those that are good. Traitors, heady, high-minded, lovers of pleasure more than lovers of God; Having a form of godliness, but denying the power thereof: from such turn away. (2 Timothy 3:1-5)

Paul said that during the last days dangerous times will come; the human race will degenerate further and further into ungodliness. Jesus said, just as it was in the days of Noah, and just as it was in the days of Lot, "Even thus will it be in the days when the Son of man is revealed" (Luke 17:30). Men will exhibit the very worst possible characteristics. Above all, they will love themselves rather than God. Worse yet, they will put on a show of godliness—the ultimate hypocrisy—while denying the power of God. Look into the eyes of men, into the windows to their souls. What do we see? Men who exhibit more and more, day by day, the characteristics Paul described? These scriptures clearly refute the theology taught by some that the world will be changing for the better as the Day of the Lord approaches.

There is no reason the Church should fall prey to the lies of the enemy. God has given us His word as a warning. "According as his divine power hath given unto us all things that pertain unto life and godliness, through the knowledge of him that hath called us to glory and virtue" (2 Peter 1:3). The Bible is clear in its teaching regarding the return of Christ; therefore, there is no reason to be deceived by false doctrine or for the confusion that engulfs believers regarding the End Times.

> For precept must be upon precept, precept upon precept; line upon line, line upon line; here a little, and there a little. (Isaiah 28:10)

Many end times arguments have one thing in common: a theory is presented, and selected scriptures, many times taken out of context, are quoted to support the theory. The result of this form of study is often a theory that contradicts the clear meaning of the Bible. This will not be the method of study of this book. Instead, groups of scriptures that relate to major topics of the End Times will be studied, and then conclusions will be drawn. There will be hundreds of scriptures reviewed concerning the End Times, not just a select few; precept will be built upon precept, line upon line.

What does the majority of the Church believe regarding the End Times? Unfortunately, this is not a frequently asked question. Most Christians appear to be disinterested in studying what the Bible has to say concerning the events of the Seventieth Week of Daniel. In general, they would rather ignore the subject, choosing rather to sidestep any lack of understanding or confusion concerning the events surrounding the return of Christ.

Regardless of the general attitude of apathy toward the many significant events of the End Times, there does appear to be a great deal of interest in the timing of the Rapture. When will the Rapture take place? Will it be a secret Rapture? Will the Rapture allow the Church to escape the wrath of the Antichrist? Of course, these are important questions. The answers determine, to a great degree, whether believers will be impacted by the momentous events of the End Times. Once these questions are addressed; however, many have little interest in studying other end times' events.

Recently, I was having dinner with a Christian couple who have been family friends for many years. During dinner, I mentioned I was writing a book on the End Times. The wife asked, "Where do you think we are at?" Before I attempted to answer her question, I first asked a few questions to determine her basic understanding of the events surrounding the return of Christ. To my amazement, she said she really did not know much of anything about the End Times. You must understand this statement came from a woman who has been a solid Christian for decades, and a regular attendee of conservative, evangelical Christian churches. This incident is symptomatic of what I believe is a lack of understanding within much of the Christian community of even the most basic facts concerning the End Times. However, you will note that even though she had very little understanding of the events of the End Times, she was keenly interested in the timing of the Rapture, which is what I assumed she was referring to when she asked her question.

Christians frequently ask whether you believe in a pretribulation, midtribulation, or posttribulation Rapture.[8] They are asking, when will the Rapture take place, relative to the last seven years. This rather narrow question is asked because most end times' studies have been constrained by an over-emphasis on the timing of the Rapture. In answer to this question, an overwhelming number would probably say they believe in a pretribulation rapture. In other words, they believe Jesus Christ will Rapture His Church before a final seven-year tribulation period.[9] The phrase tribulation period will be examined in the chapters that follow, and in more detail in Chapter 3.

For many, not believing in the theory of a pretribulation rapture is unthinkable, if not blasphemous. Pretribulationism is overwhelmingly embraced by the Christian community. Often times, discussions of the timing of the Rapture, other than those of a pretribulation nature, are not conducted with sensitivity and understanding for those who hold other views. This lack of compassion has led many to avoid discussions of biblical prophecies concerning the End Times, especially if they do not conform to the generally accepted interpretation.

The theory of a pretribulation rapture has enjoyed almost universal acceptance for over one hundred years. Therefore, pretribulationists are not accustomed to experiencing significant and sustained challenges to their theory. However, in recent years many books and articles have been written challenging this theory. Consequently, pretribulationists have said they feel they are under relentless assault, describing many of these challenges as being vicious and mean-spirited.

Tim LaHaye, in his book, *The Rapture*, expresses the concern of many pretribulationists for what they see as a negative tone in the challenges directed at their theory.

---

[8] The use of the words pretribulation, midtribulation and posttribulation might lead the reader to infer that this book will promote the concept of a tribulation period. That is not the case, which will become apparent later in the introduction, and in the chapters that follow.

[9] The phrase 'tribulation period' is not found in the Bible. It is a term invented by those who believe in a pretribulation rapture to further their theory. More will be said about a tribulation period in the chapters that follow.

> Over the years, most of those who have held a different view have been gracious toward those of us who believe in a pre-Trib Rapture, allowing for our differences to coexist peacefully. After all, agreeing on the fact that He *is* coming is more crucial than agreeing on *when* He is coming. But within the last few years, that live-and-let-live attitude has changed. There are some Christians who have taken it upon themselves to attack the pre-Tribulation Rapture—sometimes in a vicious and carnal manner.[10]

Unkind attacks against those with differing interpretations of the timing of the Rapture are unfortunate, and differences should not cause division among believers; love and compassion should be exhibited by those who call themselves a Christian. However, this understanding and compassion should be reciprocal. LaHaye had the following to say about an author who challenged the pretribulation theory.

> A formerly reliable publisher of pre-Trib material...who claims he was a pre-Tribulationist for 30 years...formulates the most confusing interpretation of end-time events put together, a concept that no one except this author would come to on his own—unless he just wanted to be different. It certainly does not represent the conclusions of an earnest prophecy student humbly trying to unravel the prophetic sequence of end-time events from a literal reading of Scripture...Because the author failed to have his manuscript evaluated by other biblical literalists with a better grasp of Greek, Hebrew, and prophecy before he rushed into print, it may well serve as an instrument of confusion, robbing some of the blessed hope, the promise of the at-any-moment return of our Savior. Fortunately, this mishmash of concepts does not seem to have caught on in the church, for if it had, it would help deaden the

---

10 Tim LaHaye, *The Rapture* (Eugene, Oregon, 2002) p. 98.

> body of Christ. One of the first things that troubled me... was his dogmatic arrogance.[11]

This characterization of an opposing writer's work certainly lacks the love and compassion one should afford a fellow Christian. Let us hope those who hold differing views will refrain from such comments in the future.

Since the Church overwhelmingly believes there will be a pretribulation rapture, it does not have much of an interest in studying the events of the End Times. For those who support this interpretation, there really is no compelling reason for further study, since they believe the Church will be raptured before the last seven years even begin. They believe the faithful will be in heaven while the world endures a seven-year tribulation period. Why be concerned about the events of the End Times if we will not be here to experience them?

The Church most certainly will enter the last seven years, the Seventieth Week of Daniel. It would not make sense for the Lord to devote hundreds of verses explaining the events of the End Times, and tell us to watch for His coming, if believers would be caught up in a secret Rapture before the End Times even begin. Therefore, a thorough study of the prophecies concerning the End Times is extremely important, and timely, considering how close the Lord's return appears to be. This book will focus on the scriptures, and will avoid any personal criticism of those who hold differing views. However, scriptures will not be compromised, since they are the foundation from which we gain our understanding of end times' events.

With few exceptions, those who teach the doctrine of a pretribulation rapture have thoroughly examined the scriptures, and believe what they offer is sound doctrine. These men and women are brothers and sisters in Christ. They will be respected for their diligence, but this book will take strong exception to their doctrine. And there must be strong exception taken to pretribulationism, because it is a false doctrine. It is a false doctrine because it contradicts the Bible. This is not a personal

---

[11] Ibid., pp. 189-190. Ibid.

attack on those who teach a pretribulation rapture, it is a criticism of their doctrine.

In the following chapters there will be considerable space devoted to refuting the doctrine of a pretribulation rapture. Why? Why not just teach what I believe to be sound doctrine, and let the Christian community judge its merits? Why not refrain from what may appear to be a controversial and divisive discussion? Because the doctrine of a pretribulation rapture is overwhelmingly *the* doctrine of the Church. It is the doctrine that is taught by most pastors, church leaders, and is enthusiastically embraced by the vast majority of congregations and denominations. It is the doctrine promoted in the majority of books and other media that deal with end times' prophecies. Few teach, or even acknowledge, any other doctrine. With such a vast majority teaching and believing in a doctrine detrimental to the body of Christ, it is necessary to refute their arguments.

If a refutation of the pretribulation rapture doctrine were avoided simply because of its controversial and potentially divisive nature, then the Church would need to avoid a discussion of many doctrinal issues. Avoiding discussions of controversial subjects is not how sound doctrine is established. Sound doctrine is established when Christians examine the word of God together, and seek the guidance of the Holy Spirit (Acts 15:1-29). Refuting pretribulationism cannot be avoided because of the enormous impact it has had, and will continue to have.

Take a look at the prophecy section in Christian bookstores. It might be difficult to find a single book dealing with end time prophecy that does not promote pretribulationism. This lack of a significant challenge to the dominant interpretation means most Christians are well acquainted with pretribulationism, and probably believe it to be true, but because it is so badly flawed, and so widely believed, it must be challenged.

> For though we walk in the flesh, we do not war after the flesh: (For the weapons of our warfare are not carnal, but mighty through God to the pulling down of strong holds;)

> Casting down imaginations, and every high thing that exalteth itself against the knowledge of God, and bringing into captivity every thought to the obedience of Christ. (2 Corinthians 10:3-5)

Paul was not shy about exposing what he believed to be false doctrine; doctrinal purity was his passion. He would boldly confront the false doctrine of any group or individual— even a fellow apostle—without wavering (Galatians 2:11-21). Pretribulationism is a theory that contradicts the Bible, and must be exposed as false doctrine.

> For the time is come that judgment must begin at the house of God: and if it first begin at us, what shall the end be of them that obey not the gospel of God? (1 Peter 4:17)

Jesus Christ came the first time not to judge the world, but to save the world (John 12:47). He will come the second time as a judge (Revelation 19:11), and when He comes, His judgment will begin with the Church. During the Great Tribulation, the faith of believers will be put to the test unlike any other time in history. Unfortunately, the Church that enters the End Times will be a compromising Church (2 Timothy 4:3-4). It will overwhelmingly believe the Lord would never allow His people to be subjected to the pain, suffering, and possible martyrdom of the Great Tribulation. The result of this false belief will be the great apostasy—the greatest falling away the Church will ever experience (2 Thessalonians 2:3). However, the Lord has always been faithful to warn His people that judgment is coming. Those who believe in the escapist doctrine of a pretribulation rapture have been forewarned. In these last days, God will use many to teach, preach, and write the truth concerning His second coming.

The End Times: The Seventieth Week of Daniel

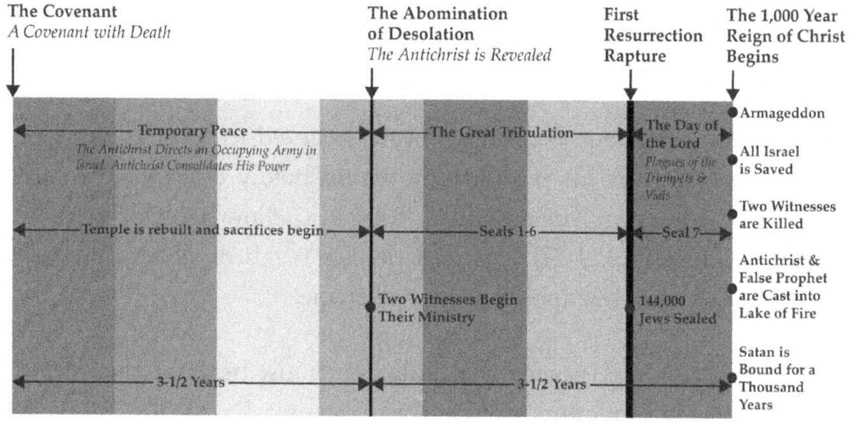

Brief Outline of the End Times

Prior to an examination of the Seventieth Week of Daniel in the chapters that follow, it will be helpful to provide a brief outline of the major events of the End Times.

There will be a seven-year period during which the events of the End Times will take place. It will be a week of years, as described in the book of Daniel, and it will be referred to as the Seventieth Week of Daniel. The Seventieth Week of Daniel will begin when a covenant, or peace treaty, is signed between Israel and many nations, lasting for a period of seven years. The individual who confirms, or ratifies, this covenant between Israel and many nations will be the Antichrist. The Covenant will allow Israel to build their temple in Jerusalem, and animal sacrifices will begin again in this third Jewish temple. Israel's enemies will be given a portion of the land of Israel as a provision of the Covenant. The Antichrist will be hailed as a messiah for bringing peace to the Middle East, although it will be a temporary peace. He will enforce this temporary peace treaty with an occupying army under his direction. Israel will regret signing this covenant, "a covenant with death," because the Antichrist will use it as an instrument in his plan to destroy Israel.

In the midst of these last seven years, after three and a half years, the Antichrist will break the Covenant. He will break the Covenant when he enters the Jewish temple in Jerusalem, sits down on the Mercy Seat of the Ark of the Covenant, and declares that he is God on earth. The temple will then be desolate to the worship of God by Israel, and animal sacrifices will cease. This despicable act of the Antichrist is the Abomination of Desolation. The Abomination of Desolation is the event that begins the Great Tribulation. At the time the Antichrist desecrates the temple, he will surround Jerusalem with his armies and attack the nation of Israel. This attack will mark the beginning of a time of trouble for Israel, "such as was not since the beginning of the world to this time, no, nor ever shall be" – the Great Tribulation. The Antichrist will subject the entire world to his will using political and military force and demonic deception. He will demand, through his False Prophet, the world worship him or be killed. During the Great Tribulation, the wrath of the Devil, there will be wars, devastating famine, and the death of billions. The Church will still be on the earth during the Great Tribulation, will be intensely persecuted by the Antichrist, and multitudes will be martyred.

As the Great Tribulation comes to an end, cosmic disturbances[12] will take place in the heavens. The sun and moon will be darkened and the stars will fall from heaven. Following these cosmic disturbances, the Lord Jesus Christ will come in the clouds of heaven with power and great glory, and the Church will be gathered together, or raptured.

Immediately following the Rapture, the Lord will pour out His Indignation upon the unbeliever. The Indignation, or wrath of God, is the, "great and the terrible day of the Lord." The wrath of God is contained in the plagues of the trumpets and vials. At the end of the Day of the Lord, at the end of the Seventieth Week of Daniel, Jesus Christ will come on a white horse with an army of angels to slay the armies of the world Satan has gathered together at Armageddon. Following the utter defeat of Satan and his army in Jerusalem, Jesus Christ will set his feet upon the Mount of Olives, pass through the Golden Gate, and begin His glorious millennial reign.

---

[12] Rosenthal, *The Pre-Wrath Rapture of the Church*, p.35.

CHAPTER 1

ISRAEL AND THE END TIMES

> Seventy weeks are determined upon thy people and upon thy holy city, to finish the transgression, and to make an end of sins, and to make reconciliation for iniquity, and to bring in everlasting righteousness, and to seal up the vision and prophecy, and to anoint the most Holy. (Daniel 9:24)

Many have said we should look to Israel for much of our understanding of the events of the End Times, and well we should. God has chosen Israel as His people; He has an abiding love for them that will never diminish (1 Kings 6:13). He has promised He will never reject nor forsake them (2 Samuel 7:24; 1 Chronicles 17:22). God will bless those who bless Israel, and curse those who curse Israel (Genesis 12:3). God has chosen to work through the nation of Israel to accomplish many of His purposes here on earth. The Seventieth Week of Daniel will be the culmination of God's dealings with the nation of Israel for their sin (Daniel 9:24-27). To ignore the fact that God will fulfill His plan for Israel during the End Times would mean we would miss the significance of many end times' events.

Since his fall, Satan has fought against God. God chose Israel as His people; therefore, Satan has done everything in his power to destroy them. The history of the Jews records unending persecutions, all of them masterminded by the Devil. Jesus Christ will return one day for His people and Satan has been plotting a way for the Lord to come up empty handed. However, Satan will not succeed in destroying Israel because God promised He would preserve a faithful remnant of Israel according to His grace (Romans 11:5).

It is essential to any study of Israel and the End Times to examine the ninth chapter of Daniel. This chapter explains many of the reasons why God planned the Seventieth Week of Daniel, and it describes the major events that will take place during this very significant time. In it, God reveals His ultimate will for Israel, which in turn will have a significant impact on the Church, and the world. The incredible depth and attention to detail in God's plan for Israel is simply awe inspiring. This chapter will include a comprehensive analysis of Daniel chapter 9, as well as other scriptures that relate to Israel and the End Times. This relatively brief chapter will lay the groundwork for an understanding of the information contained in the chapters that follow.

The Seventy Years of Daniel

> In the first year of Darius the son of Ahasuerus, of the seed of the Medes, which was made king over the realm of the Chaldeans; In the first year of his reign I Daniel understood by books the number of the years, whereof the word of the Lord came to Jeremiah the prophet, that he would accomplish seventy years in the desolations of Jerusalem. (Daniel 9:1-2)

At the time this passage was written, the Jews had been defeated by the armies of the king of Babylon, and were carried away into captivity in Babylon. Daniel understood from the book of Jeremiah that the Jews would be in captivity in Babylon for seventy years, serving the king of Babylon (Jeremiah 25:11). Why did God choose to send the Jews into captivity for seventy years?

> We have sinned, and have committed iniquity, and have done wickedly, and have rebelled, even by departing from thy precepts and from thy judgments: Neither have we

> hearkened unto thy servants the prophets, which spake in thy name to our kings, our princes, and our fathers, and to all the people of the land…Neither have we obeyed the voice of the Lord our God, to walk in his laws, which he set before us by his servants the prophets…Therefore hath the Lord watched upon the evil, and brought it upon us: for the Lord our God is righteous in all his works which he doeth: for we obeyed not his voice. (Daniel 9:5, 6, 10, 14)

Daniel understood the Jews were in captivity in Babylon as punishment for their sins. They had rebelled against God and had ignored the words of His prophets. God saw the evil the Jews had committed, and in His righteousness, He brought their sins upon them.

The understanding of why God sent the Jews into captivity in Babylon for seventy years can also be found in the way God measures time. God is sovereign, but He often operates within definable patterns. In relation to time, God often measures in groups of sevens:[13]

The creation:

> And on the seventh day God ended his work which he had made; and he rested on the seventh day from all his work which he had made. And God blessed the seventh day, and sanctified it: because that in it he had rested from all his work which God created and made. (Genesis 2:2-3)

God created the heavens and the earth in six days. On the seventh day, He rested from His work.

The Sabbath day:

> Six days thou shalt work, but on the seventh day thou shalt rest: in earing time and in harvest thou shalt rest. (Exodus 34:21)

---

[13] Gary R. Wood, *Six Days to the Rapture*, Tape 2.

God's people could work for six days. On the seventh day they were to rest from their labors.

The Sabbath year:

> Six years thou shalt sow thy field, and six years thou shalt prune thy vineyard, and gather in the fruit thereof; But in the seventh year shall be a Sabbath of rest unto the land, a Sabbath for the Lord: thou shalt neither sow thy field, nor prune thy vineyard. (Leviticus 25:3-4)

God's people could plant and harvest for six years. In the seventh year they were to let their fields rest – a Sabbath year.

Hebrew servants freed:

> At the end of seven years let ye go every man his brother an Hebrew, which hath been sold unto thee; and when he hath served thee six years, thou shalt let him go free from thee. (Jeremiah 34:14a)

God's people were commanded to have mercy upon their Hebrew servants. Hebrew servants who had been sold to their brothers could serve them for six years. In the seventh year, they were instructed to set them free – a time of rest.

In all these examples God retained the seventh period of time for Himself. This was the Lord's Day.

> And them that had escaped the sword carried he away to Babylon; where they were servants to him and his sons until the reign of the kingdom of Persia: To fulfill the word of Jeremiah, until the land had enjoyed her Sabbaths: for as long as she lay desolate she kept Sabbath, to fulfill threescore and ten years. (2 Chronicles 36:20-21)

For the four hundred and ninety years after they entered the Promised Land, the Jews disobeyed God's commands in regard to the observance of these periods of rest. They were instructed to plant and harvest for six years, and let the land rest during the seventh year. Instead, they planted and harvested continuously for the next four hundred and ninety years. They failed to obey God's command to let the land rest every seventh year. Therefore, after four hundred and ninety years had passed, there were threescore and ten years of Sabbaths, or seventy years of Sabbaths, that had not been kept holy unto the Lord (490 years divided by 7 = 70 years). As a result, He sent the Jews into captivity in Babylon for a period of seventy years. It appears they gave the Lord no other option than exile to fulfill His commandment to observe the Sabbath.

The Jews were sent into captivity in Babylon for failing to observe the Lord's command to let the land rest every seventh year. However, this was not the only reason God sent them into captivity. Israel was disobedient to God in so many other ways. The list of iniquities is extensive and includes worshipping of idols, rejecting and killing His prophets, and worshipping the queen of heaven. They became progressively more disobedient, and fell into greater depths of sin.

The Jews fulfilled this seventy-year sentence of captivity in Babylon for their sins. However, these seventy years of captivity were not the only consequences for their sins, as we will see in the following verses.

The Seventy Weeks of Daniel

> Seventy weeks are determined upon thy people and upon the holy city, to finish the transgression, and to make an end of sins, and to make reconciliation for iniquity, and to bring in everlasting righteousness, and to seal up the vision and prophecy, and to anoint the most Holy. (Daniel 9:24)

The angel Gabriel told Daniel seventy *weeks* were determined, or decreed, upon the people, Israel, and upon the holy city, Jerusalem. This is a different period of time than the seventy *years* of captivity in Daniel 9:2. According to that verse, the Jews were sent into captivity in Babylon for a period of seventy years for their sins. Though the seventy years of captivity were fulfilled, there was an additional time of punishment that was determined or decreed upon the Jews for their multitude of sins. This is the seventy week period referred to in Daniel 9:24.

Why were these additional seventy weeks determined upon the Jews and what events will take place during this time? First, God pronounced these additional seventy weeks were for the purpose of restricting or restraining Israel's sins against God. Second, this period was proclaimed to make an end of their sins; their offences against God will come to an end when these seventy weeks conclude. Third, it was declared to make reconciliation for their iniquity; the sins of Israel will be pardoned, or forgiven. Fourth, this period was commanded to bring everlasting righteousness to the Jews; after their sins have been forgiven, all of Israel will be saved (Romans 11:25-27). Fifth, it was decreed to seal up the vision and the prophecy; Daniel's vision and prophecy will be fulfilled. Finally, the seventy weeks of Daniel were proclaimed to anoint the most Holy, Jesus Christ, at His second coming. He will return to slay the wicked, to establish His kingdom here on earth, and to rule and reign for a thousand years. Jesus Christ's second coming will take place during these seventy weeks.

During these seventy weeks, Israel's sins will be restrained, come to an end, and be forgiven. As a nation, they will be saved, and Daniel's visions will be fulfilled with the second coming of Jesus Christ. Therefore, it was God's determination that the seventy years of captivity in Babylon were not sufficient to make atonement for their multitude of sins; these additional seventy weeks were also necessary. During these seventy weeks, God will accomplish much more than just reparation for Israel's sins.

The angel Gabriel told Daniel, from a specific point in time, there would be seventy weeks, until the end of time, as we know it. Well over seventy weeks have elapsed since Daniel received this message; therefore, Gabriel could not have meant seventy weeks of days. It is apparent there must be more than one way of measuring a week than a period of seven days.

The Hebrew word for a week, as mentioned in Daniel 9:24, is *Shabua.*

> *Shabua'* (shaw-boo'-ah) - sevened, i.e. a week (spec. of years): - seven, week.[14]

A Hebrew week can be measured in seven *days*, with each day of the week equaling twenty-four hours. It can also be measured in seven *years*, each day of the week equaling a year.

There are other verses in the Old Testament where a week, a *shabua*, is a period of seven years. For example, in Genesis 29, Jacob agrees to serve Laban for a period of a one week for the right to marry his younger daughter, Rachel. We discover in verse 27 this week is a period of seven years. The week of verse 27 is a *shabua.*

Just as the week in Genesis 29:27 is seven years, the week, or *shabua,* mentioned in Daniel 9:24 is also seven years – each day of the week equaling a year. Therefore, each of the seventy weeks of Daniel 9:24 represent seven-year periods of time. The seventy weeks of Daniel represent a four hundred and ninety year period of time.

The Sixty-Nine Weeks of Daniel

Daniel 9:25

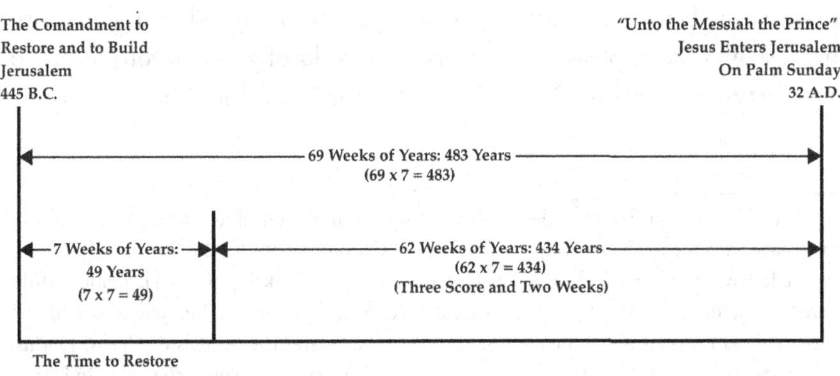

[14] James Strong, *Dictionary of The Hebrew Bible* (Lake Wylie, SC, 1988) p. 111.

Daniel 9:25 begins the explanation of the events that take place during the seventy weeks of Daniel.

> Know therefore and understand, that from the going forth of the commandment to restore and to build Jerusalem unto the Messiah the Prince shall be seven weeks, and threescore and two weeks: the street shall be built again, and the wall, even in troublous times. (Daniel 9:25)

Have the seventy weeks of Daniel 9:24 begun? The seventy weeks have begun; they began with the commandment to restore and to build Jerusalem.[15] It says, "from the going forth of the commandment to restore and to build Jerusalem unto the Messiah the Prince shall me seven weeks, and threescore and two weeks." Seven weeks of years, added to threescore and two weeks of years, equals sixty-nine weeks of years, or four hundred and eighty-three years (69 x 7 years = 483 years).[16] There were sixty-nine weeks of years, or four hundred and eighty-three years, between the commandment to restore and build Jerusalem and the entry of Jesus Christ into Jerusalem on Palm Sunday.

It is important to note this scripture separates the sixty-nine weeks of years into two distinct parts: seven weeks of years and sixty-two weeks of years. The first seven weeks of years, or forty-nine years (7 X 7 years = 49 years), was the time from the commandment to restore and build Jerusalem until that task was accomplished. The sixty-two weeks of years, or four hundred and thirty-four years (62 X 7 years = 434 years), was the time that elapsed

[15] Three separate commandments were given to restore and to build Jerusalem. Cyrus king of Persia gave a decree in the first year of his reign (2 Chronicles 36:22, 23, Ezra 1:1-3). Darius the Mede gave another decree (Ezra 6:1). Lastly, Artaxerxes, king of Persia, made a third decree (Nehemiah 2:1-8). All three of these decrees were acted upon. The Jews restored and built Jerusalem according to the commandment of God, and the decrees of Cyrus, Darius, and Artaxerxes (Ezra 6:14). However, the decree by Artaxerxes is the one referred to in Daniel 9:25, which was made in 445 B.C. The period of time from Artaxerxes decree to Christ's entry into Jerusalem on Palm Sunday was 483 years.

[16] The span of time from 445 BC to 32 AD is 477 years, not 483 years. The difference of six years is attributable to the fact that, unlike the Gregorian year, the Jewish year consists of 360 days.

from the completion of that restoration until Jesus Christ's triumphant entry into Jerusalem on Palm Sunday.

> And after threescore and two weeks shall Messiah be cut off, but not for himself: and the people of the prince that shall come shall destroy the city and the sanctuary; and the end thereof shall be with a flood, and unto the end of the war desolations are determined. (Daniel 9:26)

This sixty-two week period, or four hundred and thirty-four years (62 weeks X 7 = 434 years), began after Jerusalem had been built, and ended with Jesus Christ's entry into Jerusalem on Palm Sunday, followed by the Messiah being cut off, the crucifixion of Jesus Christ. "The people of the prince that shall come," were the Romans, and the prince was their general, Titus. The destruction of the city, Jerusalem, and the sanctuary, the second Jewish temple, took place in 70 A.D. by Roman armies under Titus' direction. Titus was a type of the Antichrist. The result of the destruction of Jerusalem and the temple was the scattering of the Jews to the ends of the earth (Leviticus 26:33; Deuteronomy 28:64-67). This scattering is commonly referred to as the Great Diaspora, or great dispersion.

The sixty-nine weeks of years have been fulfilled. However, in Daniel 9:24 God said seventy weeks of years were determined or decreed upon Israel, and upon the holy city, Jerusalem. Therefore, there is one week of years, or seven years, that is yet to be fulfilled. When will this last week of years, these seven years, be fulfilled, and why was it not fulfilled immediately after the first sixty-nine weeks of years had passed?

The Seventieth Week of Daniel

This seventieth week of years, or seven years, is suspended in time, waiting to be fulfilled, at the proper time. This is the Seventieth Week of Daniel. It will be the last seven years of earth's history as we know it.

Why did God allow a considerable gap in time between the sixty-ninth week and the seventieth week?

> I say then, Have they [Israel] stumbled that they should fall? God forbid: but rather through their fall salvation is come unto the Gentiles, for to provoke them to jealousy. Now if the fall of them be the riches of the world, and the diminishing of them the riches of the Gentiles; how much more their fulness?...For if the casting away of them be the reconciling of the world, what shall the receiving of them be, but life from the dead? For if the firstfruit be holy, the lump is also holy: and if the root be holy, so are the branches. And if some of the branches be broken off, and thou, being a wild olive tree, wert grafted in among them, and with them partakest of the root and fatness of the olive tree; Boast not against the branches. But if thou boast, thou bearest not the root, but the root thee. Thou wilt say then, The branches were broken off, that I might be grafted in. Well; because of unbelief they were broken off, and thou standest by faith. Be not highminded, but fear:...For I would not, brethren, that ye should be ignorant of this mystery, lest ye should be wise in your own conceits; that blindness in part is happened to Israel, until the fulness of the Gentiles be come in. And so all Israel shall be saved: as it is written, There shall come out of Sion the Deliverer, and shall turn away ungodliness from Jacob: For this is my covenant unto them, when I shall take away their sins. (Romans 11:11-12, 15-20, 25-27)

At the end of the sixty-ninth week, Jesus Christ was rejected by Israel, and crucified. Because Israel had rejected the ultimate sacrifice for their sins, God turned to the Gentiles. As this passage in Romans explains, the natural branches, Israel, were broken off, and the wild branches, the Gentiles, were grafted in. The Gentiles obtained mercy because of Israel's unbelief. Israel rejected salvation through Jesus Christ, and it was offered to the Gentiles. It was God's hope Israel would be jealous of the favor He showed the Gentiles, and they would be motivated to accept Jesus Christ as well.

A spiritual blindness has come upon the people of Israel because of their rejection of Christ's sacrifice (2 Corinthians 3:14-16). This blindness began at the end of the sixty-ninth week and has continued to this day. It will continue until all the Gentiles whose names are written in the book of life have been saved. The beginning of the Seventieth Week of Daniel will signal that the time of the Gentiles is coming to a close. God cast away Israel so the Gentiles might be saved, but God did not forget His covenant with them. God's dealings with Israel for their sins will conclude at the end of the Seventieth Week of Daniel, at which time all Israel will be saved.

Therefore, the purpose for the considerable gap of time between the sixty-ninth week and the seventieth week is to allow sufficient time for every Gentile who will be saved, to be saved, and to motivate Israel to also turn to the Lord. Surely we can agree with Paul in Romans 11:32-33, "For God hath concluded them all in unbelief, that he might have mercy upon all. O the depth of the riches both of the wisdom and knowledge of God! how unsearchable are his judgments, and his ways past finding out!" And in 2 Peter 3:9, "The Lord is not slack concerning his promise, as some men count slackness; but is longsuffering to us-ward, not willing that any should perish, but that all should come to repentance."

Israel suffers for two very distinct periods of time for their disobedience to God—seventy years of captivity in Babylon and an additional seventy weeks of years, which ends when Jesus Christ sets His feet upon the Mount of Olives, and ushers in His millennial reign. The seventy years of captivity in Babylon were prescribed to fulfill the seventy years of Sabbaths that were not observed for the four hundred and ninety years after Israel entered the Promised Land. God determined that Israel should suffer another seventy weeks of years, and then the end would come.

All of creation is waiting with great anticipation for the Seventieth Week of Daniel to begin. This last seven year period of time will bring a conclusion to the momentous events described by God's prophets since the beginning of time, and it will usher in the millennial reign of Jesus Christ.

CHAPTER 2

The Covenant, the Abomination of Desolation, and the Great Tribulation

The Seventieth Week of Daniel, the last seven years of earth's history as we know it, is suspended in time, waiting to be fulfilled, at the proper time. When will the Seventieth Week of Daniel begin, and what event will trigger its beginning? Only God knows when it will begin; any attempt to predict when it might begin would be foolish. Many have tried, alluding to a possible date or season, but their efforts have only served to discredit Christianity. Many who study end times' prophecies say current world events strongly indicate the Seventieth Week of Daniel will probably begin within a few months or a few years. While current events do seem to indicate it is very near, one of the pitfalls that must be avoided is attempting to fit world events into biblical prophecy, rather than allowing the Bible to validate those events. The event that will trigger the beginning of the Seventieth Week of Daniel is the confirmation of the Covenant and it is described in the book of Daniel.

The Covenant

> And he shall confirm the covenant with many for one week. (Daniel 9:27a)

The person referred to in this verse is the Antichrist. He is referred to in other scriptures as the Beast, the man of sin, and the son of perdition. The word "confirm" is derived from the Hebrew word *gabar. Gabar* can be translated in several different ways, including to confirm, to strengthen, or to prevail. The word "covenant" comes from the Hebrew word *beriyth*, which can be translated in several different ways as well, including a covenant, a confederacy or a compact. Today, we would probably be more apt to refer to a Middle East covenant as a peace treaty. The word "many" in the context of this verse implies many peoples, powers, or nations. The phrase "one week" is the week that is the focus of this book. It is the week of years that is the last seven years of earth's history, as we know it; it is the Seventieth Week of Daniel.

The Antichrist will confirm, or strengthen, a covenant or peace treaty with many for a period of seven years. The many referred to in this verse appear to be Israel and many powers or nations, the powers or nations being Israel's enemies. The signing of this Covenant will signal the beginning of the Seventieth Week of Daniel. Therefore, as we look toward peace negotiations in the Middle East, we should be intently looking for a covenant, or peace treaty, between Israel and many powers or nations, lasting for a period of seven years.

Will the entire world know when the Antichrist confirms the Covenant, or will it be a secret covenant? Scripture does not answer this question; we simply know there will be a covenant. Logic, however, would lead us to believe the signing of the Covenant will not be kept a secret. In this media-obsessed world we live in very little escapes the public eye. Practically any event of significance that takes place in Israel and the Middle East is considered newsworthy. It is difficult to open a newspaper, read a magazine, or watch the news on television without encountering one or more stories relating to events in Israel and the Middle East. Peace in the Middle East has been the goal of world leaders for decades. Imagine the news coverage when, at long last, a powerful and charismatic world leader convinces Israel and her enemies to sign a peace treaty. The media coverage would be unprecedented.

The following is a possible scenario that could lead to the signing of the Covenant.

As hostilities in the Middle East escalate, fighting between Israel and her enemies become more intense. More and more blood is running in the streets, and tensions are extremely high. Both sides appear to be on the brink of annihilating one another. Neither is willing to back down from their demands. Negotiations continue, brokered by various world leaders, but each time they fail to achieve the peace they are so desperately seeking. The possibility of peace appears to be fading, if not entirely impossible. The world is at a loss as to what can be done. There is growing concern among world leaders the increased fighting in Israel and the Middle East will have disastrous effects on the entire world: politically, militarily, and economically. The combatants do not hesitant to involve other nations in their conflict – especially if they feel it will advance their cause.

World leaders suggest various proposals for peace; however, all are eventually rejected, either by Israel, her enemies, or both. Finally, after exhausting all other options, a group of world leaders approach a particular individual. He is a man of great influence and charisma. They believe both Israel and her enemies will see him as a neutral negotiator, since he is neither a Jew nor an Arab. He is a religious and political man, and would be able to relate to the religious and political dynamics of the situation. Because of his tremendous stature and charisma, he is a man who the world leaders feel will be able to convince Israel and her enemies to negotiate for peace one more time.

A meeting is arranged between this influential and charismatic individual, Israel, and her enemies. He proposes a set of conditions for peace that will satisfy, to some extent, both sides. Some in Israel have searched for a way to build the temple on Temple Mount in Jerusalem. As negotiations proceed,

Israel will be allowed to build the temple. But above all else, the people of Israel want peace - the peace they have longed for and fought for since Israel became a nation. It is peace that is of utmost importance to the Israeli people - a relief from the constant pain and turmoil of fighting and wars that have plagued their nation since its inception. The Arabs living in Israel believe they have a rightful claim to the land of Palestine. Therefore, they are given a portion of Israel's land for a Palestinian State (Daniel 11:39).

This religious and political man realizes the situation is so tenuous a permanent peace treaty is unrealistic at this juncture. It is his opinion neither side is of the frame of mind to permanently set aside their differences until they have an opportunity to see if a temporary peace agreement will work. He proposes a short-term arrangement, a peace treaty that will last for only seven years, and suggests both sides can live with the proposed arrangement for such a relatively short period of time. More permanent arrangements can be agreed upon later. As part of the Covenant, a military force under his direction, consisting of neutral armies, will occupy Israel to enforce the peace. Both sides are concerned about the intensification of hostilities, and the increasing loss of lives, and both acknowledge the possible outcome of further escalation in the fighting. Israel would finally have the long-desired peace and security they had hoped and prayed for, in addition to the reconstruction of the temple. Israel's enemies would get a portion of the land they believe rightfully belongs to them. The parties will agree to the Covenant, and the world will rejoice.

Finally, there will be peace in the Middle East. The world will no longer have to deal with the constant tensions, fighting, and bloodshed that have beset this region for so long. This man is hailed by Israel, its enemies, and the entire world as a messiah because he was able to bring peace when it appeared all hope was lost. Many will say Jesus Christ could not bring peace to Israel, but this man has. However, in just a few short years, Israel will regret they made a covenant with the Devil, "a covenant with death" (Isaiah 28:15, 18).

The Middle East will enjoy the peace it has sought for so long, but it will be a short-lived peace. After the Covenant is signed, the temple will be built,[17] and animal sacrifices will begin again. An occupying army under the direction of the Antichrist will maintain the peace – a temporary peace that will continue for three and a half years.

The Abomination of Desolation

> And in the midst of the week he shall cause the sacrifice and the oblation to cease, and for the overspreading of abominations he shall make it desolate, even until the consummation, and that determined shall be poured upon the desolate. (Daniel 9:27b)

In the midst, or middle, of the Seventieth Week of Daniel, after three and a half years, the Antichrist will break the Covenant with Israel. He will enter the temple in Jerusalem, sit down on the Mercy Seat of the Ark of the Covenant, and declare he is God – the most abominable act that could be committed against the Jewish people. By entering the temple he will defile it, making it desolate to the worship of God, and sacrifices will cease. This disgusting and detestable act on the part of the Antichrist is referred to as the Abomination of Desolation (Matthew 24:15; Mark 13:14).

The possible end times' scenario continues.

Beginning with the signing of the Covenant, there will be peace in Israel. The Jews will have dwelled safely in their land for three and a half years (Ezekiel 38:8, 14). The temple will have been built, and sacrifices and oblations will have begun again. However, that peace will come to a sudden and abrupt halt. The Antichrist, who confirmed the Covenant, and has been enforcing the peace with an occupying army, will break the Covenant and betray Israel. He will direct his army to surround Jerusalem, and take control of the city and the temple (Luke 21:20).

[17] It may not be necessary for Israel to build an elaborate temple, similar to the second temple that was destroyed in 70 AD. The end times' temple could be made of curtains, similar to the tabernacle Moses constructed in the wilderness (Exodus 26), which could be erected in a relatively short time.

Then he will commit the most reprehensible act imaginable to Israel. The Antichrist will enter the temple in Jerusalem, sit down on the Mercy Seat of the Ark of the Covenant and declare he is God. Nothing could be more shocking and cruel for the Jews; their glorious temple now desolate to worship.

> Now We beseech you, brethren, by the coming of our Lord Jesus Christ, and by our gathering together unto him, That ye be not soon shaken in mind, or be troubled, neither by spirit, nor by word, nor by letter as from us, as that the day of Christ is at hand. Let no man deceive you by any means: for that day shall not come, except there come a falling away first, and that man of sin be revealed, the son of perdition; Who opposeth and exalteth himself above all that is called God, or that is worshipped; so that he as God sitteth in the temple of God, showing himself that he is God. (2 Thessalonians 2:1-4)

In this passage, Paul is writing to the Thessalonian church concerning their gathering together unto the Lord. He tells them not to be disturbed or frightened by reports that the day of Christ, the gathering together or Rapture of the church, has already taken place. He says that day will not come until there is a falling away and the Antichrist is revealed. When the Antichrist sits down in the temple and declares he is God is the day his identity is disclosed. The Antichrist opposes and exalts himself above God by sitting in the temple and declaring he is God - an act called the Abomination of Desolation, which begins the Great Tribulation.

The Great Tribulation

Before we begin a discussion of the Great Tribulation, it is important to understand the meaning of the terms tribulation, Great Tribulation, and Indignation.[18]

[18] Wood, *Six Days to the Rapture*, Tape 2.

> These things I have spoken unto you, that in me ye might have peace. In the world ye shall have tribulation: but be of good cheer; I have overcome the world. (John 16:33)

The word tribulation comes from the Greek *thlipsis,* which translates as pressure, affliction, anguish, persecution, or trouble.[19] Tribulation refers to times of trouble that are familiar to Christians. Examples of tribulation Christians experience in this world include pressure, affliction, persecution, pain, and death, as well as disasters such as earthquakes, floods, tornadoes, hurricanes, and war. We have experienced, and will continue to experience, ordinary tribulation. The apostle John, in the book of Revelation said, "I John, who also am your brother, and companion in tribulation" (Revelation 1:9).

> For then shall be great tribulation, such as was not since the beginning of the world to this time, no, nor ever shall be. (Matthew 24:21)

> And there shall be a time of trouble, such as never was since there was a nation even to that same time. (Daniel 12:1)

> Alas! for that day is great, so that none is like it: it is even the time of Jacob's trouble. (Jeremiah 30:7a)

The term Great Tribulation refers to a very specific tribulation – that which is *megas,* mighty or strong. This is a tribulation, "such as was not since the beginning of the world to this time, no, nor ever shall be." A tribulation so great it has never occurred before and will never be experienced again. While Christians experience ordinary tribulation on a daily basis, this tribulation will be far greater in magnitude. Thus, the affliction, persecution, death, earthquakes, floods and wars will be exceedingly magnified.

---

[19] James Strong, *Dictionary of the Greek Testament* (Lake Wylie, SC, 1988) p. 36.

The Church, the nation of Israel, and the other inhabitants of the earth will go through the Great Tribulation. Not one nation, race, religion, or individual will be exempt from the trials and testing of the Great Tribulation (Revelation 13:7).

> If any man worship the beast and his image, and receive his mark in his forehead, or in his hand, The same shall drink of the wine of the wrath of God, which is poured out without mixture into the cup of his indignation; and he shall be tormented with fire and brimstone in the presence of the holy angels, and in the presence of the Lamb. (Revelation 14:9b-10)

The Indignation of God is far different than ordinary tribulation or the Great Tribulation. The Indignation of God is the anger, rage, punishment, and vengeance of God directed toward the unrepentant sinner. It is the unrestrained, full strength wrath of God. The wrath of God will be, "poured out without mixture into the cup of his indignation." During the Indignation of God, supernatural events will take place, including one third of the sea turning to blood (Revelation 8:8), one third of the animals in the sea dying (Revelation 8:9), and locusts with stings in their tails tormenting mankind for five months (Revelation 9:3-10). These are the plagues of the trumpets and vials, as mentioned in the book of Revelation. The Lord is a righteous God. During this period, mankind will reap destruction for the sins he has sown.

The Church will not experience the Indignation of God. The Indignation, or wrath of God, is reserved for the unbeliever. The Indignation of God, the Day of the Lord, will be discussed in more detail in Chapter 4.

Pretribulationists have mistakenly combined two separate events, the Great Tribulation and the Indignation of God, together into one larger period of time, and have called it the great tribulation, which they identify as the second half of the tribulation period. They say, since God will not subject the Church to the wrath of God during the great tribulation, then the Church will not go through any portion of it. The following is an example of a typical pretribulation rapture teaching where the great tribulation and the Indignation of God are combined, and are collectively called the great tribulation. "In the meantime, after the church is raptured, the world will suffer the unprecedented time of the wrath of God which our Lord called the Great Tribulation (Matthew 24:21)."[20] Matthew 24:21 certainly does contain a description of the Great Tribulation. However, there is no mention in this verse, or any other verse in Matthew 24, that the Great Tribulation is the wrath of God. The Great Tribulation and the Indignation of God are not the same events, nor do they occur during the same period of time. They are two completely separate events, which will occur at two distinct moments in time, during which God will accomplish two very different objectives. God will not subject the Church to His Indignation and wrath during the Day of the Lord, but He will cleanse and purify the Church during the Great Tribulation.

The possible end times' scenario continues.

After he breaks the Covenant, the Antichrist, empowered by Satan, literally unleashes all of hell upon the Jews. He directs his armies to attack Jerusalem and the Jews. There is trembling and fear in the streets of Jerusalem (Jeremiah 30:5, 6). The Lord said those in Judaea, which includes Jerusalem, are to flee into the mountains. Those on the housetop and in the field should abandon everything. Woe to the pregnant and mothers with infants who will also have to flee in those days (Matthew 24:16-20).

The Great Tribulation will be unlike any tribulation that has ever occurred (Matthew 24:21). Stop and think for a moment about the greatest inhumanities of man. Next, consider that the Great Tribulation will be far greater than any tribulation that has ever taken place. The world was revolted by the Nazi persecution of the Jews during World War II. Unfortunately, the havoc the Antichrist will wreak on the Jews during the Great Tribulation will be far greater. It will be the worst nightmare Israel could have ever imagined. Many of the Jews will flee Judaea during the Great Tribulation, many will not. Those who heed the word of the Lord

---

[20] LaHaye, *The Rapture*, p. 34.

and flee from the Antichrist and his armies into the wilderness will go to a place prepared by God where they will be protected and nourished by Him (Revelation 12:6, 14-16). Those who remain in Judaea will experience the full wrath of the Antichrist.

The Church, which will still be on the earth during the Great Tribulation, will not be exempt from the fury of the Antichrist. In addition to the Jews, Christians will also be a prime target of the Devil. The Antichrist will, "make war with the remnant of her seed, which keep the commandments of God, and have the testimony of Jesus Christ" (Revelation 12:17). Christians, along with the Jews and the unbelievers, will be given the choice of bowing to the Beast or following the Lord.

> For, lo, the days come, saith the Lord, that I will bring again the captivity of my people Israel and Judah, saith the Lord: and I will cause them to return to the land that I gave to their fathers, and they shall possess it. And these are the words that the Lord spake concerning Israel and concerning Judah. For thus saith the Lord; We have heard a voice of trembling, of fear, and not of peace. Ask ye now, and see whether a man doth travail with child? Wherefore do I see every man with his hands on his loins, as a woman in travail, and all faces are turned into paleness? Alas! For that day is great, so that none is like it: it is even the time of Jacob's trouble; but he shall be saved out of it. (Jeremiah 30:3-7)

Some have said the Jews will never be taken captive again, but this is a mistaken notion. "I will bring again the captivity of my people, Israel and Judah, saith the Lord." The Jews that were scattered to the ends of the earth during the Great Diaspora, beginning in 70 AD, are returning to the land God gave to their fathers. This future captivity of the Jews will take place during the Great Tribulation. Verse 7 identifies the time of this future captivity as the Great Tribulation by saying, "that day is great, so that none is like it: it is even the time of Jacob's trouble." Many of the Jews will be taken captive by the Antichrist and his armies, and will experience the events of the Great Tribulation. Therefore, it is the nation of Israel that is the primary focus of the Great Tribulation; it is specifically the time of Jacob's, or Israel's, trouble. However, it is important to understand the Great Tribulation is not just a time of great distress for Israel, but for the Church as well. Pretribulationists teach that the phrase "Jacob's trouble" infers the Great Tribulation is meant for Israel alone, and not for the Church. They say the Church is not here for the Great Tribulation because it will be removed prior to that event in a pretribulation rapture. However, it is quite clear from scripture the Church will also experience the events of the Great Tribulation (Revelation 7:9-17, 12:17).

Why will the Jews be taken captive again? Seventy weeks are determined upon the nation of Israel (Daniel 9:24). The last of these seventy weeks, the Seventieth Week of Daniel, is yet to be fulfilled. This final period of time, these last seven years, are appointed unto the Jews for the sins they had committed. The entire seventy weeks must be fulfilled, including this future seven-year period. The Jews will be taken captive again during the End Times as part of the reconciliation for their sins.

The Book with the Seals

> But thou, O Daniel, shut up the words, and seal the book, even to the time of the end: many shall run to and fro, and knowledge shall be increased. (Daniel 12:4)

Daniel received several visions from the Lord. Contained within these visions were details of major world events that would take place over the course of history. These visions also describe events that will take place during the time of the end, or the End Times. Much of our understanding of the End Times comes from the visions recorded in the book of Daniel. Daniel is told to, "shut up the words, and seal the book, even to the time of the end." The "words" are the End Times' visions Daniel received from God, which are contained in the book. The book must be sealed, or closed up, and must remain sealed, until the time of the end. Therefore, the End Times' events contained in the book cannot take place until it is unsealed, and not one seal is to be removed, or broken, until the time of the end. Gabriel tells Daniel in Daniel 8:17, "O son of man: for at the time of the end shall be the vision."

How long is the time of the end, or how long will it last once it has begun?

> Then I Daniel looked, and, behold, there stood other two, the one on this side of the bank of the river, and the other on that side of the bank of the river. And one said to the man clothed in linen, which was upon the waters of the river, How long shall it be to the end of these wonders? And I heard the man clothed in linen, which was upon the waters of the river, when he held up his right hand and his left hand unto heaven, and sware by him that liveth for ever that it shall be for a time, times, and an half; and when he shall have accomplished to scatter the power of the holy people, all these things shall be finished. (Daniel 12:5-7)

One man asked, "How long shall it be to the end of these wonders?" This man is asking, how long will these wonders last, once they begin? The wonders are the End Times' events of Daniel's visions that are sealed in the book in verse 4. The time of the end is when the seals will be removed from the book. The wonders - these end times' events - will last, "for a time, times, and an half," ("time" = one year, "times" = two years, "half" = ½ year) or three and a half years. The "wonders" of the time of the end will last for three and a half years, during which the seals will be removed from the book.

When will the time of the end, or the End Times, begin?

> And I heard, but I understood not: then said I, O my Lord, what shall be the end of these things? And he said, Go thy way, Daniel: for the words are closed up and sealed till the time of the end. Many shall be purified, and made white, and tried; but the wicked shall do wickedly: and none of the wicked shall understand; but the wise shall

> understand. And from the time that the daily sacrifice shall be taken away, and the abomination that maketh desolate set up, there shall be a thousand two hundred and ninety day. (Daniel 12:8-11)

In verse 11 Daniel is told, "And from the time that the daily sacrifice shall be taken away, and the abomination that maketh desolate set up, there shall be a thousand two hundred and ninety days." 1,290 days equals 3 ½ years, based upon the Jewish calendar.[21] The daily sacrifices are taken away in the temple in Jerusalem when the Antichrist commits the Abomination of Desolation (Daniel 9:27). The Abomination of Desolation takes place at the mid-point of the Seventieth Week of Daniel. Thus, the time of the end consists of the one thousand two hundred and ninety days that begin with the Abomination of Desolation, which is the second half of the Seventieth Week of Daniel. The time of the end concludes at the end of the Seventieth Week of Daniel.

When the seals are removed, events contained in this book take place - the events of the time of the end. When the first seal is removed from the book the Beast enters the temple and commits the Abomination of Desolation. The Abomination of Desolation is the event that begins the Great Tribulation.

> And I saw in the right hand of him that sat on the throne a book written within and on the backside, sealed with seven seals. And I saw a strong angel proclaiming with a loud voice, Who is worthy to open the book, and to loose the seals thereof? And no man in heaven, nor in earth, neither under the earth, was able to open the book, neither to look thereon. And I wept much, because no man was found worthy to open and to read the book, neither to look thereon. And one of the elders saith unto me, Weep

[21] 3 ½ years is approximately 1,260 days, based upon the Jewish calendar. Verse 11 mentions 1,290 days. Please see *The Pre-Wrath Rapture of the Church* by Marvin Rosenthal for an explanation of a 30 day extension of time for mourning. In addition, verse 12 mentions 1,335 days. Rosenthal also explains an additional 45 day extension of time for cleansing. The explanation of these two extensions of time begins on page 273.

> not: behold, the Lion of the tribe of Judah, the Root of David, hath prevailed to open the book, and to loose the seven seals thereof. (Revelation 5:1-5)

In Revelation chapter 5 we see this very same sealed book that was described in Daniel 12:4. The book in Revelation chapter 5 is sealed, just as the book in Daniel 12:4 is sealed, and it is sealed with seven seals. The events of the time of the end are contained in this book. The events of the Great Tribulation and the Indignation of God are events that take place during the time of the end. These events unfold as the seven seals are removed. These are the events of, "a time of trouble, such as never was since there was a nation even to that same time" (Daniel 12:1), – the Great Tribulation. These are also the events of the time of, "the wrath of God, which is poured out without mixture into the cup of his indignation" (Revelation 14:10), – the Day of the Lord. Therefore, the events of the seven seals are contained in this book, which are described both in Daniel 12:4 and in Revelation 5:1-5, and they take place during the second half of the Seventieth Week of Daniel.

As Jesus Christ removes the seals from the book, events take place. There are seven seals; these seals are removed during the last three and a half years of the Seventieth Week of Daniel. The first five of these seven seals will be removed during the Great Tribulation.

The First Seal: A White Horse (Conquest)

> And I saw when the Lamb opened one of the seals, and I heard, as it were the noise of thunder, one of the four beasts saying, Come and see. And I saw, and behold a white horse: and he that sat on him had a bow; and a crown was given unto him: and he went forth conquering, and to conquer. (Revelation 6:1, 2)

The rider of the white horse, the Antichrist, will conquer the Jews and the entire world. The crown represents the power and authority he will be given. He conquers by deception (Matthew 24:5; Luke 21:8). He will overpower many in Israel and will take them captive (Jeremiah 30:3-7). The Antichrist will also overcome many in the Church through his deception (2 Thessalonians 2:1-4), and he will rule the world.

The Antichrist is a false imitation of Jesus Christ. Jesus Christ will come on a white horse at the end of the Seventieth Week of Daniel (Revelation 19:11). The Antichrist will also arrive on a white horse, but as a false Christ, and he will deceive many. In fact, he will be the most convincing false Christ the world has ever known. He will precede the coming of Jesus Christ, and will attempt to deceive the world into believing he is the Christ.

The Second Seal: A Red Horse (War)

> And when he had opened the second seal, I heard the second beast say, Come and see. And there went out another horse that was red: and power was given to him that sat thereon to take peace from the earth, and that they should kill one another: and there was given unto him a great sword. (Revelation 6:3, 4)

The rider of the red horse, the Antichrist, is given a great sword – a weapon which represents military power. He will use overwhelming military force to wage war on those who resist his absolute power. The color of the horse is representative of the blood that will be spilled as devastating wars rob the world of any hope of a resumption of the peace the Antichrist will shatter when he desolates the temple.

The Third Seal: A Black Horse (Famine)

> And when he had opened the third seal, I heard the third beast say, Come and see. And I beheld, and lo a black horse; and he that sat on him had a pair of balances in his hand. And I heard a voice in the midst of the four beasts say, A measure of wheat for a penny, and three measures

> of barley for a penny; and see thou hurt not the oil and the wine. (Revelation 6:5-6)

The rider of the black horse, the Antichrist, will assume total control of the world's economy. He will determine who can buy or sell; no one will be allowed to buy or sell unless they have taken his mark, his name, or his number. Part of his economic control will include the world's food supply. Since he will have total control of that aspect of the economy, the Antichrist will sell food for practically any price he chooses.

The Antichrist is described as holding a pair of balances, an apparatus for weighing goods in order to determine their value. This is an indication he will determine the value of all goods and services, including the world's food supply. The word "measure" in Revelation 6:6 is translated from the Greek *choinix*. A *choinix* is a unit of measure and it is equal to approximately a quart. During the Great Tribulation, "A measure of wheat will sell for a penny." The word "penny" is translated from the Greek *denarion*, from which comes the word *denarius*. A *denarius,* a Roman coin, was the equivalent of a day's wage (Matthew 20:1-16). Therefore, these verses are predicting a quart of wheat will sell for a day's wage. In other words, the wage for a day's labor will not be sufficient to purchase even the barest of necessities. The result will be a horrific famine that will engulf the entire world.

The Fourth Seal: A Pale Horse (Death)

> And when he had opened the fourth seal, I heard the voice of the fourth beast say, Come and see. And I looked, and behold a pale horse: and his name that sat on him was Death, and Hell followed with him. And power was given unto them over the fourth part of the earth, to kill with sword, and with hunger, and with death, and with the beasts of the earth. (Revelation 6:7-8)

The rider of the pale (green) horse, the Antichrist, will muster the forces of hell to inflict death upon multitudes. The wars of the second seal, "to kill with sword," and the famines of the third seal, "and with hunger," will result in the death of billions. "And with the beasts of the earth," indicates the Antichrist will employ every imaginable method at his disposal to inflict death upon those who refuse to worship him.

The Fifth Seal: Martyrdom

> And when he had opened the fifth seal, I saw under the altar the souls of them that were slain for the word of God, and for the testimony which they held: And they cried with a loud voice, saying, How long, O Lord, holy and true, dost thou not judge and avenge our blood on them that dwell on the earth? And white robes were given unto every one of them; and it was said unto them, that they should rest yet for a little season, until their fellowservants also and their brethren, that should be killed as they were, should be fulfilled. (Revelation 6:9-11)

Under the fifth seal, multitudes of Christians who have not taken the Antichrist's mark, or bowed down and worshipped his image, will be martyred. These martyrs in heaven (2 Corinthians 5:6-9), who wear white robes, which indicate righteousness, will cry out to God to avenge their death. They will be told to rest for a season until their brothers who are to be martyred are also killed.

The Great Tribulation: The Wrath of the Devil

We see from the events of the Great Tribulation, the first five seals, the Antichrist will conquer Israel and the world through deception, and will subject the world to war, famine, and death. The Great Tribulation is the wrath of the Devil. He will accomplish his will through the Antichrist during the Great Tribulation.

The Day of the Lord, which will follow the Great Tribulation, is the wrath of God. It is very important not to confuse the wrath of the Devil with the wrath of God. The phrase Great Tribulation refers to the works of the Devil, never to the works of God. During the Great Tribulation, the Devil will do everything in his power to destroy Israel, the Church, and the rest of mankind.

> Woe to the inhabiters of the earth and of the sea! for the devil is come down unto you, having great wrath, because he knoweth that he hath but a short time. (Revelation 12:12b)

The Devil is cast down from heaven at the beginning of the Great Tribulation, and he will unleash great wrath because he knows he only has a short time, the time of the Great Tribulation.

The Day of the Lord refers to the works of God, never to the works of the Devil. The Devil has no part in the Day of the Lord. The Day of the Lord is a day when, "the Lord alone shall be exalted" (Isaiah 2:17). During that day, God will pour out His wrath on the unbeliever (Revelation 14:10).

> And there appeared a great wonder in heaven; a woman clothed with the sun, and the moon under her feet, and upon her head a crown of twelve stars: And she being with child cried, travailing in birth, and pained to be delivered. And there appeared another wonder in heaven; and behold a great red dragon, having seven heads and ten horns, and seven crowns upon his heads. And his tail drew the third part of the stars of heaven, and did cast them to the earth: and the dragon stood before the woman which was ready to be delivered, for to devour her child as soon as it was born. And she brought forth a man child, who was to rule all nations with a rod of iron: and her child was caught up unto God, and to his throne. And the woman fled into the wilderness, where she hath a place prepared of God, that they should feed her there a thousand two hundred and threescore days. And there was war in heaven: Michael and his angels fought against

> the dragon; and the dragon fought and his angels, And prevailed not; neither was their place found any more in heaven. And the great dragon was cast out, that old serpent, called the Devil, and Satan, which deceiveth the whole world: he was cast out into the earth, and his angels were cast out with him. And I heard a loud voice saying in heaven, Now is come salvation, and strength, and the kingdom of our God, and the power of his Christ: for the accuser of our brethren is cast down, which accused them before our God day and night. And they overcame him by the blood of the Lamb, and by the word of their testimony; and they loved not their lives unto the death. Therefore rejoice, ye heavens, and ye that dwell in them. Woe to the inhabiters of the earth and of the sea! For the devil is come down unto you, having great wrath, because he knoweth that he hath but a short time. And when the dragon saw that he was cast unto the earth, he persecuted the woman which brought forth the man child. And to the woman were given two wings of a great eagle, that she might fly into the wilderness, into her place, where she is nourished for a time, and times, and half a time, from the face of the serpent. And the serpent cast out of his mouth water as a flood after the woman, that he might cause her to be carried away of the flood. And the earth helped the woman, and the earth opened her mouth, and swallowed up the flood which the dragon cast out of his mouth. And the dragon was wroth with the woman, and went to make war with the remnant of her seed, which keep the commandments of God, and have the testimony of Jesus Christ. (Revelation 12:1-17)

These scriptures, full of vivid symbols, describe a woman clothed with the sun, and a great red dragon. This passage, as well as many other prophetic passages in the Bible, contains a large number of symbols. Why does God use symbols when He could use plain language to describe end times' events?

Gary Matsdorf explains how symbols effectively convey a message that otherwise would not have the same impact.

> Symbols are an excellent means of expressing powerful spiritual truths that are almost inexpressible. Symbols can describe the indescribable. Symbolic pictures, once they are understood, are difficult to forget. A symbol can graphically describe something that would otherwise need to be explained in numerous words.[22]

The woman clothed with the sun is the nation of Israel. The crown of twelve stars represents the twelve tribes of the nation of Israel. The man-child is Jesus Christ. The great red dragon is the Devil. The third parts of the stars of heaven are the angels that rebelled with Satan against God. The remnant of the woman's seed is the Church, the rest of her offspring, "which keep the commandments of God, and have the testimony of Jesus Christ."

The portion of these verses that relates to the Great Tribulation is this: there was war in heaven between Michael and his angels, and the Devil and his angels. The Devil and his angels lose the battle, and are cast out of heaven and down to the earth. God said woe to those on the earth because, "the Devil is come down unto you, having great wrath, because he knoweth that he hath but a short time." Only a short time to do what?

Robert Van Kampen describes the Devil's ultimate purpose during the Great Tribulation.

> To prevent the obedient line of Israel, unwilling to worship Antichrist, from receiving Christ as their true Messiah and King, thereby finishing the mystery of God (Rev. 10:7, Rom. 11:25,26) and completing the spiritual Kingdom of God (Dan. 9:24, Rev. 11:15), which will bring an end to the rule of Satan upon earth (Dan. 2:44).[23]

---

[22] Gary Matsdorf, Sermon from Tape, 1996.
[23] Van Kampen, *The Sign*, pp. 261-262.

The Devil will be cast down to the earth at the beginning of the Great Tribulation with the full knowledge he has only a short amount of time to accomplish his task, and he will make every attempt to destroy Israel. During the Great Tribulation, Jacob's trouble, Israel will suffer the worst persecution she has ever experienced. The Devil, through his Antichrist, will unleash all of hell against Israel. This will be, "a time of trouble, such as never was since there was a nation even to that same time" (Daniel 12:1).

The great red dragon will also make war with, "the remnant of her seed, which keep the commandments of God, and have the testimony of Jesus Christ." These are the rest of her offspring – the Church of Jesus Christ. Therefore, the Church, along with Israel, will experience the events of the Great Tribulation (Revelation 13:7). Christians entering the Great Tribulation will endure wars, famines of tremendous magnitude, and the possibility of martyrdom. However, the Church that will be on earth during the Great Tribulation will be an overcoming Church; it should not despair or be fearful. Believers will overcome the Devil by the blood of the Lamb, and by the word of their testimony (Revelation 12:11).

Kept from the Hour

> Because thou hast kept the word of my patience, I also will keep thee from the hour of temptation, which shall come upon all the world, to try them that dwell upon the earth. (Revelation 3:10)

Pretribulationists claim Revelation 3:10 is a defining scripture which clearly supports their theory. Let us see if the clear meaning of this powerful verse can be understood. In this passage, Jesus Christ is speaking to the church at Philadelphia. In verse 8 He commends this church because they have kept His word and have not denied His name. Then, in verse 10, He says because they have kept the word of His patience, He will keep them from the hour of temptation that will come upon the entire world. What does the Lord mean when He says He will keep them from the hour of temptation, and what is the hour of temptation?

Van Kampen explains the straightforward meaning of Revelation 3:10.

> "Keep," in this context, translates a Greek verb that carries the basic idea of protection while within a sphere of danger, and "from", a bad translation of the Greek work *ek*, has the basic meaning of deliverance "out of" or "out from within" this dangerous time. In other words, taking the original Greek in its most customary meaning, God promises faithful churches that because of their perseverance, He will guard them while they are within this "hour of testing," promising them eventual safe deliverance "out from within" this time of great danger. What exactly is the sphere of danger that faithful churches (true Christians) are promised protection from? Most students of prophecy agree that "the hour of testing" can only refer to the Great Tribulation—the unparalleled affliction that Antichrist will unleash against those who refuse to worship him.[24]

What a wonderful promise from the Lord – protection while within this time of danger, and eventual safe deliverance out of the Great Tribulation. The hour of temptation is the Great Tribulation. In Luke 21:36 Christ said, "Watch ye therefore, and pray always, that ye may be accounted worthy to escape all these things that shall come to pass, and to stand before the Son of man." There will be a surviving remnant of the Church that will be raptured after the Great Tribulation because Paul says in 1 Thessalonians 4:15, "we which are alive and remain unto the coming of the Lord shall not prevent them which are asleep." Therefore, God will allow many in the Church to escape the Great Tribulation – "all these things" – and they will be alive and will remain unto the coming of the Lord. We know Christians will suffer persecution, and even death, during this period. There will be those who will give up their lives for the name of Christ when the Antichrist assails the Church (Revelation 6:9). However, the Lord has promised the Church there will also be those who are given safe deliverance out of the Great Tribulation.

---

[24] Ibid., pp. 34-35.

Whether we are to give our lives for the name of Christ, or we are given safe deliverance out of the Great Tribulation, we should not fear. It would be good for the Church to contemplate Romans 8:35-39 in relation to the intense persecution of this very trying time.

> Who shall separate us from the love of Christ? shall tribulation, or distress, or persecution, or famine, or nakedness, or peril, or sword? As it is written, For thy sake we are killed all the day long; we are accounted as sheep for the slaughter. Nay, in all these things we are more than conquerors through him that loved us. For I am persuaded, that neither death, nor life, nor angels, nor principalities, nor powers, nor things present, nor things to come, Nor height, nor depth, nor any other creature, shall be able to separate us from the love of God, which is in Christ Jesus our Lord. (Romans 8:35-39)

Pretribulationists believe the Lord will keep the Church from the hour of temptation. However, they say the hour of temptation is not the Great Tribulation, but the Day of the Lord, and the Day of the Lord, which is the wrath of God, encompasses the entire seven years of the tribulation period. LaHaye said, in reference to Revelation 3:10, "God is saying, 'I will keep you out of the wrath to come."[25] Therefore, pretribulationists contend the Church must be raptured before the tribulation period begins. They say the Church will not go through the test of a tribulation period, nor does it need to. LaHaye goes on to say, "Since our Lord faithfully promised to keep His Bride, the church, *out of* the 'hour of trial which shall come upon the whole world, to test those who dwell on the earth' (the church doesn't need to be tested—we have already made our decision for Christ), it is a reasonable act of faith that we take Him at His word."[26]

Unfortunately, pretribulationists fail to distinguish between the wrath of the Devil, the Great Tribulation, and the wrath of God, the Day of the Lord. Temptation infers there will be a test. There will certainly be a test associated

---

[25] LaHaye, *The Rapture*, p. 50.

[26] Ibid., p. 54.

with the Great Tribulation. That test will be whether to bow down to the Antichrist, or to follow the Lord. Some will pass the test and worship Jesus Christ, and some will fail and worship the Antichrist. However, there is no test associated with the Day of the Lord. There is not one Day of the Lord passage where there is any mention of a test. The test will end with the Great Tribulation. Those who pass the test of the Great Tribulation will be raptured into heaven. The Day of the Lord will follow the Great Tribulation and the Rapture of the Church. During the Day of the Lord, God will pour out His wrath on those who failed the test of the Great Tribulation.

In the preceding paragraph, regarding the testing of the Church, LaHaye was quoted as saying, "the church doesn't need to be tested—we have already made our decision for Christ." Taken at its worst, this quote would imply once a person comes to a saving faith in Jesus Christ the Lord should shield them from the trials and testing of this world. The assumption will be made the writer does not believe the Lord has exempted Christians from trials and testing of our faith, since the Bible clearly promises a life full of persecution and trials of our faith.

> Confirming the souls of the disciples, *and* exhorting them to continue in the faith, and that we must through much tribulation enter into the kingdom of God (Acts 14:22). (See also 2 Timothy 3:12; 2 Corinthians 6:4-5; 1 Peter 1:7, 4:12-14)

Paul makes this quite clear when he says we must enter the kingdom of God through much tribulation.

However, LaHaye clearly implies at some times, or in some situations, Christians should be exempt from a testing of our faith. It was written within the context of a discussion of the End Times; therefore, the assumption will be made the writer was inferring Christians will be exempt from testing during that period. However, this line of thinking could not be further from the truth of the gospel, irrespective of the time frame or situation. We are most certainly exempt from the wrath of God that will come upon the earth, but the Bible does not say the Church does not need to be tested simply because we have made a decision for Christ. Unfortunately, this comment is indicative of the overall philosophy of pretribulationists. The root of the theory of a pretribulation rapture is the escape of the Church from the trials and testing of the End Times. Let us hope the Church will be more concerned for the integrity of the word of God than for the comfort of this escapist theory.

> For this we say unto you by the word of the Lord, that we which are alive and remain unto the coming of the Lord shall not prevent them which are asleep. For the Lord himself shall descend from heaven with a shout, with the voice of the archangel, and with the trump of God: and the dead in Christ shall rise first: Then we which are alive and remain shall be caught up together with them in the clouds, to meet the Lord in the air: and so shall we ever be with the Lord. Wherefore comfort one another with these words. (1 Thessalonians 4:15-18)

The Church will be protected while in this time of danger, and then will be given eventual safe deliverance out of the Great Tribulation. There will be those who will be martyred, and there will be those who will survive, which is exactly what these scriptures teach. The phrase, "we which are alive and remain," carries the meaning of that survival; those who are raptured will be alive and will have survived the Great Tribulation.

> Then if any man shall say unto you, Lo, here is Christ, or there; believe it not. For there shall arise false Christs, and false prophets, and shall show great signs and wonders; insomuch that, if it were possible, they shall deceive the very elect. Behold, I have told you before. Wherefore if they shall say unto you, Behold, he is in the desert; go not forth: behold, he is in the secret chambers; believe it not. (Matthew 24:23-26)

Here is a warning for the Church that will enter the Great Tribulation. At the beginning of that time, Satan will be cast down to the earth having great wrath, knowing he has only a short time. He will persecute the woman, Israel, and the remnant of her seed, the rest of her offspring, the Church of God. Those who reside in Judaea are told to flee into the mountains (Matthew 24:16). The persecution of the Jews by the Antichrist will be so intense that the only way for many of the Jews to survive will be to escape into relatively uninhabited areas. It would probably be wise for the Church to do the same. These scriptures are speaking to the Church that will attempt to escape from the wrath of the Antichrist. Jesus said if any man says, "here is Christ," do not believe him. If any man says, "he is in the desert," do not go into the desert. If any man says, "he is in the secret chambers," do not go into the secret chambers. These scriptures are a warning to the Church not to be deceived.

Even though we will flee from the Antichrist, this does not mean the Church will be cowering in fear. Fleeing into the mountains or deserts will be a form of protection from the attacks of the Antichrist. When the Jews were plotting to kill Paul he escaped from them when the disciples lowered him down a wall in a basket at night (Acts 9:23-25). In Acts 14:1-7, the apostles were preaching the gospel and performing signs and wonders in Iconium. Those who opposed their ministry planned to stone them. The apostles discovered their plan, and fled to Lycaonia where they continued to preach the gospel. During the Great Tribulation, the Church will valiantly rise to the challenge, witness to the unsaved and to wavering believers, and will be responsible for the salvation of multitudes. However, there will be the need for Christians to flee the attacks of the Antichrist in order to continue to minister, as well as to survive the Great Tribulation.

> For as the lightning cometh out of the east, and shineth even unto the west; so shall also the coming of the Son of man be. (Matthew 24:27)

> For as the lightning, that lighteneth out of the one part under heaven, shineth unto the other part under heaven; so shall also the Son of man be in his day. (Luke 17:24)

Through signs and lying wonders, Satan will attempt to deceive Christians into believing the second coming of the Lord is at hand. Christians should not be misled by these deceptive signs and wonders performed by the Antichrist. We will know the Lord is coming to Rapture His Church when we see the heavens illuminated by lightening coming out of the east and shining to the west. When the Church sees the magnificent brilliance of the coming of the Lord, then and only then will we know the time is at hand. The second coming of Jesus Christ, His appearance or epiphany, will be a magnificent brightness, one that will illuminate the darkness.

When will the Great Tribulation end?

> Immediately after the tribulation of those days shall the sun be darkened, and the moon shall not give her light, and the stars shall fall from heaven, and the powers of the heavens shall be shaken. (Matthew 24:29)

> And I beheld when he had opened the sixth seal, and, lo, there was a great earthquake; and the sun became black as sackcloth of hair, and the moon became as blood; And the stars of heaven fell unto the earth, even as a fig tree casteth her untimely figs, when she is shaken of a might wind. And the heaven departed as a scroll when it is rolled together; and every mountain and island were moved out of their place. (Revelation 6:12-14)

"Immediately after the tribulation of those days," refers to the period immediately following the Great Tribulation. Immediately after the Great Tribulation ends, "shall the sun be darkened, and the moon shall not give her light, and the stars shall fall from heaven, and the powers of the heavens shall be shaken." The events described in these verses are the cosmic disturbances of the sixth seal. Revelation 6:12-14 describes the same cosmic disturbances as Matthew 24:29 – the events of the sixth seal. Therefore, the Great Tribulation ends with the opening of the sixth seal. We will discuss the sixth seal at greater length in Chapter 3.

The letters to the seven churches in Revelation chapters 2 and 3 clearly describe the condition of the Church in the last days. It will be a Church that is desperately in need of cleansing and repentance. The modern Church certainly fits this description.

> Husbands, love your wives, even as Christ also loved the church, and gave himself for it; That he might sanctify and cleanse it with the washing of water by the word, That he might present it to himself a glorious church, not having spot, or wrinkle, or any such thing; but that it should be holy and without blemish. (Ephesians 5:25-27)

Jesus Christ will return for a holy Church, without spot (defect, disgrace), wrinkle, or blemish (faultless, unblameable). Is the Church today without defects and faultless before the Lord?

Dave MacPherson, in his book *The Great Rapture Hoax,* gives an apt description of the modern Church.

> Multitudes of Christians today, including many who are lukewarm, are looking for an any-moment "exit us" to the Promised Land. There'll be a removal all right—a removal of all the spots and wrinkles. Right now the Church has so many spots it's beginning to look like a leopard colony![27]

The Church needs to be transformed. This much-needed transformation will require intense pressure, the kind of pressure, or heat, that separates impurities from silver and gold. The Great Tribulation will be the pressure the Lord will use to transform the Church.

> But the people that do know their God shall be strong, and do exploits. And they that understand among the people shall instruct many. (Daniel 11:32b-33a)

[27] Dave MacPherson, *The Great Rapture Hoax* (Fletcher, N.C., 1983) p. 120.

The Great Tribulation will not only be a time of intense pressure for the Church; it will be the most glorious and exciting period in the history of the church. It will be the time when the true Church will overcome the greatest testing of its faith, will fulfill its ministry, and will stand before the Lord as His completed bride. These scriptures describe believers during the Great Tribulation who will withstand the Devil, be courageous, and perform valiantly. They will discern the ultimate motives of the Antichrist, and the False Prophet, and will teach those who will listen what the Bible says about the consequences of worshipping the Antichrist.

> And now, little children, abide in him; that, when he shall appear, we may have confidence, and not be ashamed before him at his coming. (1 John 2:28)

It is the Lord's desire that when He raptures His Church we will be confidently looking for His return, and will not be ashamed. As we will see in Chapter 4, which deals with the day of God's wrath, there is a frightening consequence for those who fail the test of the Great Tribulation.

CHAPTER 3

THE DAY OF THE LORD RAPTURE

> In my Father's house are many mansions: if it were not so, I would have told you. I go to prepare a place for you. And if I go and prepare a place for you, I will come again, and receive you unto myself; that where I am, there ye may be also. (John 14:2, 3)

At the last supper, when He was about to be betrayed and crucified, the Lord told the disciples He was leaving to prepare a dwelling place for them in His Father's house. He said He would return for them and take them to heaven, there to experience eternal life. This promised return of Jesus Christ to receive us unto Himself is the Rapture of the Church.

> Knowing this first, that there shall come in the last days scoffers, walking after their own lusts, And saying, Where is the promise of his coming? For since the fathers fell asleep, all things continue as they were from the beginning of the creation. (2 Peter 3:3, 4)

Unfortunately, within the Church today, there is a lack of interest in a study of the End Times. There are some who have a keen interest, but they appear to be the exception. Skeptics, who doubt the Lord's return is very near, are saying, "Where is the promise of his coming?" Others are weary of waiting for an imminent return of the Lord. They have been hoping the Rapture would take them away from a world that is growing increasingly hostile to their profession of faith. Possible seasons or predicted dates have come and gone without fulfillment.

Today, most discussions of the End Times seem to be confined to when the Rapture will take place, and whether the Church will have to endure the Great Tribulation. As for a scholarly study of Bible prophecy concerning the End Times, there appears to be little interest. And why should there be? If the prevailing belief is that we will be raptured prior to the last seven years, and not have to endure the pain, suffering, and persecution of the Great Tribulation, then where is the motivation to study the End Times? If the Church will be in heaven with the Lord during the End Times, why would believers have much interest in a study of this period?

From biblical times until the early nineteenth century the church was clearly unified in their belief we would enter a period of severe testing – the Great Tribulation.[28] The early church believed the Antichrist would assault them, followed by their deliverance at the Rapture, with the coming of Jesus Christ. However, the beliefs of the early church were not systematized and labeled with any doctrinal name. In the early nineteenth century; however, systematized doctrinal explanations of the End Times and timing of the Rapture began to arise. The following are the most common today.

Before the tribulation period: these are the pretribulationists. Pretribulationists believe Jesus Christ will Rapture His Church before the tribulation period. Beginning in the early nineteenth century John Darby and the Plymouth Brethren, and Edward Irving and the Catholic Apostolic Church, championed the doctrine of a pretribulation rapture. Then in the early twentieth century the Scofield Reference Bible, first published in 1909, was instrumental in popularizing the doctrine of a pretribulation rapture. C.I. Scofield clearly taught a pretribulation rapture in his comments that were placed next to relevant scriptures, a practice that lent tremendous credibility to his pretribulational view.

---

[28] Please see quotes of early church theologians from Dave MacPherson's, *The Great Rapture Hoax*, at the end of this chapter.

Pretribulationists believe the second coming of Jesus Christ is imminent, and has been imminent, since the day He left the earth and was received into a cloud. They teach no prophesied events must take place before the Lord can return; He can come at any moment, in an instantaneous, secret, signless Rapture. The last seven years, which they call the tribulation period, is the time when God will pour out His wrath. Since the Church is not appointed to wrath, it must be raptured prior to the tribulation period. John Walvoord, Dwight Pentecost, and Tim LaHaye are prominent proponents of this view.

At the midpoint of the tribulation period: these are the midtribulationists. Midtribulationists believe Jesus Christ will Rapture His Church in the middle of the tribulation period. In the mid-twentieth century, Norman Harrison and his book, *The End: Rethinking The Revelation,* was instrumental in advocating this view of the Rapture. Midtribulationists believe the intense suffering of the Great Tribulation will take place in the second half of the tribulation period. In some ways the midtribulation Rapture view is a compromise between the pretribulation and posttribulation views.

At the end of the tribulation period: these are the posttribulationists. Posttribulationists believe Jesus Christ will Rapture His Church at the end of the tribulation period. There are many variations of posttribulationism. Robert Gundry in his book, *The Church and the Tribulation,* espoused this view. Posttribulationism has been embraced by the Church longer than pretribulationism or midtribulationism.

This book agrees with the beliefs concerning the End Times that were generally embraced by the church from biblical times until the nineteenth century. However, the beliefs of the early church should not serve to validate any particular doctrine concerning the timing of the Rapture; the teaching that agrees with scriptures is the valid teaching.

> But I would not have you to be ignorant, brethren, concerning them which are asleep, that ye sorrow not, even as others which have no hope. For if we believe that Jesus died and rose again, even so them also which

> sleep in Jesus will God bring with him. For this we say unto you by the word of the Lord, that we which are alive and remain unto the coming of the Lord shall not prevent them which are asleep. For the Lord himself shall descend from heaven with a shout, with the voice of the archangel, and with the trump of God: and the dead in Christ shall rise first: Then we which are alive and remain shall be caught up together with them in the clouds, to meet the Lord in the air: and so shall we ever be with the Lord. Wherefore comfort one another with these words. (1 Thessalonians 4:13-18)

Paul instructed the church not to be concerned or to mourn for those who have died in faith. He said if we believe Jesus Christ was resurrected, then we can believe the Lord will raise those who died in faith. In fact, those Christians who are alive at the second coming of the Lord will not precede those who died in faith prior to the Rapture. The dead in Christ will rise first, then Christians who are alive at the time of the Rapture will be caught up (catch away, pluck, pull, take by force) together with them in the clouds to meet the Lord in the air. This is the Rapture of the Church.

> And when he had spoken these things, while they beheld, he was taken up; and a cloud received him out of their sight. And while they looked stedfastly toward heaven as he went up, behold, two men stood by them in white apparel; Which also said, Ye men of Galilee, why stand ye gazing up into heaven? this same Jesus, which is taken up from you into heaven, shall so come in like manner as ye have seen him go into heaven. (Acts 1:9-11)

These scriptures tell us in what manner Jesus is going to return at the Rapture, "He was taken up and a cloud received him out of their sight." He left in a cloud and this is how He will return – in clouds. Jesus Christ will come, "in the clouds of heaven with power and great glory" (Matthew 24:30). "Behold, he cometh with clouds; and every eye will see Him" (Revelation 1:7). Some believe Jesus is going to return at a secret moment and only those who will be raptured will see Him. This is incorrect; every living soul on the face of the earth will see Him coming in the clouds.

The End Times in the Gospels

Many Christians would be surprised if they were told a description of the events of the End Times could be found in a clear and concise manner in the gospels. In fact, the gospels are one of the best sources for understanding the events of the End Times. God intended these events to be clearly understood, and the End Times' message is contained in the gospels in probably its simplest form. Three of the gospels – Matthew, Mark, and Luke – clearly describe the events leading up to the Rapture, and the Rapture itself, in exactly the same order. Of these three gospels, Matthew's account of the second coming of the Lord and the Rapture of the Church is the most complete. His account of the last days and the Rapture can easily be understood if we interpret these scriptures in a literal and sequential manner.

> When ye therefore shall see the Abomination of Desolation, spoken of by Daniel the prophet, stand in the holy place, (whoso readeth, let him understand:) Then let them which be in Judaea flee into the mountains: Let him which is on the housetop not come down to take any thing out of his house: Neither let him which is in the field return back to take his clothes. And woe unto them that are with child, and to them that give suck in those days! But pray ye that your flight be not in the winter, neither on the sabbath day: For then shall be great tribulation, such as was not since the beginning of the world to this time, no, nor ever shall be. And except those days should be shortened, there should no flesh be saved: but for the elect's sake those days shall be shortened. Then if any man shall say unto you, Lo, here is Christ, or there; believe it not. For there shall arise false Christs, and false prophets, and shall show great signs and wonders; insomuch that, if it were possible, they

> shall deceive the very elect. Behold, I have told you before. Wherefore if they shall say unto you, Behold, he is in the desert; go not forth: behold, he is in the secret chanbers; believe it not. For as the lightning cometh out of the east, and shineth even unto the west; so shall also the coming of the Son of man be. For wheresoever the carcase is, there will the eagles be gathered together. Immediately after the tribulation of those days shall the sun be darkened, and the moon shall not give her light, and the stars shall fall from heaven, and the powers of the heavens shall be shaken: And then shall appear the sign of the Son of man in heaven: and then shall all the tribes of the earth mourn, and they shall see the Son of man coming in the clouds of heaven with power and great glory. And he shall send his angels with a great sound of a trumpet, and they shall gather together his elect from the four winds, from one end of heaven to the other. (Matthew 24:15-31)

The following is a sequential outline of the primary end times' passages found in Matthew chapter 24.

The Abomination of Desolation will take place, which was mentioned by Daniel the prophet (Daniel 9:27; 11:45; 12:11). When the Abomination of Desolation occurs those who are in Judaea are told to escape into the mountains. No one should return to their house or field to take anything with them. God said it will be a very difficult time for those who are pregnant, and for those who have infants. After the Abomination of Desolation there will be great tribulation, a tribulation so great none like it has taken place since the beginning of the world, and none like it will ever take place again. The days of the Great Tribulation will be shortened or no person will survive (Amos 8:9). During the days of the Great Tribulation, false Christ's and false prophets will arise and will perform lying signs and wonders in an attempt to deceive the elect. Immediately after the Great Tribulation has ended, cosmic disturbances will take place – the sun and the moon will be darkened and the stars will fall from heaven (Isaiah 13:10). All the people of the earth will mourn, as they see Jesus Christ come in the clouds of heaven with power and great glory. There will be the sound of a great trumpet and Jesus Christ will Rapture His Church.

The reader will note in this description of the events of the End Times and the Rapture of the Church there are no facts to support a pretribulation rapture. This presents an obvious dilemma for pretribulationists – how do they deal with these scriptures that present a Rapture *after* the Great Tribulation? Pretribulationists assert these scriptures are not describing the Rapture of the Church, but the Rapture of Israel at the Battle of Armageddon.

The Bible must be interpreted literally, and in the most natural and unstrained manner. Pretribulationists are certainly not taking Matthew chapter 24 at its face value when they suggest it is describing the Rapture of Israel at Armageddon. When scripture is used to support a particular view of the End Times that does not conform to a literal interpretation of the Bible, other complications usually surface. How many raptures are there? Is there one Rapture for the Church prior to a tribulation period, and then another for Israel at the end of this period? The Bible is very clear – there is one and only one Rapture, or resurrection, of the just. This concept of multiple raptures will be covered at length later in this chapter with a discussion of the resurrections of the dead.

As was discussed in Chapter 2, Revelation 5:1-5 describes a book that is sealed with seven seals. The events of the End Times are contained in this book. These events unfold as the seven seals are removed from the book. The first five of these seven seals will be removed during the Great Tribulation. When the first seal is removed the rider of the white horse, the Antichrist, deceives the world into believing he is a messiah and he conquers the entire world. When the second seal is removed the rider of the red horse, the Antichrist, plunges the world into devastating wars. When the third seal is removed the rider of the black horse, the Antichrist, puts a stranglehold on the worlds food supply and multitudes are engulfed in a worldwide famine. When the fourth seal is removed the rider of the pale horse, the Antichrist, uses the powers at his disposal to inflict death upon billions. When the fifth seal is removed multitudes of Christians who have not worshipped the Antichrist will be martyred.

The Sixth Seal: Cosmic Disturbances

> And I beheld when he had opened the sixth seal, and, lo, there was a great earthquake; and the sun became black as sackcloth of hair, and the moon became as blood; And the stars of heaven fell unto the earth, even as a fig tree casteth her untimely figs, when she is shaken of a mighty wind. And the heaven departed as a scroll when it is rolled together; and every mountain and island were moved out of their places. And the kings of the earth, and the great men, and the rich men, and the chief captains, and the mighty men, and every bondman, and every free man, hid themselves in the dens and in the rocks of the mountains; And said to the mountains and rocks, Fall on us, and hide us from the face of him that sitteth on the throne, and from the wrath of the Lamb: For the great day of his wrath is come; and who shall be able to stand? (Revelation 6:12-17)

Under the sixth seal, cosmic disturbances take place: there is a great earthquake, the sun is darkened, and the moon turns to blood. The stars fall to the earth and every mountain and island is moved. The entire world will fall into total darkness as the sun, moon, and stars are extinguished.

When these cosmic disturbances take place, men escape into the caves and rocks of the mountains to hide themselves from God (Isaiah 2:19-21). These men are unbelievers. Even unbelievers will understand it is God Almighty who is responsible for these cosmic disturbances. The sign of Christ's coming and the end of the world will be so spectacular every man, believer or unbeliever, will acknowledge it is God Almighty who is at work. Mankind will clearly see the great day of God's wrath has arrived. Because these unbelievers do not know God, and have rebelled against Him, their reaction to these miraculous signs in the heavens will be to shrink away and hide themselves from Him in the caves and rocks of the mountains. They will be terror stricken as they anticipate the wrath of God that is about to be poured out on them. Luke described this as a time of, "distress of nations, with perplexity; the sea and the waves roaring; Men's hearts failing them for fear, and for looking after those things which are coming on the earth" (Luke 21:25b; 26a).

The 144,000 Jews

> And I saw another angel ascending from the east, having the seal of the living God: and he cried with a loud voice to the four angels, to whom it was given to hurt the earth and the sea, Saying, Hurt not the earth, neither the sea, nor the trees, till we have sealed the servants of our God in their foreheads. And I heard the number of them which were sealed: and there were sealed an hundred and forty and four thousand of all the tribes of the children of Israel. (Revelation 7:2-4)

After the cosmic disturbances of the sixth seal, but before the seventh seal is opened, two events of tremendous significance will take place. The first event will be the sealing of the servants of God. Four angels will hold the four winds of the earth. Another angel, having the seal of God, will instruct the four angels not to hurt the earth until he has sealed the servants of God in their foreheads. The hurting of the earth, the Indignation or wrath of God, will take place under the seventh seal. The servants of God who will be sealed are the 144,000 Jews. They must be sealed before the Indignation of God is poured out under the seventh seal. They will go through the Indignation of God, but will be protected, sealed, from God's wrath. We will discuss the sealing of the 144,000 Jews in greater detail in Chapter 6.

The Raptured Church

The second event to take place after the cosmic disturbances of the sixth seal could not be more glorious. Christians will not react to these cosmic disturbances in the same manner as unbelievers. Since we will be eagerly awaiting the appearance of our Lord (Titus 2:13; 2 Timothy 4:8; 1 Peter 1:7), we will be watching, expecting the coming of Jesus Christ (Luke 21:28). We will not be ashamed, but will be confidently looking to the heavens for His coming (1 John 2:28). This will be a day of great gladness and joy.

What will the unbelievers see when they peer out from the caves and rocks of the mountains? What will the believers see when they look expectantly toward the heavens for the return of the Lord? They will both see the same glorious sight.

> For as the lightning cometh out of the east, and shineth even unto the west; so shall also the coming of the Son of man be. (Matthew 24:27)

> For as the lightning, that lighteneth out of the one part under heaven, shineth unto the other part under heaven; so shall also the Son of man be in his day. (Luke 17:24)

The earth that has been enveloped in total darkness by the cosmic disturbances of the sixth seal, will now be gloriously illuminated as the Lord returns to Rapture His Church. The sky will be lit as though lightning had flashed from the east to the west, from one horizon to the other. The coming of the Lord will transform total darkness into total light.

> After this I beheld, and, lo, a great multitude, which no man could number, of all nations, and kindreds, and people, and tongues, stood before the throne, and before the Lamb, clothed with white robes, and palms in their hands...And one of the elders answered, saying unto me, What are these which are arrayed in white robes? and whence came they? And I said unto him, Sir, thou knowest. And he said to me, These are they which came out of great tribulation, and have washed their robes, and made them white in the blood of the Lamb. Therefore are they before the throne of God, and serve him day and

> night in his temple: and he that sitteth on the throne shall dwell among them. They shall hunger no more, neither thirst any more; neither shall the sun light on them, nor any heat. For the Lamb which is in the midst of the throne shall feed them, and shall lead them unto living fountains of waters: and God shall wipe away all tears from their eyes. (Revelation 7:9, 13-17)

These scriptures say, "a great multitude, which no man could number, of all nations, and kindreds, and people, and tongues, stood before the throne, and before the Lamb, clothed with white robes (cleansed), and palms in their hands (triumphant)." Who is this great multitude? One of the elders in heaven says, "These are they which came out of great tribulation." The elder goes on to say, "They shall hunger no more, neither thirst any more; neither shall the sun light on them, nor any heat." This great multitude will go through the Great Tribulation and be persecuted, oppressed, and buffeted. However, God will rescue them from the Great Tribulation, and they will stand cleansed and triumphant before God, who will wipe away every tear from their eyes. Who is this great multitude? *It is the Raptured Church!*

This great multitude stands before the throne, cleansed, and triumphant. This great multitude is standing; they have bodies.[29] They are alive, and have survived the Great Tribulation, and have been resurrected in the Rapture. They are standing before the throne of God in their resurrected, immortal bodies (1 Corinthians 15:53-55).

One of the elders asks John to identify the great multitude standing in heaven in white robes. John admits he does not recognize this group. And why would he? It is a massive group, "which no man could number," and diverse, coming from, "all nations, and kindreds, and people, and tongues." Then the elder declares this group has come out of the Great Tribulation. They came suddenly, all at once. There is no sense of a

---

[29] The bodies of these standing before the throne is contrasted with those in heaven in Revelation 6:9 who are described as souls—without their immortal, incorruptible bodies, those who have died in faith prior to the Rapture.

continual coming. This great multitude, in its entirety, has just arrived in heaven.[30] The Church will go through the Great Tribulation, and then be raptured, in its entirety, before the Indignation or wrath of God is poured out under the seventh seal.

The progression is natural and unstrained. The events of the Great Tribulation take place under the first five seals (Revelation 6:1-11). Then cosmic disturbances take place as the sixth seal is opened, and unbelievers hide themselves from the wrath of God that is about to come upon the earth (Revelation 6:12-17). Before the wrath of God is poured out under the seventh seal, the 144,000 Jews are sealed (Revelation 7:1-4), and the Church is raptured (Revelation 7:9-17). With the opening of the seventh seal, God's Indignation, or wrath, begins (Revelation 8). The Church will not be on the earth for the wrath of God.

The Seventh Seal: The Plagues of the Trumpets and Vials

> And when he had opened the seventh seal, there was silence in heaven about the space of half an hour. And I saw the seven angels which stood before God; and to them were given seven trumpets...And the seven angels which had the seven trumpets prepared themselves to sound. The first angel sounded, and there followed hail and fire mingled with blood, and they were cast upon the earth: and the third part of trees was burnt up, and all green grass was burnt up. (Revelation 8:1, 2, 6, 7)

---

[30] We know from 1 Thessalonians 4:13-18 that the church that is alive at the time of the Rapture will be preceded by the dead in Christ. Therefore, even though the dead in Christ are not specifically mentioned in Revelation 7:9, they must be included in this great multitude standing before the throne in heaven. In addition, promises made to these saints in Revelation 7 are the same promises God made to the Church as a whole. For example, in Revelation 21:4, in a reference to the church dwelling in the new Jerusalem, it says at that time, "God shall wipe away all tears from their eyes."

Under the seventh seal, seven trumpets are given to seven angels. The wrath of God is contained in the seven trumpets. The opening of the seventh seal marks the beginning of the Day of the Lord.

> Likewise also as it was in the days of Lot; they did eat, they drank, they bought, they sold, they planted, they builded; But the same day that Lot went out of Sodom it rained fire and brimstone from heaven, and destroyed them all. Even thus shall it be in the day when the Son of man is revealed. (Luke 17:28-30)

The events of the first trumpet in Revelation 8:7 are the same events described in Luke 17:28-30. Revelation 8:7 says, "The first angel sounded and there followed hail and fire mingled with blood, and they were cast upon the earth." The first trumpet immediately follows the Rapture of the Church in Revelation 7:9-17. Luke 17:29 says, "But the same day that Lot went out of Sodom it rained fire and brimstone from heaven." These two scriptures are describing the exact same event, the beginning of the wrath of God under the seventh seal. Then in Luke 17:30 it says, "Even thus shall it be in the day when the Son of man is revealed." Fire and brimstone will fall to the earth the day the Son of man is revealed. The Son of man, Jesus Christ, will be revealed at the Rapture. The Rapture will take place first, then the Day of the Lord's wrath will begin with the opening of the seventh seal, and hail and fire from heaven will be cast upon the earth.

> And as it was in the days of Noe, so shall it be also in the days of the Son of man. They did eat, they drank, they married wives, they were given in marriage, until the day that Noe entered into the ark, and the flood came, and destroyed them all. (Luke 17:26-27) (See also Matthew 24:37-39)

The day Noah entered the ark can be compared to the day of Jesus Christ and the Rapture of His Church. On the day Noah and his family entered the ark the flood came and destroyed the inhabitants of the earth. The righteous were preserved, and the unrighteous were destroyed by the flood. On the day Jesus Christ raptures His Church God will pour out His wrath upon the inhabitants of the earth. In the same manner, the righteous will be preserved and the unrighteous will suffer the plagues of the wrath of God.

The purpose of describing the events of the first trumpet is to establish that the Day of the Lord begins with the opening of the seventh seal, which contains the seven trumpets. Trumpets two through seven will be discussed in Chapter 4.

> And I looked, and behold a white cloud, and upon the cloud one sat like unto the Son of man, having on his head a golden crown, and in his hand a sharp sickle. And another angel came out of the temple, crying with a loud voice to him that sat on the cloud, Thrust in thy sickle, and reap: for the time is come for thee to reap; for the harvest of the earth is ripe. And he that sat on the cloud thrust in his sickle on the earth; and the earth was reaped. (Revelation 14:14-16)

The reaping of the earth with a sharp sickle is a symbolic description of the Rapture of the Church. The "harvest of the earth" is the Church, which is "ripe," which means it is mature, or perfected (Ephesians 4:13). This is the harvest of the just, the righteous. The Rapture will take place prior to the Day of the Lord's wrath.

> And another angel came out of the temple which is in heaven, he also having a sharp sickle. And another angel came out from the altar, which had power over fire; and cried with a loud cry to him that had the sharp sickle, saying, Thrust in thy sharp sickle, and gather the clusters of the vine of the earth; for her grapes are fully ripe. And the angel thrust in his sickle into the earth, and gathered the vine of the earth, and cast it into the great winepress of the wrath of God. And the winepress was trodden without the city, and blood came out of the winepress,

> even unto the horse bridles, by the space of a thousand and six hundred furlongs. (Revelation 14:17-20)

This passage describes the harvest of the unjust, the unrighteous, the unbelievers, during the Day of the Lord. The harvest of the unjust during the Day of the Lord will follow the harvest of the just at the Rapture. We know these scriptures are describing the harvest of the unjust because those who are harvested are, "cast into the great winepress of the wrath of God." The Day of the Lord is the wrath of God. The harvest of the unjust will take place during the Day of the Lord when God pours out His Indignation, or wrath, on the unbeliever.

What is evident from the preceding scriptures is the just will be delivered at the Rapture, followed by the judgment of the unjust during the Day of the Lord's wrath.

Let us review again the significance of the Seventieth Week of Daniel. This is a seven-year period that is called a week. God created the earth in six days, and on the seventh day He rested; this was the Lord's Day (Genesis 2:2). God said Israel could work six days, but on the seventh day they should rest; this was the Lord's Day (Exodus 34:21). God said Israel could plant and harvest for six years, but in the seventh year the land should be allowed to rest; this was a Sabbath rest for the Lord, the Lord's Day (Leviticus 25:2-4). God said if the Jews possessed Hebrew servants for six years, then in the seventh year they should be set free. (Jeremiah 34:14) In all of these examples of God's dealings with Israel He worked in periods of seven days, or seven years. God said the last day or last year – the seventh – is His. This seventh day, or seventh year, is the Lord's Day, or the Day of the Lord.

The Rapture will take place within this seven day/year timetable. At the end of the sixth day/year, as the seventh day/year is about to begin, the Rapture will occur. Therefore, the Rapture can be described as the sixth day Rapture, or the Day of the Lord Rapture. The seventh day/year is the Indignation, or wrath of God, the Day of the Lord.

The Day of The Lord Rapture

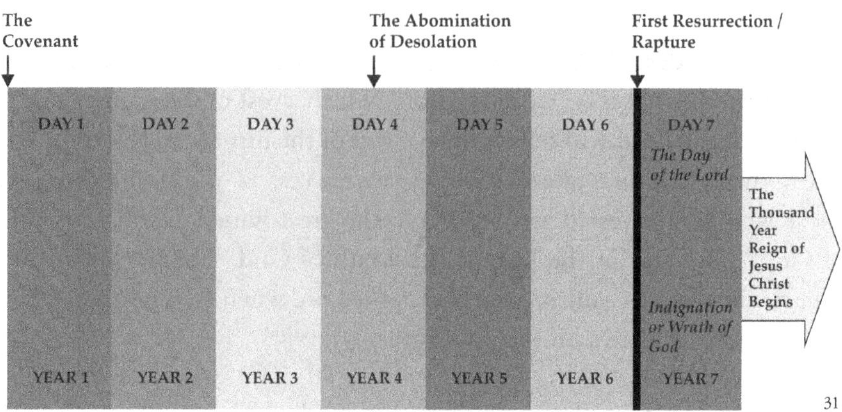

[31]

The Two Second Comings of Jesus Christ

Pretribulationists teach that the Lord will come once *for* the saints, and a second time *with* the saints. They say His first coming takes place prior to the seven-year tribulation period. The purpose of His first coming is to Rapture the Church into heaven. He will come *for* the saints at the Rapture. They say the second time He comes is at the end of the tribulation period. The purpose for the second time He comes will be to destroy the armies that have assembled at Armageddon, rescue Israel and the tribulation saints, and establish His Millennial kingdom. He will come *with* the saints who are in heaven as His army to fight the Antichrist and his armies at Armageddon.

The following quotes are examples of pretribulation teachings on the two second comings of Jesus Christ.

Dave Hunt, in "The Berean Call," says:

> If it [the Rapture] occurs at the beginning of the tribulation period, then clearly Christ's Second Coming

[31] Wood, *Six Days to the Rapture*, Page 42.

> at the end of the Tribulation to rescue Israel in the midst of Armageddon is a separate event...The descriptions in Scripture of the Rapture and Second Coming respectively are so different in so many details that they could not possibly be describing the same occurrence.[32]

Tim LaHaye says:

> While critics complain that the pre-Trib theory is not covered in a single passage, we have noted that Titus 2:13 gives the titles for the two events (the blessed hope and the glorious appearing);[33]
>
> They [the Rapture and the glorious appearing] are obviously two separate events!...Only by robbing these passages [1 Thessalonians 4:16-17] of their obvious meaning can we ignore the two comings of Christ, one for His church and another for the world.[34]

These quotes describe two comings of Jesus Christ. No matter what they call them - the blessed hope and the glorious appearing, or the Rapture and the second coming - they are proposing two second comings of Christ. How many second comings of Jesus Christ are described in the Bible? Are there two second comings of the Lord, one to Rapture the Church at the beginning of a tribulation period, and another for the world at the end of this period? There is only one second coming of Jesus Christ recounted in the Bible, and it does not take place at the beginning of the last seven years, which they call the tribulation period.

Let us see if the Bible makes it clear that there is only one second coming of Jesus Christ through a examination of the resurrections of the dead.

---

[32] Dave Hunt, "The Berean Call" (October, 2003).

[33] LaHaye, *The Rapture*, p. 85.

[34] Ibid., p. 36.

The Resurrections of the Dead

> And many of them that sleep in the dust of the earth shall awake, some to everlasting life, and some to shame and everlasting contempt. (Daniel 12:2)

This verse is describing two groups of individuals, who have died, and have come back to life. It is describing two resurrections of the dead. The first resurrection is to everlasting life, the second resurrection is to shame and everlasting contempt.

> Verily, verily, I say unto you, The hour is coming, and now is, when the dead shall hear the voice of the Son of God: and they that hear shall live. For as the Father hath life in himself; so hath he given to the Son to have life in himself; And hath given him authority to execute judgment also, because he is the Son of man. Marvel not at this: for the hour is coming, in the which all that are in the graves shall hear his voice, And shall come forth; they that have done good, unto the resurrection of life; and they that have done evil, unto the resurrection of damnation. (John 5:25-29)

These verses are describing the same two resurrections that were mentioned in Daniel 12:2. The time is coming when all who have died will come back to life. Those who have done good will come back to life in the first resurrection – the resurrection of life. Those who have done evil will come back to life in the second resurrection – the resurrection of damnation.

> And have hope toward God, which they themselves also allow, that there shall be a resurrection of the dead, both of the just and unjust. (Acts 24:15)

Again, we are told of two resurrections of the dead. The first resurrection is the resurrection of the just (Luke 14:14). The second resurrection is the resurrection of the unjust. The resurrections of the dead mentioned in these passages are mass resurrections. These resurrections of the dead are not individual resurrections, such as the resurrections of Lazarus (John 11:43-44), or the two witnesses (Revelation 11:12).

There are *two, and only two,* mass resurrections of the dead, and they are described in three books of the Bible. These scriptures are describing the exact same events, these two resurrections. One resurrection is for everyone who is just, and one resurrection is for everyone who is unjust. No unjust person is resurrected in the first resurrection – the resurrection of the just – *not one.* No just person is resurrected in the second resurrection – the resurrection of the unjust – *not one.*[35]

> And I saw the souls of them that were beheaded for the witness of Jesus, and for the word of God, and which had not worshipped the beast, neither his image, neither had received his mark upon their foreheads, or in their hands; and they lived and reigned with Christ a thousand years. But the rest of the dead lived not again until the thousand years were finished. This is the first resurrection. Blessed and holy is he that hath part in the first resurrection: on such the second death hath no power, but they shall be priests of God and of Christ, and shall reign with him a thousand years. (Revelation 20:4b-6)

The apostle John is describing two resurrections of the dead. In the first resurrection, the souls of those who were beheaded for the witness of Jesus, and did not worship the Beast, or receive his mark, are resurrected. John says, "This is the first resurrection." The first resurrection of the dead is the Rapture of the Church, the resurrection of the just. The Rapture will include all who have died in faith, as well as Christians who are, "alive and remain unto the coming of the Lord" (1 Thessalonians 4:15). Those who are raptured in the first resurrection will live and reign with Christ a thousand years – the millennial reign of Jesus Christ. The Church will be on the earth when the Antichrist is in power because John sees Christians who die at the hands of the Antichrist during the Great Tribulation.

---

[35] Wood, *Six Days to the Rapture,* Tape 8.

Those who die as martyrs during the Great Tribulation are part of the first resurrection.

These souls, beheaded for the witness of Jesus, and then resurrected, are the Christians who will be killed by the Antichrist during the Great Tribulation. In verse 5 John says, "This is the first resurrection." We know the first resurrection takes place at the Rapture. Some say these are the 144,000 Jews who have not taken the mark of the Beast, and will be resurrected at a later time. Those who are resurrected are not the 144,000 Jews (Revelation 7:9). These Christians are beheaded for the witness of Jesus, and they are resurrected in the first resurrection. They must be resurrected in order to rule and reign with Christ for a thousand years, which agrees with Revelation 6:11 and 7:9. They are clothed in white robes (purified), and have palms in their hands (triumphant), and they came out of the Great Tribulation.

"But the rest of the dead lived not again until the thousand years were finished." The rest of the dead, those who do not participate in the first resurrection – the Rapture of the Church – will not live again until after the millennial reign of Christ. John says those who do not take part in the first resurrection of the dead will be under the power of the second death. What is the second death?

> And I saw a great white throne, and him that sat on it, from whose face the earth and the heaven fled away; and there was found no place for them. And I saw the dead, small and great, stand before God; and the books were opened: and another book was opened, which is the book of life: and the dead were judged out of those things which were written in the books, according to their works. And the sea gave up the dead which were in it; and death and hell delivered up the dead which were in them: and they were judged every man according to their works. And death and hell were cast into the lake of fire. This is the second death. And whosoever was not found written in the book of life was cast into the lake of fire. (Revelation 20:11-15)

This is the Great White Throne judgment. This is the second resurrection of the dead – the resurrection of the unjust. This is the second death. Hell will give up its dead and they will stand before God, and books will be opened, including the book of life. The unjust will be judged according to their works. Their names will not be found written in the book of life, and they will be cast into the lake of fire. Those who participate in the second death are unbelievers, those who are damned to the fires of hell, damned to eternal separation from God. This means from the time of the first resurrection, the Rapture, until the end of the thousand years, not one dead person is resurrected, as far as mass resurrections are concerned.

Pretribulationists say the Rapture of the Church will take place before the beginning of the Great Tribulation, but Revelation 20:4 says Christians are beheaded during the Great Tribulation.

> After this I beheld, and, lo, a great multitude, which no man could number, of all nations, and kindreds, and people, and tongues, stood before the throne, and before the Lamb, clothed with white robes, and palms in their hands…And one of the elders answered, saying unto me, What are these which are arrayed in white robes? and whence came they? And I said unto him, Sir, thou knowest. And he said to me, These are they which came out of great tribulation, and have washed their robes, and made them white in the blood of the Lamb. Therefore are they before the throne of God, and serve him day and night in his temple: and he that sitteth on the throne shall dwell among them. They shall hunger no more, neither thirst any more; neither shall the sun light on them, nor any heat. For the Lamb which is in the midst of the throne shall feed them, and shall lead them unto living fountains of waters: and God shall wipe away all tears from their eyes. (Revelation 7:9, 13-17)

John sees a vision of, "a great multitude, which no man could number, of all nations, and kindreds, and people, and tongues, stood before the throne, and before the Lamb, clothed with white robes, and palms in their hands." John is told, "These are they which came out of great tribulation." Who is this great multitude? It is the Raptured Church! They are clothed in white robes with palms in their hands. Clearly, the Church will go through the Great Tribulation, and then will be raptured before the wrath of God is poured out during the Day of the Lord.

In which resurrection are these Christians, who are beheaded during the Great Tribulation, resurrected? The first resurrection, or Rapture, takes place after the Great Tribulation (Revelation 7:9). They must be raised from the dead after they are beheaded, but before the end of the Seventieth Week of Daniel, before the thousand years begin. The second resurrection does not take place until the end of the thousand years, but we know not one just person is resurrected in the second resurrection. Therefore, those who are beheaded during the Great Tribulation will be resurrected in the first resurrection, the Rapture of the Church.

Pretribulationists teach the Church will be raptured before the tribulation period, and multitudes of unbelievers who have been left behind will be saved during this period. They say these unbelievers, who were resistant to the gospel prior to the Rapture, will be shocked when Christians unexpectedly disappear. Many of these unbelievers will realize the message of the Bible concerning the End Times and the Rapture of the Church was true, and they will accept Jesus Christ. They say these unbelievers, these tribulation saints, who have been left behind, and who are saved during the tribulation period, will be raptured at the end of this period.

The following quote from Hunt is typical of pretribulation teaching regarding those who are left behind.

> In contrast, at the Second Coming there is no resurrection until Antichrist is defeated, he and the false prophet have been, "cast alive into a lake of fire" (Rv 19:20) and Satan has been bound in the "bottomless pit [for] a thousand years" (20:1-3) –none of which is even remotely related to the Rapture of believers to heaven. Then, to "the

> first resurrection" which occurred at the Rapture are added a unique group: "them that were beheaded for the witness of Jesus, and for the word of God, and which had not worshiped the beast, neither his image, neither had received his mark upon their foreheads, or in their hands…they lived and reigned with Christ a thousand years" (4,5).[36]

Pretribulationists teach the Rapture of the Church will occur at the beginning of the tribulation period. In addition, a "unique group" of believers will be saved during the tribulation period, and then are resurrected at the end of it. This "unique group" is added to those who went up in the first resurrection. LaHaye further identifies those referred to as tribulation saints when he says, "Also, keep in mind that the saints who are martyred during the Tribulation are not part of the church."[37] Not part of the Church? How can a believer in Jesus Christ, a saint, one who is saved and is martyred for his faith, not be a part of the Church? What criteria do pretribulationists believe qualify someone for being part of the Church? In a previous quote from LaHaye in this chapter he mentions, "the two comings of Christ, one for the church and the other for the world." LaHaye would want us to believe at the "Second Coming" there will be a resurrection of a "unique group" of believers, who "are not part of the church," a group he describes as "the world." Revelation 20:4, 5 clearly identifies those who are, "beheaded for the witness of Jesus, and for the word of God, and which had not worshipped the Beast, neither his image, neither had received his mark upon their foreheads, or in their hands," as those who are caught up in the first resurrection, the Rapture of the Church. Verse 5 identifies these who are raptured in verse 4 as, "the first resurrection." There is no biblical basis whatsoever for a second resurrection of a "unique group" of believers who "are not part of the church."

When a particular theory of the End Times contradicts the Bible, as pretribulationism does, there is always a need to create alternative

[36] Hunt, *The Berean Call*, October, 2003.

[37] LaHaye, *The Rapture*, p. 63.

explanations for scriptures that contradict the theory. Such is the case with Revelation 20:4-6. These scriptures are clearly describing Christians who have been martyred for their faith during the Great Tribulation, and then are raptured in the first resurrection. Pretribulationists recognize Revelation 20:4-6 describes a group who is resurrected, but who must first endure the tribulation period. Since they believe the Church is raptured before the tribulation period, they are compelled to relegate these "tribulation saints" to a status which is outside of the Church.

How many first resurrections are there? There is only one first resurrection described in the Bible, and it is called the resurrection of the just. There can only be one first resurrection; there can only be one Rapture. Therefore, when pretribulationists teach two second comings they are teaching a theory comprised of human conclusions and their own logic, and not the clear meaning of the Bible.

Will unbelievers who are left behind at the Rapture get another opportunity to accept Jesus Christ and be raptured? Let us see how the parables of Noah, Lot and the ten virgins confirm the fact that there will only be one resurrection of the just.

> And as it was in the days of Noe, so shall it be also in the days of the Son of man. They did eat, they drank, they married wives, they were given in marriage, until the day that Noe entered into the ark, and the flood came, and destroyed them all. (Luke 17:26-27) (See also Matthew 24:37-39)

The day Noah boarded the ark can be compared to the day when the Son of man is revealed, and He raptures the Church. The inhabitants of the world during Noah's time were going about their daily lives. They were wicked and corrupt men whose hearts were full of evil, and the earth was filled with their violence (Genesis 6:5, 11-12). On the same day Noah and his family boarded the ark the flood came and destroyed these evil men. The door of the ark was shut, and those outside of the ark perished. Those who were outside of the ark did not have another opportunity to get on board. They were left behind, and they perished. As the End Times approach men will likewise be going about their daily lives. In the last days men will be wicked and corrupt just as in Noah's day (2 Timothy 3:1-5). On the same day Jesus Christ raptures His Church He will pour out His wrath upon the inhabitants of the earth. Those who are left behind will not have another opportunity to be saved and raptured.

> Likewise also as it was in the days of Lot; they did eat, they drank, they bought, they sold, they planted, they builded; But the same day that Lot went out of Sodom it rained fire and brimstone from heaven, and destroyed them all. Even thus shall it be in the day when the Son of man is revealed (Luke 17:28-30).

The Bible compares the day Lot went out of Sodom to the day when the Son of man is revealed and raptures the Church. The inhabitants of the world during Lot's time were going about their daily lives. The men of Sodom were wicked, and they were great sinners before the Lord (Genesis 13:13). On the same day Lot left Sodom it rained fire and brimstone from heaven and destroyed these wretched men. Lot and his family were guided out of Sodom by angels, and those who were left behind in the city perished. The inhabitants of Sodom did not have an opportunity to escape the fire and brimstone from heaven. As the End Times approach men will likewise be going about their daily lives. In the last days men will be wicked, and they will be great sinners before the Lord, just as in the days of Lot. On the same day Jesus Christ raptures His Church He will pour out His wrath upon the inhabitants of the earth, and hail and fire mingled with blood will be cast upon the earth (Revelation 8:7). Jesus Christ will Rapture His Church, and those who are left behind will not have another opportunity to be saved and raptured.

> Then shall the kingdom of heaven be likened unto ten virgins, which took their lamps, and went forth to meet the bridegroom. And five of them were wise, and five were foolish. They that were foolish took their lamps, and took no oil with them: But the wise took oil in their

> vessels with their lamps. While the bridegroom tarried, they all slumbered and slept. And at midnight there was a cry made, Behold, the bridegroom cometh; go ye out to meet him. Then all those virgins arose, and trimmed their lamps. And the foolish said unto the wise, Give us of your oil; for our lamps are gone out. But the wise answered, saying, Not so; lest there be not enough for us and you: but go ye rather to them that sell, and buy for yourselves. And while they went to buy, the bridegroom came; and they that were ready went in with him to the marriage: and the door was shut. Afterward came also the other virgins, saying, Lord, Lord, open to us. But he answered and said, Verily I say unto you, I know you not. (Matthew 25:1-12)

In the parable of the ten virgins, five were wise, and five were foolish. The five wise virgins represent believers, the bride of Christ. The five foolish virgins represent unbelievers, those who have rejected the Lord. In this parable, the bridegroom is Jesus Christ. The day of the bridegroom's coming can be compared to the day when the Son of man is revealed, and He raptures the Church. While the five foolish virgins went to buy oil the bridegroom came. On the same day, the five wise virgins went in to the marriage, and the door was shut. Those who were outside when the door was shut were not allowed to enter, even though they pleaded for the door to be opened. The five foolish virgins did not have another opportunity to go into the marriage. The Lord will say to these unbelievers, "I know you not." Jesus Christ will Rapture His Church, and those who are left behind will not have another opportunity to be saved and raptured.

The Parousia of Jesus Christ

> For this we say unto you by the word of the Lord, that we which are alive *and* remain unto the coming (parousia)of the Lord shall not prevent them which are asleep. For the Lord himself shall descend from heaven with a shout, with

> the voice of the archangel, and with the trump of God: and the dead in Christ shall rise first: Then we which are alive and remain shall be caught up together with them in the clouds, to meet the Lord in the air: and so shall we ever be with the Lord (1 Thessalonians 4:15-17).

> And I saw heaven opened, and behold a white horse; and he that sat upon him was called Faithful and True, and in righteousness he doth judge and make war. His eyes were as a flame of fire, and on his head were many crowns; and he had a name written, that no man knew, but he himself. And he was clothed with a vesture dipped in blood: and his name is called The Word of God. And the armies which were in heaven followed him upon white horses, clothed in fine linen, white and clean (Revelation 19:11-14).

1 Thessalonians 4:15-17 describes the catching away, or Rapture, of the Church. This is the second coming, or *parousia,* of Jesus Christ. The Rapture of the Church is immediately followed by the great and the terrible Day of the Lord, during which God will pour out His wrath on the unbeliever. Revelation 19:11-14 describes Jesus Christ as He returns on a white horse, at the end of the Day of the Lord, to slay the wicked. Some would say two comings of Christ have been described in these verses, one at the Rapture and one at the end of the Day of the Lord, separated by a period of one year. However, when Christ comes to Rapture His Church, He will not return to heaven, to remain there until He comes again. There is only one coming, or *parousia,* of the Lord, during which He will Rapture the Church, pour out His wrath during the Day of the Lord, and defeat the armies of the world that have gathered at Armageddon. To understand why there is only one second coming of the Lord it is important to understand the meaning of *parousia.*

> *Parousia* - a being near, i.e. advent (often, return; spec. of Christ to punish Jerusalem, or finally the wicked); (by impl.) phys. aspect:-coming, presence.[38]

[38] Strong, *Dictionary Of The Greek Testament,* p. 56.

Rosenthal explains the *parousia* of Jesus Christ.

> *Parousia* (coming) is derived from two Greek words, *para*, meaning *with* and *ousia* meaning *being*. *Parousia*, then, denotes two things: an arrival and a consequent presence with...The coming (*parousia*) of Christ will include His continuing presence to Rapture the church and His Day of the Lord judgment of the wicked. The other words employed to describe His coming or revelation focus on one aspect of His coming, whereas *parousia* is speaking of the totality of that glorious *series* of events. Christ's coming (*parousia*) will be seen in the heavens (that is, His glory-not His bodily form), and there will be a continuous presence for the purpose of rapturing the Church and judging the wicked...The Lord's coming is consistently portrayed as a singular event...And in every case, His return is in the singular; not *comings* but *coming*. There is not even a hint—anywhere—of two separate comings. That is simple, unadorned, biblical fact.[39]

There is only one coming, one *parousia,* of the Lord. It is a singular event, a coming, not comings. It is an arrival and continuing presence during which He will Rapture the Church, and pour out His wrath during the Day of the Lord, a one year period of time.

Pretribulationists teach two second comings. The first coming is *for* the saints at the beginning of the tribulation period, and the second coming is *with* the saints at the end of this period, when the saints, as the armies of God, follow the Lord on white horses. The Bible, however, does not teach two second comings. There is only one second coming; it does not take place at the beginning of a tribulation period and the Church is not the army that follows Christ on white horses.

---

[39] Rosenthal, *The Pre-Wrath Rapture of the Church*, pp. 217, 222, 223.

Angels or Saints with Jesus Christ at His Coming?

> And I saw heaven opened, and behold a white horse; and he that sat upon him was called Faithful and True, and in righteousness he doth judge and make war. His eyes were as a flame of fire, and on his head were many crowns; and he had a name written, that no man knew, but he himself. And he was clothed with a vesture dipped in blood: and his name is called The Word of God. And the armies which were in heaven followed him upon white horses, clothed in fine linen, white and clean. (Revelation 19:11-14)

Pretribulationists use Revelation 19:11-14 to justify their teaching that the Church will be raptured prior to the tribulation period. They say the Lord will come *for* the saints at the beginning of this period, and then Jesus Christ will return *with* the saints at the end of this period. They say the armies following Christ on white horses are, "clothed in fine linen, white and clean," just like the saints, the bride of Christ, who in Revelation 19:8 are also, "arrayed in fine linen, clean and white: for the fine linen is the righteousness of saints." However, the armies following Christ on white horses are not the Raptured Church. Just because these armies on white horses wear white linen does not mean they are the Church. The armies in Revelation 19:11-14 are not the only group in the Bible who are clothed in white linen. In Revelation 15:6, the seven angels who possess the seven plagues of God are also, "clothed in pure and white linen," and they are not this army. Therefore, apparel does not necessarily identify the armies that follow the Lord.

> For the Son of man shall come in the glory of his Father with his angels (aggelos); and then he shall reward every man according to his works. (Matthew 16:27)

> When the Son of man shall come in his glory, and all the holy angels with him, then shall he sit upon the throne of his glory. (Matthew 25:31)

> Whosoever therefore shall be ashamed of me and of my words in this adulterous and sinful generation; of him also shall the Son of man be ashamed, when he cometh in the glory of his Father with the holy angels. (Mark 8:38)

> And to you who are troubled rest with us, when the Lord Jesus shall be revealed from heaven with his mighty angels. In flaming fire taking vengeance on them that know not God, and that obey not the gospel of our Lord Jesus Christ: Who shall be punished with everlasting destruction from the presence of the Lord, and from the glory of his power; When he shall come to be glorified in his saints, and to be admired in all them that believe (because our testimony among you was believed) in that day. (2 Thessalonians 1:7-10)

The armies that follow the Lord from heaven are mighty and holy angels. They are angels, and not the Church, not because of their clothing, but because of what is described in Matthew 16:27, Matthew 25:31, Mark 8:38, and 2 Thessalonians 1:7-10. When Jesus Christ is revealed from heaven, and takes vengeance on those that do not know God, He will be accompanied by His mighty and holy angels. The Church will be glorifying and admiring the Lord at His coming. Jesus Christ will return on a white horse with His army of holy angels, who will be clothed in fine linen, white and clean.

The Bible clearly says the raptured saints will rule and reign with Jesus Christ on earth for a thousand years (Revelation 20:6). If the raptured saints are not the army that accompanies Christ when He comes from heaven on a white horse to judge and make war (Revelation 19:11-14), then when do we return to the earth?

Many Mansions in my Father's House

> Then we which are alive and remain shall be caught up together with them in the clouds, to meet the Lord in the air: and so shall we ever be with the Lord. (1 Thessalonians 4:17)

When the Church is raptured during the Seventieth Week of Daniel we will meet the Lord in the air. This scripture promises, beginning with the Rapture, we will never be separated from the Lord. Where will we go after we are raptured, after we meet the Lord in the air, to always be with the Lord?

> In my Father's house are many mansions: if it were not so, I would have told you. I go to prepare a place for you. And if I go and prepare a place for you, I will come again, and receive you unto myself; that where I am, there ye may be also. (John 14:2-3)

After Jesus Christ's first coming He returned to heaven to prepare a place for His Church. Jesus said there are many mansions (residences, abodes) in His Father's house. The place He is preparing for us are dwellings in His Father's house. Jesus said after He returns to receive us unto Himself, the Rapture of the Church, we will never be separated from Him.

> And I John saw the holy city, new Jerusalem, coming down from God out of heaven, prepared as a bride adorned for her husband. And I heard a great voice out of heaven saying, Behold, the tabernacle of God is with men, and he will dwell with them, and they shall be his people, and God himself shall be with them, and be their God…And there came unto me one of the seven angels which had the seven vials full of the seven last plagues, and talked with me, saying, Come hither, I will show thee the bride, the Lamb's wife. And he carried me away in the spirit to a great and high mountain, and showed me that great city, the holy Jerusalem, descending out of heaven from God. (Revelation 21:2-3, 9-10)

After the armies of world are defeated by Jesus Christ and his army of holy angels, and the Beast and the False Prophet are cast alive into the lake of the fire, New Jerusalem will come down to the earth out of heaven. The Lord will inhabit the New Jerusalem, and we will dwell there with Him. In fact, the Church will have been dwelling in the New Jerusalem ever since the Rapture, ever since we met the Lord in the air. One of the angels told John he would show him the bride of Christ. The angel then carried John to a mountain and showed him the New Jerusalem. The angel was not showing John the New Jerusalem and implying the city was the bride of Christ. The angel was showing John the bride of Christ, the saints of God, who were dwelling in the New Jerusalem. Therefore, when the Church is raptured we will go to the New Jerusalem, the Father's house, where there are many mansions. We will return to earth when the New Jerusalem, our heavenly dwelling place, comes down to the earth from God out of heaven at the beginning of the Millennium.

The Restrainer

> Now we beseech you, brethren, by the coming of our Lord Jesus Christ, and by our gathering together unto him, That ye be not soon shaken in mind, or be troubled, neither by spirit, nor by word, nor by letter as from us, as that the day of Christ is at hand. Let no man deceive you by any means: for that day shall not come, except there come a falling away first, and that man of sin be revealed, the son of perdition; Who opposeth and exalteth himself above all that is called God, or that is worshipped; so that he as God sitteth in the temple of God, shewing himself that he is God…And now ye know what withholdeth that he might be revealed in his time. For the mystery of iniquity doth already work: only he who now letteth will let, until he be taken out of the way. (2 Thessalonians 2:1-4, 6-7)

These are some of the most quoted verses by those who believe in a pretribulation rapture to suggest believers will be gathered together, or raptured, before a tribulation period. "And now we know what withholdeth that he (the Antichrist) might be revealed in his time." Someone is withholding the Antichrist from being revealed – from being disclosed.

Verse 7 says, "For the mystery of iniquity doth already work: only he who now letteth (withholds, restrains, prevents) will let, until he be taken out of the way." Who is withholding, restraining, or preventing the Antichrist from being revealed in his time, and when is this restrainer taken out of the way?

Pretribulationists teach that the restrainer is the Holy Spirit, the one who is withholding or preventing the Antichrist from being revealed in his time. They say the Holy Spirit will leave the earth before the tribulation period, and when He leaves He must take the Church with Him, because the Holy Spirit cannot be taken from believers. Furthermore, they interpret the meaning of the Holy Spirit being taken out of the way to be His departure from the earth. Since the Lord would not take the Holy Spirit from believers, then believers would be raptured when the Holy Spirit is taken out of the way, and then the Antichrist could be revealed. However, pretribulationists cannot produce one scripture to substantiate their claim that the Holy Spirit is the restrainer. They simply say the Holy Spirit appears as the most logical candidate to be the restrainer.

The identification of the Holy Spirit as the restrainer, and His removal at the beginning of a tribulation period, presents a dilemma for Pretribulationists. They say many will be saved after the Rapture of the Church and the removal of the Holy Spirit during the tribulation period. They call these who are left behind, and are saved after the Rapture, the tribulation saints. Since it is the work of the Holy Spirit to convict mankind of their sin, and the Holy Spirit has been removed in a pretribulation rapture, who will be responsible for convicting the tribulation saints of their need for salvation? Pretribulationists say it will be the work of the 144,000 Jewish evangelists. Unfortunately, there is not one verse in the Bible that states, or even implies, the 144,000 Jews of the book of Revelation function as evangelists. Revelation simply says the 144,000 Jews are sealed for protection during the Day of the Lord's wrath, and they are the first fruits of many more Jews who will be saved at the end of the Seventieth Week of Daniel. The 144,000 Jews are not evangelists, and there is absolutely no biblical basis for the pretribulationists contention that the Holy Spirit is the restrainer of 2 Thessalonians 2:6-7.

2 Thessalonians 2:3 explicitly says the gathering together, or Rapture of the Church, does not take place until *after* the Antichrist is revealed. The revealing of the Antichrist takes place at the midpoint of the Seventieth Week of Daniel, and is the event that begins the Great Tribulation. Therefore, the Church will enter the Great Tribulation in the middle of the Seventieth Week of Daniel. Pretribulationists do not understand who is taken out of the way, and when he is taken out of the way.

> But the prince of the kingdom of Persia withstood me one and twenty days: but, lo, Michael, one of the chief princes, came to help me; and I remained there with the kings of Persia…But I will show thee that which is noted in the scripture of truth: and there is none that holdeth with me in these things, but Michael your prince. (Daniel 10:13, 21)

> And at that time shall Michael stand up, the great prince which standeth for the children of thy people: and there shall be a time of trouble, such as never was since there was a nation even to that same time: and at that time thy people shall be delivered, every one that shall be found written in the book. (Daniel 12:1)

Michael the archangel is, "the great prince which standeth for the children of thy people." Michael has been the one who stands for, helps, and protects the "children of thy people," the nation of Israel. He is the helper, the protector of Israel. He is the one that holds, or restrains, the one who withstands her enemies and strengthens Israel. Michael is the one who is responsible for restraining the demonic forces of the Devil that come against Israel.

Daniel 12:1 says, "And at that time shall Michael stand up," referring to the beginning of the Great Tribulation. In the preceding verse, Daniel 11:45, the Antichrist desecrates the temple, which is the Abomination of Desolation. Then Daniel 12:1 says, "at that time shall Michael stand up." The "time" when Michael stands up is when the Antichrist commits the

Abomination of Desolation. Michael will stand up when the Antichrist enters the temple and commits the Abomination of Desolation, which is the event that begins the Great Tribulation. The meaning of "stand up" cannot be that Michael continues to restrain Israel's enemies, or strengthens Israel, because it is at this time the Great Tribulation begins. This will be the worst time the nation of Israel will ever experience. It will be the time of Jacob's trouble (Jeremiah 30:7). If stand up meant that Michael would continue to protect Israel, then there would be no opportunity for Satan to unleash his wrath upon Israel during the Great Tribulation.

Stand up, *amad*, means to stand still, tarry, or cease. Therefore, Michael will stand still, tarry, or cease from protecting Israel. He will no longer help or protect the children of Israel. The result for Israel will be, "a time of trouble, such as never was since there was a nation even to that same time." It will be the time of Jacob's trouble, the Great Tribulation. Michael will cease to restrain the Devil from unleashing his fury against Israel, which will allow, "that Wicked shall be revealed" (2 Thessalonians 2:8), the Antichrist.

Who then is withholding, restraining, or preventing the Antichrist from being revealed in his time? Michael the archangel! Michael is the restrainer, the one withholding or preventing the Antichrist from being disclosed to the world.

Verse 7 says, "only he who now letteth (withholds) will let, until he be taken out of the way." The Greek word for, "out of the way," is *Mesos.*

> *Mesos* (mes'-os) - middle (as adj. or [neut.] noun): -among, x before them, between, + forth, mid [-day, -night], midst, way.[40]

This verse says he who is withholding, will withhold, until he is taken out of the middle, between, midst, or way. Michael the archangel stands between Israel and the demonic forces which are attempting to destroy her. It is Michael, and not the Holy Spirit, who will be taken out of the middle,

[40] Strong, *Dictionary Of The Greek Testament*, p. 47.

or midst, from between Israel and the Devil, and then the Antichrist will be revealed. Michael will not be taken out of the way at the beginning of a tribulation period, but at the midpoint of the Seventieth Week of Daniel.

> And there was war in heaven: Michael and his angels fought against the dragon; and the dragon fought and his angels, And prevailed not; neither was their place found any more in heaven. And the great dragon was cast out, that old serpent, called the Devil, and Satan, which deceiveth the whole world: he was cast out into the earth, and his angels were cast out with him. And I heard a loud voice saying in heaven, Now is come salvation, and strength, and the kingdom of our God, and the power of his Christ: for the accuser of our brethren is cast down, which accused them before our God day and night. And they overcame him by the blood of the Lamb, and by the word of their testimony; and they loved not their lives unto the death. Therefore rejoice, ye heavens, and ye that dwell in them. Woe to the inhabiters of the earth and of the sea! for the devil is come down unto you, having great wrath, because he knoweth that he hath but a short time. And when the dragon saw that he was cast unto the earth, he persecuted the woman which brought forth the man child. And to the woman were given two wings of a great eagle, that she might fly into the wilderness, into her place, where she is nourished for a time, and times, and half a time, from the face of the serpent. (Revelation 12:7-14)

There was war in heaven; Michael the archangel and his angels fought against the Devil and his angels. Predictably, Michael and his angels won the fight. The Devil and his angels were cast out of heaven and down to the earth. The Devil was thrust out of heaven and he persecuted the woman (Israel) who brought forth the man child (Jesus Christ). Revelation 12:7-14 is describing a battle in heaven that will take place in the future. This battle will take place during the End Times, at the midpoint of the

Seventieth Week of Daniel. The intense persecution of Israel begins when the Antichrist commits the Abomination of Desolation, the event that begins the Great Tribulation. Once the Devil is cast out from heaven Michael will no longer restrain or withhold the Devil. Michael is taken out of the way, and the Antichrist is then revealed. The Devil is cast down to the earth, "having great wrath, because he knoweth that he hath but a short time" (Revelation 12:12) – the short time being the final three and a half years of the Seventieth Week of Daniel. The result is Jacob's trouble, the Great Tribulation. The Antichrist, empowered by the Devil, will only maintain his covenant with Israel as long as Michael the archangel restrains him from carrying out his ultimate plan, which is the destruction of Israel. However, after Satan is cast out of heaven, at which time he realizes he has only a short time to destroy Israel, Michael the archangel will no longer restrain him, and he will be relatively unhindered in his assault on Jerusalem and his pursuit of the Jews.

Let us see how the Lord's dealings with Israel during the time of Jacob's trouble, the Great Tribulation, compare with His dealings with His servant Job.

> Now there was a day when the sons of God came to present themselves before the LORD, and Satan came also among them. And the LORD said unto Satan, Whence comest thou? Then Satan answered the LORD, and said, From going to and fro in the earth, and from walking up and down in it. And the LORD said unto Satan, Hast thou considered my servant Job, that there is none like him in the earth, a perfect and an upright man, one that feareth God, and escheweth evil? Then Satan answered the LORD, and said, Doth Job fear God for nought? Hast not thou made an hedge about him, and about his house, and about all that he hath on every side? thou hast blessed the work of his hands, and his substance is increased in the land. But put forth thine hand now, and touch all that he hath, and he will curse thee to thy face. And the LORD said unto Satan, Behold, all that he hath is in thy power;

> only upon himself put not forth thine hand. So Satan went forth from the presence of the LORD. (Job 1:6-12)
>
> Again there was a day when the sons of God came to present themselves before the LORD, and Satan came also among them to present himself before the LORD. And the LORD said unto Satan, From whence comest thou? And Satan answered the LORD, and said, From going to and fro in the earth, and from walking up and down in it. And the LORD said unto Satan, Hast thou considered my servant Job, that there is none like him in the earth, a perfect and an upright man, one that feareth God, and escheweth evil? and still he holdeth fast his integrity, although thou movedst me against him, to destroy him without cause. And Satan answered the LORD, and said, Skin for skin, yea, all that a man hath will he give for his life. But put forth thine hand now, and touch his bone and his flesh, and he will curse thee to thy face. And the LORD said unto Satan, Behold, he is in thine hand; but save his life (Job 2:1-6).

Job was a perfect and an upright man who feared God and turned away from evil. The Lord had a hedge around this righteous man, his family, and his possessions. The Lord took down the hedge, His protection, to the degree Satan could touch Job's life. God did not abandon Job. God was still in control of Job's life. He only gave Satan a space to work. Satan could do no more to Job than what God allowed.

Just like God took down the hedge and allowed Satan to work in Job's life, God will have Michael stand still or cease to protect Israel. Michael will no longer withhold or restrain the Devil from his pursuit of Israel. God will not abandon Israel, but He will remove His protection, to a degree, for a period of time, for a particular purpose.

The Holy Spirit cannot be taken from the earth in a pretribulation rapture because He is God, and because He is God, He is omnipresent, being everywhere at the same time. The Holy Spirit is very active on the earth after the Antichrist is revealed. There are many who will be saved during the Great Tribulation (Joel 3:14). This will be the work of the Holy Spirit, who will still be on the earth, convicting men of their sins and their need for salvation through Jesus Christ.

Pretribulation Myths

The topic of this book is the End Times, the Seventieth Week of Daniel. The Rapture of the Church is the subject of just one chapter in this book, although a very significant one. An examination of the timing of the Rapture is an important part of any study of the End Times. Because of its importance, it is necessary to examine the biblical contradictions contained in the theory of a pretribulation rapture – and there are many biblical contradictions inherent in pretribulationism. These contradictions help to establish that pretribulationism is a false doctrine. The following are just a few of the many contradictions of pretribulationism.

Imminence

Imminence is very important to the pretribulation rapture theory. John F. Walvoord, one of the leading proponents of a pretribulation rapture, said imminence is the, "heart of Pretribulationism."[41] Pretribulationists teach that the Rapture of the Church can occur at any moment and no prophesied events must take place before that time. They say we will not know the series of events preceding the Rapture, or the approximate time of the Lord's return. The Church will be totally surprised by the Rapture; it will be a signless event. The Lord will return for a sleeping Church, in a secret moment, and will catch us unaware. One of the popular, yet misunderstood, phrases they use to describe this event is His coming for the Church, "as a thief in the night" (1 Thessalonians 5:2). They say the Lord will come when we are not expecting him, "at an hour when ye think not" (Luke 12:40). The teaching of an imminent return of the Lord rejects

[41] Walvoord, *The Rapture Question*, p. 55.

the clear teaching of the Bible that the Church will know the series of events preceding the Rapture, and the approximate timing of that event. The scriptures pretribulationists use to support imminence are actually a call to the Church for watchfulness and preparedness.

Pretribulationists teach that the belief in an imminent return of the Lord has brought hope and comfort to the Church, and a motivation for Godly living. LaHaye believes an imminent Rapture will positively affect the Christian lifestyle. He says, "You're a little more careful. A little more aware. A little more guarded. A little more thoughtful. A little more prepared."[42]

LaHaye also contends that without the hope of an imminent Rapture, the Church will lose its focus.

> "What happens when you take away the certainty that Jesus Christ could appear at any moment? It takes the edge off your guard. In a spiritual sense, you may not be able to sleep profoundly, but you will think that you can certainly afford a few lapses, a few catnaps. 'Yes, my Lord is coming and I need to be ready...but I'll have plenty of notice—at least three-and-a-half years. Yes, I need to keep watch, but nothing is going to surprise me, because I have a list of events that have to happen before my Lord appears.'"[43]

He also believes those who are opposed to an imminent pretribulation rapture are "causing many innocent victims to abandon their expectation of the Rapture in their lifetime and in the process have not only stolen their hope but, in some cases, their zeal for service."[44] He goes on to say the assaults from those who oppose the theory of an imminent rapture are hope stealers. "Anytime we destroy a saint's belief that Christ will Rapture His Church before the Antichrist appears on the scene, we strip

---

[42] LaHaye, *The Rapture*, p. 22.
[43] Ibid., p. 73.
[44] Ibid., p. 10.

him of the hope that traditionally has helped the church live a life of expectancy."[45]

As a Christian, I take strong exception to the implication I need the hope of an imminent Rapture to stay focused on the Lord's return, and to be zealous for service to Him – that without this belief I will not be as careful, as aware, as guarded, as thoughtful, or as prepared. My carefulness, awareness, thoughtfulness, or preparedness is not based upon whether the Lord might return at any moment, but upon my relationship with Jesus Christ, my love for the Lord, and my desire to obey His commands. I do not believe in an imminent return of the Lord, and yet I am eagerly waiting and looking for the signs and events which precede the Rapture. I am following the instruction of the Lord to be ever watchful and prepared for His return, whenever it may occur (Matthew 25:13; Mark 13:35; 1 Thessalonians 5:6). In the meantime, my relationship with the Lord will not diminish, and I will not be without hope, nor will my zeal for service diminish.

LaHaye made another flawed assumption regarding the attitude of those who are not looking for an imminent Rapture. In reference to a pastor who did not believe in a pretribulation rapture, and did not want LaHaye to preach it in his church, LaHaye surmised, "Apparently he was looking forward to going through it."[46] This is a presumptuous notion. Just because this pastor disagreed with his theory of an imminent Rapture, LaHaye assumed he was looking forward to going through the tribulation period? It is unfortunate anyone would conclude a church leader or other Christians are looking forward to going through a time of great distress just because they do not believe in the theory of a pretribulation rapture.

He continues, "But the relentless attacks of recent years (including some vicious distortions of the facts) have prompted many to question its (imminent Rapture) truth. This has led to confusion for some and complacency for others."[47] Actually, it is the theory of a pretribulation

[45] Ibid., p. 221.
[46] Ibid., p. 10.
[47] Ibid., p. 19.

rapture that has the most potential for causing complacency in the Church. If a Christian believed withstanding the wrath of the Devil during the Great Tribulation was not a possibility, then where would be the motivation to be prepared for a time of trouble, "such as was not since the beginning of the world"?

LaHaye also says, "Recent assaults on the pre-Tribulation Rapture view have left many Christians confused and in some cases disillusioned. Some have even abandoned this blessed hope, discarding their belief that the Lord could return at any moment."[48] Confused and disillusioned about an imminent Rapture? If we can be confused and disillusioned about the timing of the Rapture, then we are placing our hope in something the Lord never commanded us to put our hope in.

Let us examine scriptures pretribulationists use in defense of their belief in imminence.

As A Thief in the Night

> But of the times and the seasons, brethren, ye have no need that I write unto you. For yourselves know perfectly that the Day of the Lord so cometh as a thief in the night (1 Thessalonians 5:1-2).

Pretribulationists quote these verses repetitively in an attempt to convince the Church Jesus Christ will come for His bride at a moment when we are not expecting Him, as a thief in the night. We need to ask, to whom is the Lord directing these verses.

> For when they shall say, Peace and safety; then sudden destruction cometh upon them, as travail upon a woman with child; and they shall not escape. But ye, brethren, are not in darkness, that that day should overtake you as a thief. Ye are all the children of light, and the children of

[48] Ibid., p. 18.

> the day: we are not of the night, nor of darkness. Therefore let us not sleep, as do others; but let us watch and be sober (1 Thessalonians 5:3-6).

Verse 3 gives us the answer. The Lord is saying He will come as a thief in the night for those who say peace and safety, and they will not escape sudden destruction. The world will be saying peace and safety when the Antichrist signs the Covenant between Israel and its enemies at the beginning of the Seventieth Week of Daniel. Israel, unbelievers, and many Christians will believe the Antichrist is a man of peace. Much to their surprise, after three and a half years, the Antichrist will break the Covenant when he sits down in the temple and declares himself God, and then attacks Israel and the rest of the world. Daniel 8:25 says the Antichrist, "by peace shall destroy many." The peace and safety of the first three and a half years will be followed by sudden destruction during the Great Tribulation and the Day of the Lord. Those who are deceived will worship the Antichrist, take his mark, and will suffer the wrath of God during the Day of the Lord. Those in the Church who have been watching and are prepared for what the Bible says about the events of the End Times will not be deceived. We will not be saying peace and safety, and we will escape the Day of the Lord's wrath when Jesus Christ comes to Rapture His Church.

A thief comes, "to steal, and to kill, and to destroy" (John 10:10), and darkness is, "the power of Satan" (Acts 26:18). The Lord will not come to steal, and to kill, and to destroy the Church, Christians are not under the power of Satan, and Jesus Christ will not return for His Church, "as a thief in the night." Jesus Christ will return as a thief in the night for unbelievers, for those who say "peace and safety" when there is no peace, for the children of the night and the children of the darkness. We are, "the children of the light, and the children of the day," who will be watching and prepared for the Lord's return.

> But the day of the Lord will come as a thief in the night; in the which the heavens shall pass away with a great noise, and the elements shall melt with fervent heat, the earth also and the works that are therein shall be burned up.

> Seeing then that all these things shall be dissolved, what manner of persons ought ye to be in all holy conversation and godliness, Looking for and hasting unto the coming of the day of God, wherein the heavens being on fire shall be dissolved, and the elements shall melt with fervent heat? (2 Peter 3:10-12)

Likewise, in 2 Peter 3, the Lord clearly says during the Day of the Lord's wrath, when the heavens will pass away and the earth will be burned up, He will come as a thief in the night. These events will come upon the unbelievers, those who have missed the Rapture, those who will face the terrifying events of the Day of the Lord.

> And unto the angel of the church in Sardis write; These things saith he that hath the seven Spirits of God, and the seven stars; I know thy works, that thou hast a name that thou livest, and art dead. Be watchful, and strengthen the things which remain, that are ready to die: for I have not found thy works perfect before God. Remember therefore how thou hast received and heard, and hold fast, and repent. If therefore thou shalt not watch, I will come on thee as a thief, and thou shalt not know what hour I will come upon thee. (Revelation 3:1-3)

In scriptures pertaining to the Seventieth Week of Daniel and the Rapture of the Church, when the Lord says He will come as a thief, He is addressing those who are not watching, those who are sleeping spiritually (Matthew 24:4; Luke 12:39; I Thessalonians 5:2, 4; Revelation 3:3). In Revelation chapter 3, the Lord is addressing the church at Sardis and He proclaims they are spiritually dead. He warns them to be watchful, to strengthen their relationship with the Lord, to preserve what they have received and heard, and to repent. He warns them if they do not watch for Him, then he will come upon them as a thief.

A thief is a stealer. In John 10:10 Jesus said, "The thief cometh not, but for to steal, and to kill, and to destroy." If there was going to be a pretribulational Rapture, and if it would take place without any signs, then the Day of the Lord would overtake believers as a thief in the night. Clearly, that is not what the scriptures teach. Stop and consider: would the Lord use such a phrase, "as a thief in the night," to describe His coming for His beloved bride the Church? Is Jesus Christ coming, "to steal, and to kill, and to destroy," the Church? He is coming to take His bride to heaven for a glorious marriage supper. The Church will be raptured away, an event of great joy, to spend eternity with the Lord. To say the Lord will come for His bride, "as a thief in the night," is just plain wrong. It is clearly not the straightforward, literal meaning of these scriptures.

At An Hour When Ye Think Not

> Let your loins be girded about, and your lights burning; And ye yourselves like unto men that wait for their lord, when he will return from the wedding; that when he cometh and knocketh, they may open unto him immediately. Blessed are those servants, whom the lord when he cometh shall find watching: verily I say unto you, that he shall gird himself, and make them to sit down to meat, and will come forth and serve them. And if he shall come in the second watch, or come in the third watch, and find them so, blessed are those servants. And this know, that if the goodman of the house had known what hour the thief would come, he would have watched, and not have suffered his house to be broken through. Be ye therefore ready also: for the Son of man cometh at an hour when ye think not. Then Peter said unto him, Lord, speakest thou this parable unto us, or even to all? And the Lord said, Who then is that faithful and wise steward, whom his lord shall make ruler over his household, to give them their portion of meat in due season? Blessed is that servant, whom his lord when he cometh shall find so doing. Of a truth I say unto you, that he will make him ruler over all that he hath. But and if that servant say in

> his heart, My lord delayeth his coming; and shall begin to beat the menservants and maidens, and to eat and drink, and to be drunken; The lord of that servant will come in a day when he looketh not for him, and at an hour when he is not aware, and will cut him in sunder, and will appoint him his portion with the unbelievers. And that servant, which knew his lord's will, and prepared not himself, neither did according to his will, shall be beaten with many stripes. (Luke 12:35-47)

Verse 40 says, "the Son of man cometh at an hour when ye think not." Pretribulationists quote verse 40 repeatedly in an attempt to convince believers Jesus Christ will return for His Church at a time when we are not expecting Him - He will come in a secret moment and catch us unaware. However, verse 40 cannot be quoted out of context. Jesus Christ will not come for His Church at an hour when we think not. In verses 35-38, Jesus tells the church - the men that wait for their Lord, the blessed servants - to be prepared and to watch for His coming. The Lord tells us we are blessed if He finds us watching when He returns.

Then in verse 39, there is a warning for the goodman of the house. If the goodman of the house does not watch, the thief will come at an hour he would not know, and his house will be burglarized. Then verse 40 says, "Be ye therefore ready also: for the Son of man cometh at an hour when ye think not."[49] To whom is the Lord speaking when He says He will come for them at an hour when they think not? Peter asks this very question when he says, "speakest thou this parable unto us, or even to all?" The Lord answers Peter in verses 45-47 when He speaks of the evil servant (Matthew 24:48), the goodman of the house, who says the Lord is delayed in His coming. This unfaithful and unwise steward is not watching for the Lord's return, and beats his menservants and maidens, and gets drunk. The Lord will come in a day when this wicked servant is not looking for Him, and in an hour when he is not aware, and will beat him with many stripes, and

[49] Pretribulationists assert that, "Be ye therefore ready also," is directed to those in verses 35-38, the blessed servants, those who are watching for the Lord's return. It is not. It is directed to the goodman of the house, the evil servant. "Be ye therefore ready also," could also be translated as,

will give him his share with the unbelievers. The Lord was clearly speaking to the goodman of the house when He said, "Be ye therefore ready also: for the Son of man cometh at an hour when ye think not." The Son of man's coming will be a surprise to the goodman of the house, who is not watching, and he will suffer dearly for it. In contrast, the faithful and wise steward is the servant the Lord will find watching when He comes. The Lord will make this faithful and wise steward ruler over all His possessions.

In the Twinkling of an Eye

> Behold, I show you a mystery; We shall not all sleep, but we shall all be changed, In a moment, in the twinkling of an eye, at the last trump: for the trumpet shall sound, and the dead shall be raised incorruptible, and we shall be changed. (1 Corinthians 15:51-52)

Do these scriptures say we will be raptured, "In a moment, in the twinkling of an eye"? That is what pretribulationists teach. They say when the Lord returns, Christians will disappear in an instant, in a split second. In fact, they say the Rapture will happen so quickly those who are not raptured will not even see the Rapture take place. LaHaye said, "However, anyone who does not participate in the Rapture will not actually see it, for it will occur in the 'twinkling of an eye.'" The word twinkling has been defined as a, 'gleam in your eye,' which is faster than the eye can see."[50] This concept is contrary to scripture since the Bible clearly says every eye, every person, will see the Lord when He comes to Rapture His Church (Matthew 24:30; Acts 1:9-11). Revelation 1:7 says, "Behold, he cometh with clouds; and every eye shall see him, and they also which pierced him: and all kindreds of the earth shall wail because of him." Jesus Christ will arrive in the clouds to Rapture His Church, and at that time, "every eye shall see him." There will not be a secret Rapture, every person on the face of the earth will see the Lord in the clouds, and it will not take place in the "twinkling of an eye."

---

[50] LaHaye, *The Rapture*, p. 38.

It is important to understand verses 51-52 of 1 Corinthians 15 are not directly addressing the Rapture of the Church. They do not say we will be raptured in a moment, in the twinkling of an eye. They say we will be changed, or made different, in a moment, in the twinkling of an eye. Changed into what?

> For this corruptible must put on incorruption, and this mortal must put on immortality. So when this corruptible shall have put on incorruption, and this mortal shall have put on immortality, then shall be brought to pass the saying that is written, Death is swallowed up in victory. O death, where is thy sting? O grave, where is thy victory? (1 Corinthians 15:53-55)

We will be changed from our mortal, corruptible (decaying, perishable) bodies, into our immortal, incorruptible (deathless, unending existence) bodies. After our mortal bodies have been changed into our immortal bodies, we will be raptured, raised incorruptible, to meet the Lord in the air. The assumption could be made that both the changing of our bodies and the Rapture could occur in an instant. However, that is not the case, which will become apparent when we examine the following scriptures.

> Likewise also as it was in the days of Lot; they did eat, they drank, they bought, they sold, they planted, they builded; But the same day that Lot went out of Sodom it rained fire and brimstone from heaven, and destroyed them all. Even thus shall it be in the day when the Son of man is revealed. In that day, he which shall be upon the housetop, and his stuff in the house, let him not come down to take it away: and he that is in the field, let him likewise not return back. Remember Lot's wife. (Luke 17:28-32)

These verses are describing the Rapture of the Church. On the day of the Rapture, Christ instructs us not to return to our house or field to take anything with us. We are told to remember Lot's wife. The angels of the Lord had to seize Lot's family and lead them out of the city. Lot's wife looked back, and was turned into a pillar of salt (Genesis 19:26). She looked back because she did not want to leave the things of this world behind. The Lord tells us not to look back at our worldly possessions, as Lot's wife did, or go back to take them with us. It follows there cannot be an instantaneous Rapture if we will have the time to go back and take anything with us. This means there will be a period of time between the beginning of the Rapture, and when we are caught up into the clouds to meet the Lord in the air. Therefore, it will not be an instantaneous Rapture.

Can you imagine hearing the Lord's voice, hearing a great trumpet blow, seeing the Lord in the clouds, and then contemplating whether to go into your house to take anything with you such as gold or precious stones, photo albums, or the family Bible? Sadly, this is exactly what will happen. Some Christians will be so tied to the things of this earth they will go back in an attempt to take their worldly possessions with them.

We do not know the day or the hour, but we do know the events of the Rapture. The Lord will descend from heaven with a shout (1 Thessalonians 4:16, John 5:25), "with the voice of the archangel" (1 Thessalonians 4:16), and with the trumpet of God (1 Thessalonians 4:16; 1 Corinthians 15:52; Matthew 24:31). The entire world will see Jesus Christ come in the clouds (Acts 1:9-11; Matthew 24:30; Revelation 1:7). The dead in Christ, those who died in faith, will be raised incorruptible (1 Thessalonians 4:16; 1 Corinthians 14:52). Those believers that are alive at the time of the Rapture will be changed into their incorruptible, immortal, bodies (1 Corinthians 15:52). These believers will then be caught up into the clouds, with the dead in Christ, to meet the Lord in the air, and we will always be with the Lord. (1 Thessalonians 4:17). These events do not indicate a secret Rapture, nor do they indicate an instantaneous Rapture – just the opposite. There will be quite a commotion at the time of the Rapture. It will be a spectacular event.

Occasionally, there are Christians who think the Rapture has already taken place and they have been left behind. Such was the case of a Christian who left his house and family and returned after a short absence, expecting to find his family, but instead found no one at home. This Christian panicked, thinking he had missed the rapture, and had been left behind. This unfortunate situation was the result of a lack of understanding of the Bible. There are many misunderstandings regarding the Rapture of the Church and the events of the End Times.

To believe in the concept of imminence we would have to ignore other scriptures.

> Husbands, love your wives, even as Christ also loved the church, and gave himself for it; That he might sanctify and cleanse it with the washing of water by the word, That he might present it to himself a glorious church, not having spot, or wrinkle, or any such thing; but that it should be holy and without blemish. (Ephesians 5:25-27)

Jesus Christ is returning at the Rapture for, "a glorious church, not having spot (defect, disgrace), or wrinkle, or any such thing; but that it should be holy and without blemish (faultless, unblameable)." The Church is certainly not without defects or faultless. Therefore, Jesus Christ cannot Rapture His Church.

The modern Church is moving away from, instead of toward, perfection. The Church needs to be cleansed and purified to be without, "spot, or wrinkle." It will take the extraordinary events of the Great Tribulation to cleanse and purify the Church. When the Church is under the intense pressure of the events of the Great Tribulation it will truly experience its finest hour. When the Antichrist is assailing the Church with afflictions, persecution, and possible martyrdom, only then will the Church be perfected.

The Lord will use the Great Tribulation to cleanse and purify His Church. Those who have fallen into a spiritual slumber will either revive, or choose to follow the Antichrist. Those who have been deceived by false doctrines will either return to the doctrinal purity of the gospel of Jesus Christ, or will believe the lies of the Devil. There will be no middle ground, no gray areas. There will be no lukewarm Christians during the Great Tribulation.

The hot ones will be on fire for the Lord, the cold ones will follow the Antichrist. There will be those who follow the Lord with all of their being, and there will be those who follow the Antichrist.

> Wherefore he saith, When he ascended up on high, he led captivity captive, and gave gifts unto men…And he gave some, apostles; and some, prophets; and some, evangelists; and some, pastors and teachers; For the perfecting of the saints, for the work of the ministry, for the edifying of the body of Christ: Till we all come in the unity of the faith, and of the knowledge of the Son of God, unto a perfect man, unto the measure of the stature of the fulness of Christ. (Ephesians 4:8, 11-13)

Following His death and resurrection, Jesus Christ was received into heaven. Ephesians chapter 4 says at that time He gave gifts unto men. The gifts he gave to the Church were the five-fold ministry: the ministries of the apostles, prophets, evangelists, pastors, and teachers. Jesus Christ possessed all five of these ministry gifts; He was an apostle, a prophet, an evangelist, a pastor, and a teacher. The Lord distributed His ministry to these five governmental offices of the church. Five-fold ministers are responsible, "For the perfecting of the saints, for the work of the ministry, for the edifying of the body of Christ." How long will the Church need the gifts of the five-fold ministry? We will need these gifts, "Till we all come in the unity of the faith, and of the knowledge of the Son of God, unto a perfect man, unto the measure of the stature of the fulness of Christ." Has the Church attained this lofty goal? Look at the Church today. It has no doctrinal unity; it is splintered into many factions and denominations, and is sinking further and further into conformity with the world. The Church surely has not attained, "the knowledge of the Son of God, unto a perfect man, unto the measure of the stature of the fulness of Christ."

Revelation 14:14-16 describes the Rapture of the Church. The Rapture of the Church is likened to a harvest. The time for the harvest has come because the fruit is ripe. The fruit that is ripe is the Church. In the context of this verse, the phrase "ripe" means mature, ready for the harvest.

The five-fold ministry must continue its work because the Church is not mature or perfected. Jesus Christ cannot come to Rapture His Church until this work is completed. Therefore, Jesus Christ cannot Rapture His Church, and the teaching of imminence is again invalidated.

> That the trial of your faith, being much more precious than of gold that perisheth, though it be tried with fire, might be found unto praise and honour and glory at the appearing of Jesus Christ. (1 Peter 1:7)

The testing of our faith, which is a trial by fire, is ready to be revealed in the last time. This test will take place during the End Times – the Seventieth Week of Daniel. The trial by fire will be complete at the revelation of Jesus Christ, at the Rapture of the Church.

Pretribulationists have gone to great lengths to defend imminence. Unfortunately, in some cases, they have had to invent rather contorted scenarios in the defense of their theory. Dave Hunt, in his book, *How Close Are We?*, makes a valiant attempt to support imminence. First, he boldly states, "nothing at any time in history could have stood between the church and the Rapture. There are no signs and no conditions that needed to be fulfilled in the past, nor are there any today."[51] This is the classic position normally taken by pretribulationists. After making this statement, he attempts to explain how various end times' prophecies could have taken place at any moment in history, even if their fulfillment might seem impossible at any time other than during this generation.

Hunt admits this is the first generation in nineteen hundred years to possess weapons capable of wiping out all life on the earth. He then poses the question, could previous generations have developed such weapons in the seven years between the Rapture and Armageddon? Could a previous generation go from knights in armor to nuclear arms in seven years? He answers by saying, "There may be other weapons more ingenious and far more horrible which could have been developed and used more simply

---

[51] Dave Hunt, *How Close Are We?*, (Eugene, Oregon, 1993) p. 257.

and quickly. No one can dogmatically rule out such a possibility. Human genius is unpredictable."[52]

Hunt mentions the Antichrist will control all banking and commerce in the entire world. He admits this concept seemed impossible in the past. This generation has developed computers and communications satellites that could fulfill this prophecy. A cashless society employing electronic transactions is certainly a possibility today. He asks whether such sophisticated electronics could have been developed by a feudal society. Similar to his previous defense of a rapid development of weapons of mass destruction, he again proposes a hypothetical situation regarding banking and commerce. "Could it have been accomplished by previous generations? Once again, while admitting that such a feat would not seem likely under ordinary circumstances, one cannot say it would have been impossible. There may well be some other more ingenious method of accomplishing more simply the same end which could have been developed quickly had the Rapture occurred at any previous time in history."[53]

It is necessary for the Jews to return to the land of Israel, and for Israel to once again become a nation before the Seventieth Week of Daniel can begin. This is necessary because the Antichrist will confirm a covenant involving the nation of Israel at the beginning of Daniel's seventieth week. Hunt notes that our generation is the first one in history to see Israel reestablished in her land. However, Hunt says if at any point in history the Jews were still scattered around the world without a homeland, and the Antichrist were to come to power, then a provision of the Covenant involving Israel would simply include the immediate creation of the nation of Israel.

Hunt says, "If any of these elements could not be developed within a seven-year period immediately following the Rapture of the Church, then we would have lost immanency. Something would have had to occur prior to the Rapture. In fact, all of these unusual signs of the Second Coming could have developed within the seven-year period no matter at what point

[52] Ibid., p. 260.
[53] Ibid., p. 261.

in history the Rapture might have taken place."[54] He has certainly gone to great lengths to defend imminence, but no amount of suppositions will ever prove imminence. At one point he undermines his own hypothesis by saying, "Ours is the first generation for which these prophecies, seemingly impossible before, even make sense."[55]

Is the return of Jesus Christ for His Church imminent? The return of Jesus Christ is not imminent today, and has never been imminent since His first coming. There have always been, and continue to be, prophesied events that must take place before the Lord can Rapture His Church. Only after these prophesied events have taken place can the Church look to the heavens for the sign of His coming and the end of the world. There is not one scripture in the Bible that teaches an imminent return of the Lord. The scriptures pretribulationists mistakenly use to support their belief in an imminent return of the Lord actually teach preparedness and watchfulness.

> "Watch therefore: for ye know not what hour your Lord doth come." (Matthew 24:42)
>
> "Watch therefore, for ye know neither the day nor the hour wherein the Son of man cometh." (Matthew 25:13)
>
> "Watch ye therefore: for ye know not when the master of the house cometh, at even, or at midnight, or at the cockcrowing, or in the morning." (Mark 13:35)
>
> Blessed are those servants, whom the lord when he cometh shall find watching: (Luke 12:37)
>
> "Therefore let us not sleep, as do others; but let us watch and be sober." (1 Thessalonians 5:6)
>
> Remember therefore how thou hast received and heard, and hold fast, and repent. If therefore thou shalt not

[54] Ibid., p. 270.

[55] Ibid., p. 259.

> watch, I will come on thee as a thief, and thou shalt not know what hour I will come upon thee. (Revelation 3:3)

These scriptures clearly tell us we should be watching for the Lord's coming. Why would the Lord tell us to watch for His coming if there were no signs to watch for? The Lord said there would be signs of His coming (Luke 21:25). We will know He is coming soon. End times' prophecies warn us to, "watch and be sober."

The Blessed Hope

> Looking for that blessed hope, and the glorious appearing of the great God and our Saviour Jesus Christ. (Titus 2:13)

Those who believe in a pretribulation rapture are quick to question how the Rapture of the Church can be the blessed hope mentioned by Paul in Titus 2:13 if the Church must first endure the tribulation period. They question how it can be a blessed hope if the Church is on the run from the Antichrist, living in caves or holes, and hunted down and killed if they refuse to worship the Beast or his image during this period? This question reflects pretribulationists belief that God would never allow the Church to endure the trials and testing of the Great Tribulation. By taking this position they are essentially saying every Christian, from the time of Jesus Christ until the present day, who has endured intense persecution and even death for his faith, must not have been experiencing the blessings of God, and must not have been looking forward to the Rapture of the Church. This is a self-centered view that alienates them from their brothers and sisters in the Lord who were persecuted and killed as Christians throughout history, as well as those Christians who are being persecuted and killed for the name of the Lord even today. What would pretribulationists say to Moses, Job, Joseph, David, Jeremiah, and Paul? Would they tell these men of God they were not experiencing the blessings of God simply because they had experienced persecution and suffering for the Lord?

Pretribulationists declare that the Church should be looking for, "that blessed hope," of an imminent pretribulation rapture, and, "the glorious appearing," of the Lord at the end of the tribulation period to slay the wicked at Armageddon. They say these are two separate and distinct events, two second comings, separated by seven years. Firstly, they are incorrect in teaching, "the blessed hope," is a reference to the Rapture - it is not. The blessed hope of Titus 2:13 is the hope of eternal life. This fact is made abundantly clear simply by reading the preceding and following chapters. Paul said in Titus 1:2, "In hope of eternal life, which God, that cannot lie, promised before the world began." Again, in Titus 3:7, "That being justified by his grace, we should be made heirs according to the hope of eternal life." Clearly, the blessed hope is the hope of eternal life, not the hope of an imminent pretribulation rapture. Secondly, the Rapture and the second coming of the Lord are not two separate and distinct events. The Rapture and second coming are one and the same. The Bible does not teach two second comings of Jesus Christ. There is only one second coming of the Lord (Revelation 7:9-17; 20:4-6), during which He will Rapture the Church, pour out His wrath on the unbeliever, and begin His millennial reign.

Paul was instructing the church to be looking for the blessed hope of eternal life, as well as the glorious appearing of Jesus Christ, the Rapture of the Church. The glorious appearing, the *Epiphaneia* or epiphany, is the second coming of Jesus Christ – when He comes to Rapture the Church and pour out his wrath upon the unrepentant.

Furthermore, there is no diminishing of the blessed hope of eternal life, no matter when the Rapture occurs, or what we may experience here on earth. Eternal life is a blessed hope whether or not we experience the Great Tribulation and the wrath of the devil. Multiple scriptures promise the Church a life of trials and tribulations for the witness of Jesus Christ (Colossians 1:24; 2 Timothy 4:5; 1 Peter 4:13). The timing of the Rapture has nothing whatsoever to do with our hope of eternal life, nor should it diminish that hope. This is not to detract from the fact Paul also encouraged the church in his letter to Titus to be looking for the return of the Lord, as he does in many other scriptures.

Prophesied Events Prior to the Rapture

The teaching of an imminent return of the Lord does not allow for any prophesied events to take place prior to the Rapture. To hold to the teaching of imminence, pretribulationists must ignore a multitude of scriptures that clearly teach prophesied events will take place before the Rapture of the Church. There are scriptures in many books of the Bible which prophesy events that must take place before the Rapture, including Isaiah, Jeremiah, Ezekiel, Daniel, Joel, Amos, Obadiah, Zephaniah, Zechariah, Malachi, Matthew, Mark, Luke, Acts, 1 & 2 Thessalonians, 2 Peter, and Revelation.

> And he shall send Jesus Christ, which before was preached unto you: Whom the heaven must receive until the times of restitution of all things, which God hath spoken by the mouth of all his holy prophets since the world began. (Acts 3:20, 21)

God the Father will send Jesus Christ again - the second coming of the Lord. However, heaven must receive or accept Him, "until the times of restitution (restoration) of all things." The times of the restitution of all things are the End Times. Jesus Christ will remain in heaven until all the prophesied events concerning His return come to pass. This means there are prophesied events that must take place before Jesus Christ's second coming. Therefore, the teaching of imminence contradicts the Bible.

> And as he sat upon the mount of Olives, the disciples came unto him privately, saying, Tell us, when shall these things be? and what shall be the sign of thy coming, and of the end of the world? (Matthew 24:3)

This is the most obvious scripture regarding a prophesied event that must take place before Christ will return for His saints. The disciples ask Jesus, "What shall be the *sign* of thy coming?" A sign, in the context of this verse, is an indication of a coming supernatural occurrence, that occurrence being the second coming of Jesus Christ. Therefore, there will be a sign, a miracle or wonder, which will take place prior the Lord's return. This prophesied supernatural event makes the teaching of a signless Rapture untenable.

> And then shall appear the sign of the Son of man in heaven. (Matthew 24:30a)

This verse mentions the same prophesied event, "the sign of thy coming," as Matthew 24:3.

Matthew 24 speaks of three additional prophesied events that take place before the coming of the Lord and the Rapture.

> When ye therefore shall see the Abomination of Desolation, spoken of by Daniel the prophet, stand in the holy place, (whoso readeth, let him understand:). (Matthew 24:15)

The Abomination of Desolation is a prophesied event that will precede the coming of the Lord and the gathering together of His elect.

> For then shall be great tribulation, such as was not since the beginning of the world to this time, no, nor ever shall be. (Matthew 24:21)

The Great Tribulation is a prophesied event that will precede the coming of the Lord and the Rapture.

> Immediately after the tribulation of those days shall the sun be darkened, and the moon shall not give her light, and the stars shall fall from heaven, and the powers of the heavens shall be shaken. (Matthew 24:29)

Cosmic disturbances are a prophesied event that will take place prior to the coming of the Lord and the Rapture.

Of considerable relevance to our discussion of imminence is the timing of these cosmic disturbances. Joel 2:31 says, "The sun shall be turned into darkness, and the moon into blood, before the great and the terrible day of the Lord come." These cosmic disturbances take place before the Day of the Lord. Pretribulationists teach the entire seven years of the tribulation period are the Day of the Lord. Therefore, these cosmic disturbances would have to take place before the tribulation period, which would be a prophesied event that precedes the Rapture of the Church. Furthermore, we know these cosmic disturbances cannot take place prior to a tribulation period because they are associated with the opening of the sixth seal. Revelation 6:12-13 says, "And I beheld when he had opened the sixth seal, and lo, there was a great earthquake; and the sun became black as sackcloth of hair, and the moon became as blood; And the stars of heaven fell unto the earth." This is a description of cosmic disturbances which take place with the opening of the sixth seal. Even pretribulationists teach the sixth seal is opened during the tribulation period.

> Now we beseech you, brethren, by the coming of our Lord Jesus Christ, and by our gathering together unto him, That ye be not soon shaken in mind, or be troubled, neither by spirit, nor by word, nor by letter as from us, as that the day of Christ is at hand. Let no man deceive you by any means: for that day shall not come, except there come a falling away first, and that man of sin be revealed, the son of perdition; Who opposeth and exalteth himself above all that is called God, or that is worshipped; so that he as God sitteth in the temple of God, showing himself that he is God. (2 Thessalonians 2:1-4)

These scriptures tell us the gathering together will not occur until *after* two events have taken place – a falling away, or apostasy, and the revealing of the Antichrist. Pretribulationists say the gathering together of the saints mentioned in these scriptures is not the Rapture of the Church, but rather the gathering together of the Raptured saints already in heaven, who join Christ as His army at the battle of Armageddon. They say these saints were raptured at the beginning of a seven-year tribulation period, and have been in heaven with the Lord since that time. Do not be misled; there is only one gathering together of the saints, and it is the Rapture of the Church (Matthew 24:31; Mark 13:27). There is no biblical basis for using the term gathering together for any event other than the Rapture of the Church.

A more thoughtful analysis of these scriptures will lead us to conclude the gathering together described here is indeed the Rapture of the Church. Paul is addressing the Thessalonian church about *our* gathering together unto the Lord. Why would he be talking to them about *our* gathering together, the Christians who remain on earth, if this scripture is referring to those who would have already been caught up in a pretribulation raptured and would be in heaven? In verses 2 and 3 he says, "That ye be not shaken in mind, or be troubled, neither by spirit, nor by word, nor by letter as from us, as that the day of Christ is at hand. Let no man deceive you by any means." Apparently, the Thessalonian church had heard a false prophecy, an erroneous teaching, or read a letter purporting to be from Paul, that the Rapture had already taken place. This epistle was an encouragement to the Thessalonian church they had not missed the Rapture. Why would Paul encourage them not to be disturbed or frightened that the day of Christ, the Rapture, had already taken place, if this event had already taken place?

Many Christians believe the great apostasy, or defection from the truth, described in these scriptures has already taken place. Some have said the falling away began immediately after biblical times, and has continued to this day, while others believe it occurred during the Dark Ages. However, this scripture refers to a very specific falling away – *the* falling away – one that will take place at a very specific time in the future. This apostasy is described within the context of end times' events: the revealing of the Antichrist, the Abomination of Desolation, and the second coming of Jesus Christ. More specifically, it will take place during the Great Tribulation, when the Church will come under tremendous persecution from the Antichrist. In an obvious end times' passage, Joel 3:14 says, "Multitudes, multitudes in the valley of decision: for the Day of the Lord is near in the valley of decision." Multitudes will be required to make their decision to serve the Lord, or worship the Antichrist, as the Day of the Lord draws near. The Day of the Lord follows the Great Tribulation. During the Great Tribulation, Christians will be given the choice to worship the Antichrist or to confess their faith in Jesus Christ.

In *The Book of the Revelation,* William R. Newell writes,

> The falling away is, I am perfectly convinced, described in II Thessalonians 2 and Revelation 13. It is the whole world falling clear away from God to worship the Devil, -all except the elect, who were written in the Book of Life from the foundation of the world...There is coming an awful apostasy, a falling away of the human race to the god of this age. They shall worship the dragon because he will give his power to the wild-beast-Satan's burlesque of the resurrection. There is the reversal of everything that is divine. Satan has the place of God, and the Beast is Satan's Christ; and the False Prophet becomes an awful parody of the Holy Spirit. Now that is coming! And that, I think, is what God means by the apostasy.[56]

According to 2 Thessalonians 2:1-4, a second event that must take place before the Rapture is the revealing (disclosure, the removal of cover) of the man of sin – the Antichrist. These verses say this event must take place before the Rapture of the Church. This presents a dilemma for pretribulationists. If they agree with 2 Thessalonians 2:1-4, that the revealing of the Antichrist will precede the Rapture, then immanency is lost. If they suggest there is a gap of time between the revealing of the Antichrist and the beginning of the tribulation period, they are contradicting the clear meaning of these scriptures.

Has the Antichrist been revealed or disclosed? Has a charismatic world leader confirmed a covenant between Israel and its enemies, entered a rebuilt Jewish temple, and declared he is God on earth? Obviously, these events have not taken place. Therefore, Jesus Christ will not return for His Church until this event has taken place, and the teaching of an imminent return of the Lord is once again invalidated.

Some have said the Antichrist will be revealed when he confirms the Covenant at the beginning of the Seventieth Week of Daniel. That is not

---

[56] William R. Newell, *The Book of the Revelation* (Chicago, 1935) p. 388.

when he will be revealed. That is the time when he appears on the world scene as a powerful and charismatic leader who is able to keep Israel and its enemies from annihilating one another. When the Covenant is signed, many in the Church will certainly know he is the Antichrist through their understanding of Biblical prophecy, and a witness of the Spirit. Israel will not know he is the Antichrist, nor will the world, nor will many in the Church. If Israel knew he was the Antichrist, why would they sign a covenant with the Devil, "a covenant with death?" (Isaiah 28:15, 18) If the world knew this man was making a covenant he intended to break three and a half years later, thereby shattering the peace they had worked so hard to attain, would they allow him to negotiate the peace treaty in the first place? Not only will Israel and the world not know they are signing a covenant with the Devil, they will proclaim that he is a messiah.

Has the man of sin, the son of perdition, been revealed? Has his cover been taken off, and has his identity been disclosed? Clearly not. Therefore, Jesus Christ cannot return for His Church. Verse 4 tells us how the Antichrist will be revealed. It describes the Antichrist as the one, "Who opposeth and exalteth himself above all that is called God, or that is worshipped; so that he as God sitteth in the temple of God, showing himself that he is God." The Antichrist will be revealed to Israel, and to the world, when he commits the Abomination of Desolation. The Antichrist is literally and physically revealed when he sits down in the Jewish temple in Jerusalem and declares he is God on earth. This is the Abomination of Desolation, and this is the event that begins the Great Tribulation.

Why is the Timing of the Rapture Such a Controversial Subject?

The Rapture is one of the most controversial subjects in the Christian community today. A discussion of the Rapture will undoubtedly cause more emotional response than most any other biblical topic. However, this controversy is not normally about whether there will be a Rapture, or about the events of the Rapture. The controversy is almost always centered on the timing of the Rapture. Why is there such heated and sometimes bitter debate over the timing of the Rapture, when discussions covering other aspects of the Rapture, as well as most other end times' events, are either relatively ignored, or elicit little, if any, emotional response? Many Christians believe God would never allow them to suffer the trials and tribulations that will take place during the End Times. Some Christians superimpose this belief on the word of God concerning the timing of the Rapture. Our belief in the timing of the Rapture determines whether or not we will suffer total disruption of our lives, intense persecution, and possible martyrdom. This is why the timing of the Rapture is so intensely debated within the Church. It has more to do with personal well-being, aversion to pain, and a desire for physical self-preservation, than what the Bible actually says. Again, let us hope and pray Christians will cease to think more of their own well-being than the integrity of the word of God.

The thought of entering the Great Tribulation, and to suffer pain, persecution, and possible martyrdom, is not acceptable to many in the Church. Yet, all of the apostles, except one, were martyred. Thousands of Christians are killed every year for their faith. In fact, many believe the persecution of Christians today is greater than at any time in the history of the Church. This may not be so in the United States, but it is in many other countries of the world where Christians are under intense persecution for their faith. Revelation 20:4 describes Christians who, "were beheaded for the witness of Jesus." If God has allowed Christians to suffer persecution in the past, who can say God will not allow us to suffer affliction, persecution, or even martyrdom while the Devil is pouring out his wrath prior to Jesus Christ's second coming? Why would God exempt the last generation of Christians from persecution when the previous generations were not exempt? 2 Timothy 3:12 says, "Yea, and all that will live godly in Christ Jesus shall suffer persecution." In 1 Peter 4:12-13, Peter tells the church not to be surprised concerning the fiery trials that will try them, but to rejoice that they are partakers of Christ's sufferings.[57]

---

[57] Wood, *Six Days to the Rapture,* Tape 8.

Why Pretribulationism Now?

There is a very important question that must be answered at this point in our study. Why would the teaching of a pretribulation rapture emerge in the Church during the early nineteenth century? Why would this doctrine appear when, for over eighteen hundred years, the concept of the Church being raptured before entering a time of severe testing was relatively unknown in the Church?

The Lord will Rapture His Church. This is clearly what the Bible teaches in hundreds of passages, and this is what the vast majority of the Church believes. No matter what Satan does, he cannot prevent the Rapture from taking place. However, he can deceive many in the Church into believing they will be raptured before the trials and testing of the Seventieth Week of Daniel, thus rendering them less than fully prepared for the momentous events of that time.

During the days of the early church, belief in a pretribulation rapture would not have carried the same grave consequences that it does today, if we believe the return of the Lord is very near. Jesus Christ could not return during the early days of the church because all that the prophets had prophesied concerning the second coming of the Lord had not come to pass (Acts 3:20, 21). However, the timing of the Rapture matters very much to the modern Church because it appears the Lord's return is very near. These are the days when the Seventieth Week of Daniel could begin because there are no prophesied events that remain to be fulfilled before the Covenant could be signed, and the last seven years would begin.

The relatively sudden appearance, and almost universal acceptance, of the teaching of pretribulationism coincides with one very important event. That very important event is the second coming of the Lord, and the Rapture of His Church. Therefore, the apparent reason the teaching of a pretribulation rapture has surfaced in recent times is because the return of the Lord to Rapture His Church is very near, and Satan is attempting to deceive the Church into believing it will not have to endure the events of the Great Tribulation, thus rendering the Church less than fully prepared.

Perils of Pretribulationism

There were teachers during the time of Paul's ministry who troubled the church with false doctrines in an attempt to deceive it regarding the return of the Lord (2 Thessalonians 2:1-3; 2 Timothy 2:16-18). Similarly, there are teachers in the modern Church bringing in damnable heresies (2 Peter 2:1, 2). Paul said in 1 Timothy 4:1, "Now the Spirit speaketh expressly, that in the latter times some shall depart from the faith, giving heed to seducing spirits, and doctrines of devils." These are the latter times, and there are seducing spirits and doctrines of devils in the Church. These seducing spirits and doctrines of devils are causing some to depart from the faith, and will cause even more to depart from the faith in the future. When in the future will even more depart from the faith? During the End Times, the Seventieth Week of Daniel! This will be the time of the great apostasy Paul spoke of in 2 Thessalonians 2:3.

Pretribulationism is being taught in the vast majority of churches today. Therefore, the vast majority of the Church is looking for an imminent return of the Lord. They are being taught this imminent return of the Lord will take place before the last seven years begin, and they will be spared any of the trials and testing of the tribulation period, which includes the Great Tribulation. Satan knows his time is running out. He knows there will be a time when he will be able to pour out his wrath. His goal is to seduce the Church into believing a lie concerning the possibility of entering a time of great trial and testing. He is doing all he can to soften and lull the faithful into believing they will not have to fight. Satan must be overjoyed that they are not expecting a fight. The Church is being set up for a major fall. Many will not only be deceived by Satan, but will be deluded by God Himself. For those who enter the Great Tribulation and are deceived by Satan's signs and lying wonders, and choose not to believe the truth, God will, "send them strong delusion, that they should believe a lie" (2 Thessalonians 2:11).

Pretribulationists contend that no harm can come from their teaching, even if the Church is not raptured before the beginning of the tribulation period. They say pretribulationism is first and foremost a call to lead a godly life, and to be prepared for the Lord's return at any moment. Pretribulationists say if they find they are wrong about the timing of the Rapture they will simply admit their error and do their best to endure this period. It is their belief the Church will in no way be harmed if their teaching of a pretribulation rapture is proven false. Unfortunately, this assumption is naïve at best, and potentially lethal at its worst.

> But shun profane and vain babblings: for they will increase unto more ungodliness. And their word will eat as doth a canker: of whom is Hymenaeus and Philetus; Who concerning the truth have erred, saying that the resurrection is past already; and overthrow the faith of some. (2 Timothy 2:16-18)

2 Timothy is very explicit in saying profane (wicked) and vain babblings (fruitless discussions) regarding the Rapture will subvert the faith of some. The doctrine of a pretribulation rapture will be a contributing factor in the great apostasy of the Church. The great apostasy will take place when a totally surprised and unprepared Church enters the Seventieth Week of Daniel and experiences the trials and testing of the Great Tribulation. Those who are teaching a pretribulation rapture should prayerfully consider 2 Timothy 2:16-18.

Rosenthal warns:

> The church will enter the Seventieth Week of Daniel to encounter the difficulties of that period and the Antichrist himself. If it does, having been taught and convinced of an imminent pretribulation rapture, the consequences will be calamitous. The church will enter that period unprepared, spiritually naked, vulnerable, and ripe for the Antichrist's deception. The psychological implications will be disastrous. A questioning of the trustworthiness of the Word of God will naturally follow. It will be a spiritual catastrophe—a *Pearl Harbor* of incalculable proportions—a satanically planned sneak attack.

> Some will attempt to counter this charge by suggesting that the church is called upon to live holy and righteously at all times, and that, therefore, she should be prepared for any eventuality—even entering the Seventieth Week of Daniel, if that should occur. Such arguments are idealistic but not realistic. It is impossible to effectively train an army for a major battle if the soldiers are told they will never have to participate. Reservists who see little likelihood that they will ever see combat will never prepare like those knowing they may soon be sent to the front lines.[58]

Van Kampen similarly cautions,

> The church that enters the last days will undergo intense persecution that largely could be avoided if it had possessed correct understanding of those days. Scripture teaches that the church of the last days will, in general, be a compromised, confused church, and that much of its afflictions will come because of improper teaching.[59]

> And then shall that Wicked be revealed, whom the Lord shall consume with the spirit of his mouth, and shall destroy with the brightness of his coming: Even him, whose coming is after the working of Satan with all power and signs and lying wonders, And with all deceivableness of unrighteousness in them that perish; because they received not the love of the truth, that they might be saved. And for this cause God shall send them strong delusion, that they should believe a lie: That they all might be damned who believed not the truth, but had pleasure in unrighteousness. (2 Thessalonians 2:8-12)

[58] Rosenthal, *The Pre-Wrath Rapture of the Church*, pp. 281-282.

[59] Van Kampen, *The Sign*, p. 2.

There is great peril for those who have not totally given their lives to Jesus Christ and enter the Seventieth Week of Daniel unprepared. The wicked one, whose is empowered by Satan, and will be revealed after the restrainer, Michael the archangel, is taken out of the way, is the Antichrist. He will come, "with all power and signs and lying wonders." This will be a time of tremendous deception, great distress, and intense persecution. Those who enter Daniel's seventieth week will be under extreme pressure to bow down and worship the image of the Beast, or be killed. Not only will they be confronted with the power of Satan and his signs and lying wonders, but if they do not turn their hearts totally to the Lord they will be deluded by God himself to believe the lies of Satan, because they chose not to believe the truth of the gospel.

How important is a study of the End Times, the Seventieth Week of Daniel? If one holds to the doctrine of a pretribulation rapture, the importance is diminished, since the Church will be exempt from the last seven years and the work of the Devil during the Great Tribulation. However, if we believe the faithful will endure the persecution of the Antichrist during the Great Tribulation, and then rescued at the coming of the Lord prior to the Day of the Lord's wrath, then a study of the End Times is of tremendous importance. If the Church will endure suffering and persecution greater than any that has ever taken place, or ever will take place, then we need to be prepared in every way: mentally, physically and spiritually. If we are informed and prepared for the events of the End Times we will not be taken by surprise when these significant events take place.

Rosenthal further warns of the perils facing those who subscribe to the theory of a pretribulation rapture.

> Pretribulation rapturism provides a false hope, however sincerely proclaimed—an escape before the seventieth week begins. Like sugared water, it may taste good, but it has no medicinal value. Even worse, it will keep the church from what can truly help—the urgent admonition to watchfulness (Matt. 24:42-44; 25:13), faithfulness (Matt. 24:45-47), preparedness (Matt. 25:1-13), and fruitfulness

> (Matt. 25:14-30). This generation of believers could find itself inside the seventieth week, there to have occasion to resist the Antichrist and stand true to the King of Glory.[60]

From biblical times until the early nineteenth century, the church was clearly unified in its belief they would enter a time of severe testing – the Great Tribulation. The Antichrist would assault the church, followed by their deliverance at the Rapture – with the coming of Jesus Christ.

Let us look at what has been written through the ages regarding Christians and the events of the End Times. The following quotations were taken from Dave MacPherson's, *The Great Rapture Hoax*.

Tertullian, a church theologian, in the second century, said, "The souls of the martyrs are taught to wait [Rev. 6]… that the beast Antichrist with his false prophet may wage war on the church of God."

Augustine, author of *Confessions* and *City of God*, in the fourth century, said, "But he who reads this passage [Daniel 12], even half a sleep, cannot fail to see that the kingdom of Antichrist shall fiercely, though for a short time, assail the Church."

Martin Luther, the fifteenth century leader of the German Reformation, said, "[The book of Revelation] is intended as a revelation of things that are to happen in the future, and especially of tribulations and disasters for the Church."

John Knox, a sixteenth century Scottish proponent of the Reformation, said "… the great love of God towards his church, whom he pleased to forewarne of dangers to come, so many yeers before they come to passé… to wit, The man of sin, The Antichrist, The Whore of Babilon."

George Mueller, in the nineteenth century, said, "The Scripture declares plainly that the Lord Jesus will *not* come until the Apostacy shall have taken place, and the man of sin…shall have been revealed."[61]

---

[60] Rosenthal, The Pre-Wrath Rapture of the Church, p. 296.

[61] MacPherson, *The Great Rapture Hoax*, pp. 17-30.

The preceding quotes clearly indicate the early church understood the Antichrist would assail them during the Great Tribulation, followed by the return of the Lord.

Walvoord, a pretribulationist, said, "The fact is that neither posttribulationism nor pretribulationism is an explicit teaching of the Scriptures. The Bible does not, in so many words, state either."[62] This is a rather disturbing statement, considering the fact that those attempting to support a particular biblical teaching normally aspire to an, "explicit teaching of the Scriptures." The scriptures are very explicit concerning the Rapture and the events of the Seventieth Week of Daniel. It should be apparent from this discussion pretribulationism is not an explicit teaching of the scriptures. In fact, the doctrine of a pretribulation rapture has no biblical foundation whatsoever.

Walvoord goes on to say, "It is therefore not too much to say that the Rapture question is determined more by ecclesiology [study of the church] than eschatology [study of the last days]."[63] Should the timing of the Rapture be decided after we have thoroughly examined the historical teachings of the church (ecclesiology), or after a thorough study of the prophecies of the Bible regarding the End Times (eschatology)? Do we put our confidence in the opinions of men, or in the inspired, infallible word of God?

In conclusion, there is only one Rapture, there is only one first resurrection, and it is called the resurrection of the just. At the Rapture, everyone who died in faith is resurrected; there will not be one believer left in the grave. Then every believer who is alive and remains is caught up to be with the Lord in the air. Those who are caught up in the first resurrection will spend eternity with the Lord. At the end of the thousand year reign of Jesus Christ, the dead are brought before the Great White Throne judgment. This is the second resurrection, the resurrection of the unjust. The unjust are judged and their names are not found in the book of life. Their works are judged and their final punishment, the lake of fire, is determined.

---

[62] Walvoord, *The Rapture Question*, p. 148.

[63] Ibid., p. 16.

CHAPTER 4

THE DAY OF THE LORD

> Howl ye; for the day of the LORD *is* at hand; it shall come as a destruction from the Almighty. Behold, the day of the LORD cometh, cruel both with wrath and fierce anger, to lay the land desolate: and he shall destroy the sinners thereof out of it. For the stars of heaven and the constellations thereof shall not give their light: the sun shall be darkened in his going forth, and the moon shall not cause her light to shine. And I will punish the world for *their* evil, and the wicked for their iniquity; and I will cause the arrogancy of the proud to cease, and will lay low the haughtiness of the terrible. (Isaiah 13:6, 9-11)

The Lord is a righteous and just God. He is also patient and longsuffering. However, there will come a day when God will say enough – enough of the selfishness and the murders and the rebellion. He will have endured the ungodliness of unrighteous mankind long enough. There will come a day when the unrepentant will reap what they have sown. God will finally pour out His holy and righteous indignation upon a world that has gone mad (Jeremiah 51:7). He will take vengeance on those who have profaned His name and have not obeyed the gospel of Jesus Christ. He will pour out his wrath on those who have made the conscious decision to bow down and worship the Antichrist and his image, and take his mark. There will be a day when God will execute His judgment upon the ungodly in righteousness. This future day the Bible calls the Day of the Lord. The

Day of the Lord initiates the judgment of the wicked by God Almighty. The ungodly will be judged, and their fate will be the lake of fire.

The possible end times' scenario continues.

As the Great Tribulation comes to an end, there will be a great earthquake, the sun will be darkened, and the moon will become as blood. The stars of heaven will fall to the earth, and every mountain and island will be moved out of their place. Not one inhabitant on the face of the earth - Christian, Jew, or unbeliever - will miss the fact that God is at work in these cosmic disturbances, and that He is about to pour out His wrath upon the earth. Unbelievers will react to these awe-inspiring events by hiding in the dens and in the rocks of the mountains.

As these cosmic disturbances come to an end, but before the wrath of God is poured out on unbelievers, the Lord will descend with a shout, with the voice of the archangel, and with the trumpet of God. The entire world will see Jesus Christ come in the clouds. The dead in Christ, those who died in faith, will be raised, and will put on their incorruptible bodies. Those believers that are alive and remain will also be changed into their incorruptible, immortal, bodies. Then those believers who are alive and remain will be caught up into the clouds, with the dead in Christ, to meet the Lord in the air, and we will forever be with the Lord.

Immediately following the Rapture of the Church, as those who are left behind are contemplating the significance of the Rapture, an angel will sound a trumpet, and hail and fire mingled with blood will be cast upon the earth. One third of all the trees and all green grass will be destroyed by fire. This is the beginning of the Day of the Lord's wrath. This is the beginning of the great and the terrible Day of the Lord.

The Bible needs to be interpreted literally, and whenever possible, sequentially. This need for a literal and sequential interpretation of the Bible is nowhere more important than in the book of Revelation. The book introduced in Revelation chapter 5, which is sealed with the *seven seals,* cannot be opened until the time of the end. This book can only be opened by Jesus Christ. In Revelation 6:1, Jesus Christ opens the first seal of this book. The opening of the first seal initiates the time of the end, the second half of the Seventieth Week of Daniel (Daniel 12:5-9). The Abomination of Desolation and the events of the Great Tribulation take place as the first five seals are removed. When the sixth seal is opened, cosmic disturbances take place; the earth is ravaged by a great earthquake, and men recognize that the great day of the Lord's wrath is about to take place. Before the Day of the Lord begins, the 144,000 Jews are sealed, and the Church is raptured.

The Seventh Seal: The Plagues of the Trumpets and Vials

> And when he had opened the seventh seal, there was silence in heaven about the space of half an hour. And I saw the seven angels which stood before God; and to them were given seven trumpets. (Revelation 8:1-2)

When the seventh seal on the book is removed, seven angels are given *seven trumpets*. After the seventh seal is opened, but before the seven trumpets are blown, there is one-half hour of silence in heaven. This half hour of silence is observed in anticipation of the awesome events that will take place during the Day of the Lord. As the seven trumpets are blown, the events of the Day of the Lord, the Indignation or wrath of God, will take place. This is the undiluted, full strength, wrath of God – what the unbeliever will experience. These are the most frightening and devastating events ever recorded in the Bible. As the first angel sounds his trumpet, "there followed hail and fire mingled with blood, and they were cast upon the earth: and the third part of trees was burnt up, and all green grass was burnt up" (Revelation 8:7). As the second through sixth angels sound their trumpets similarly horrifying events will take place.

"But in the days of the voice of the seventh angel, when he shall begin to sound, the mystery of God should be finished, as he hath declared to his servants the prophets" (Revelation 10:7). When the seventh angel sounds his seventh trumpet, the mystery of God will be finished. Following the sound of the seventh trumpet, the apostle John, "saw another sign in heaven, great and marvelous, seven angels having the seven last plagues; for in them is filled up the wrath of God" (Revelation 15:1). These seven last plagues are contained in *seven vials.* When the first angel pours out his vial upon the earth, "there fell a noisome and grievous sore upon the men which had the mark of the Beast, and upon them which worshipped his image" (Revelation 16:2). As the second through sixth angels pour out their vials similar horrifying plagues are poured out upon the earth. With the pouring out of the seventh vial, "there came a great voice out of the temple of heaven, from the throne, saying, It is done" (Revelation 16:17).

To summarize, the opening of the *seven seals,* is followed by the blowing of the *seven trumpets,* which is followed by the pouring out of the *seven vials*, and then the end will come.

> And the times of this ignorance God winked at; but now commandeth all men every where to repent: Because he hath appointed a day, in the which he will judge the world in righteousness by that man whom he hath ordained; whereof he hath given assurance unto all men, in that he hath raised him from the dead. (Acts 17:30-31)

The Day of the Lord is mentioned in hundreds of passages and is one of the most important topics in the Bible. To gain a thorough understanding of the events of the End Times the Day of the Lord must be understood.

The Day of the Lord is referred to in a number of ways in the Bible. It is called, "The Day of the Lord's vengeance" (Isaiah 34:8), "The Day of the Lord God of hosts" (Jeremiah 46:10), "The Day of the Lord" (Ezekiel 30:3), "The great and the terrible day of the Lord" (Joel 2:31), "The great day of the Lord" (Zephaniah 1:14), "The great and dreadful day of the Lord" (Malachi 4:5), and "That great and notable day of the Lord" (Acts 2:20).

The events of the Day of the Lord will be like none that have ever occurred. An account of the Day of the Lord includes some of the most awesome events found anywhere in the Bible. The events associated with the judgment of the ungodly during the Day of the Lord are almost too incredible to comprehend. During this day a great star will fall from heaven on the waters of the earth making them bitter, and many men die from the water. Locusts with tails like scorpions will torment men for five months with the sting in their tails. Horses will spew fire, smoke, and brimstone out of their mouths killing a third of the inhabitants of the earth. An angel will pour out his vial on the earth, and men will be tormented with noisome and grievous sores. An angel will pour out his vial on the sun, and men will be scorched with fire and great heat. In no other place in the Bible are such extraordinary and such awe-inspiring events described. These unparalleled events are what the unbeliever can anticipate.

The Day of The Lord

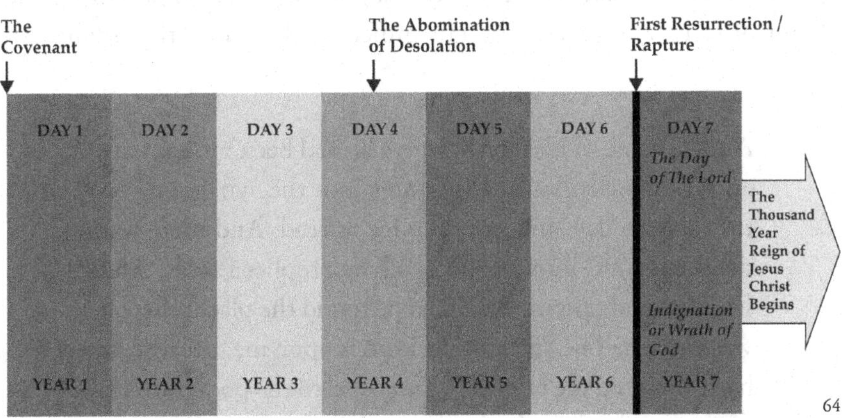

[64]

What is the Day of the Lord? First, it is a very specific period of time. God has established a pattern of reserving the seventh part for Himself, which is referred to as the Lord's Day. The Day of the Lord will be the seventh part of the last seven years of earth's history, as we know it. The Day of the Lord will be the last year of the final seven years that are the Seventieth Week of Daniel.

Secondly, it will be a series of events. The Great Tribulation will end with the opening of the sixth seal. Under the sixth seal cosmic disturbances will

[64] Wood, *Six Days to the Rapture*, Page 42.

take place. Men will look up and recognize the great day of God's wrath is coming. Before God's wrath is poured out the 144,000 Jews will be sealed, and the Church will be raptured. Immediately after the Rapture of the Church, the seventh seal will be opened, and the Day of the Lord will commence. The plagues of the trumpets and vials will take place during the Day of the Lord, which are the wrath of God. It is this outpouring of God's Indignation – the plagues of the seventh seal – which are the events of the Day of the Lord.

The Day of the Lord is more than just the period of time when the Indignation of God is poured out. As the name implies, it is literally the Day of the Lord Jesus Christ. It is the day when Jesus Christ returns to Rapture His Church; it is the day when He pours out his wrath on the unbeliever for a period of one year; it is the day when He comes on a white horse to slay the wicked; and it is the day when He sets His feet on the Mount of Olives and ushers in His millennial kingdom that shall have no end.

> And he came to Nazareth, where he had been brought up: and, as his custom was, he went into the synagogue on the sabbath day, and stood up for to read. And there was delivered unto him the book of the prophet Esaias. And when he had opened the book, he found the place where it was written, The Spirit of the Lord is upon me, because he hath anointed me to preach the gospel to the poor; he hath sent me to heal the brokenhearted, to preach deliverance to the captives, and recovering of sight to the blind, to set at liberty them that are bruised, To preach the acceptable year of the Lord. (Luke 4:16-19)

In His first coming, Jesus Christ came to preach the gospel and to bring salvation to those who would hear the word of the Lord. In John 12:47, Jesus said He came not to judge the world, but to save the world. In Luke 4:18-19, Jesus is reading from Isaiah 61:1-2. However, He chose to read verse 1 and only part of verse 2 of Isaiah chapter 61. Why did Jesus choose to omit reading the remainder of verse 2?

> The spirit of the Lord GOD is upon me; because the LORD hath anointed me to preach good tidings unto the meek; he hath sent me to bind up the brokenhearted, to proclaim liberty to the captives, and the opening of the prison to them that are bound; To proclaim the acceptable year of the LORD, and the day of vengeance of our God; to comfort all that mourn. (Isaiah 61:1-2)

Verse 2 continues with, "and the day of vengeance of our God." The day of vengeance is the Day of the Lord, the day of His wrath. It appears Jesus chose to read only the first portion of Isaiah 61:2 because the purpose of His first coming was not to judge the world, but to preach the gospel and to bring salvation. Therefore, there is yet a day when Jesus Christ will come, not to save the world, but to judge the world. This will be the Day of the Lord.

> Dearly beloved, avenge not yourselves, but rather give place unto wrath: for it is written, Vengeance is mine; I will repay, saith the Lord. (Romans 12:19)

Christians view Romans 12:19 as an admonition to refrain from taking revenge when they have been unjustly abused – and well they should. However, this scripture has significant end times' implications. The Lord is instructing Christians not to retaliate, take revenge, or vindicate themselves when they are ill-treated. Instead, they are instructed to allow the Lord the opportunity to punish evil men. The Lord will take vengeance on our adversaries when He pours out His wrath upon them for their ungodly actions. The Lord said vindication, or retribution, is His. He will recompense them for their evil. The Lord has a very specific time when He will take vengeance on the ungodly; it is the Day of the Lord.

Who will experience the vengeance of the Day of the Lord?

> For the Day of the Lord of hosts shall be upon every one that is proud and lofty, and upon every one that is lifted up; and he shall be brought low. (Isaiah 2:12)

The arrogant and haughty will be subject to the Day of the Lord. The Day of the Lord is appointed to the wicked who exalt themselves above God.

> I will also stretch out mine hand upon Judah, and upon all the inhabitants of Jerusalem...Hold thy peace at the presence of the Lord GOD: for the Day of the Lord is at hand: for the LORD hath prepared a sacrifice, he hath bid his guests. (Zephaniah 1:4a, 7)

The Day of the Lord is the culmination of God's dealings with Israel for their sins. Therefore, the nation of Israel will experience the Day of the Lord, and then be saved when they call on His name at the end of this one year period. (Zechariah 13:8-9; Malachi 3:2-3, 4:1)

The Lord is a just and a righteous God. He is also very exacting. The Jews are God's chosen people, and He has a just and righteous claim to them; they are His heritage. Isaiah 34:8 reveals much about the nature of God. This important scripture gives us tremendous insight into God's unique relationship with Israel, and the significance of the Day of the Lord.

> For it is the Day of the Lord's vengeance, and the year of recompenses for the controversy of Zion. (Isaiah 34:8)

This "Day" is the Day of the Lord – the last year of the seven years of the Seventieth Week of Daniel. This will be the year of the Lord's vengeance or revenge, during which He will pour out his wrath on the wicked. It will be the year of retribution - the time of dispensing punishment - for those who rebelled against God. More specifically, it will be the day when God punishes those who have unjustly persecuted His people, Israel. During the Day of the Lord, He will recover His claim or title to the nation of Israel because they are his heritage, His inheritance. It is amazing to consider the depth of the wisdom and the knowledge of God that is contained in this one passage.

The Church, unlike Israel and the rest of the world, will *not* be subjected to the wrath of God during the Day of the Lord. We will have been raptured just prior to the beginning of the Day of the Lord.

Pretribulationists have made perhaps their greatest mistake in assuming the entire Seventieth Week of Daniel is the Day of the Lord, which they call the tribulation period. Pretribulationists say the entire tribulation period is the Day of the Lord - the time of His wrath - and the Rapture will take place before the Day of the Lord, because Christians are not appointed to wrath (1 Thessalonians 5:9). They are partly correct; the Rapture will take place before the Day of the Lord, and Christians will not suffer His wrath. However, the Day of the Lord will not begin until the seventh year of the Seventieth Week of Daniel, and the entire seven years of the Seventieth Week of Daniel are not the Day of the Lord. This incorrect assumption has become the foundation upon which all other pretribulation doctrine must stand.

The Great Tribulation will take place during the Seventieth Week of Daniel, but it is not God's wrath, it is the Devil's wrath.[65] The Devil will be cast out of heaven, and will come down to earth having great wrath, because he knows he has only a short time in which to attempt to destroy the nation of Israel (Revelation 12:7-17). The Antichrist is an agent of the Devil. During the Great Tribulation, the Antichrist will conquer through satanic deception (white horse), will instigate devastating wars (red horse), which will cause horrific famine (black horse), which will result in the death of billions (pale horse). Under the fifth seal, the Antichrist will martyr many in the Church. These acts of the Antichrist during the Great Tribulation are not God's wrath. God is not responsible for the deception, war, famine, and death during the Great Tribulation. God will not deceive His own Church, nor is He responsible for the martyrdom of Christians. In scripture, God never takes responsibility for the events of the Great Tribulation.

In contrast, the Bible makes it very clear God is directly responsible for the plagues of the trumpets and vials during the Day of the Lord. These are the wrath of God Almighty (Isaiah 13:6, 11). The plagues of the trumpets and vials are the events that will take place during the wrath of God. These

[65] Some have called the Great Tribulation the time of man's wrath against his fellow man. It certainly is a time when men will be responsible for brutal and barbaric attacks; however, the Devil will be the instigator and the one with the master plan for destroying Israel and persecuting the Church of God.

are the events of the great and the terrible day of the Lord (Joel 2:31), the great and dreadful day of the Lord (Malachi 4:5). This is what the unbeliever can anticipate. God said He alone will be exalted in the day of His wrath (Isaiah 2:11). The Great Tribulation is not part of the Day of the Lord, and the last seven years are not the Day of the Lord. The Great Tribulation is not the wrath of God, but the wrath of the Devil, and it will take place during the Seventieth Week of Daniel, and will precede the Day of the Lord. Therefore, the Church cannot be caught up in a pretribulation rapture, and once again, pretribulationism is invalidated.

God's purpose for many End Times prophecies is to send warnings. God is sending admonitions to those who refuse to repent – warnings of what is going to happen in the end – so that when unbelievers stand before God they cannot say they did not understand. These warnings also serve to notify those in the Church who have not totally given their lives to the Lord that they need to be cleansed and purified, or they will experience the wrath of God as well. Those who refuse to submit themselves to God, and reject serving Him, need to be made aware of their future. According to Ezekiel 33, we are watchmen. Christians are responsible for making mankind aware of the events to come – events that will greatly affect both the sinner and the saint.

The Indignation of God is probably the most frightening portion of the Bible because it is the unrestrained, undiluted, full strength, wrath of God. There will be great torment and destruction for those who are present during the Day of the Lord. However, those who are watching for the glorious appearing of our Lord Jesus Christ have nothing to fear.

The Seven Trumpets

> And when he had opened the seventh seal, there was silence in heaven about the space of half an hour. And I saw the seven angels which stood before God; and to them were given seven trumpets...And the seven angels which had the seven trumpets prepared themselves to sound. (Revelation 8:1-2, 6)

With the opening of the seventh seal, the seven angels standing before God will be given seven trumpets. In Revelation chapters 8 and 9, when the first six angels blow their trumpets, God will pour out His wrath on the earth. These trumpet judgments will be swift and terrible.

> And the angel which I saw stand upon the sea and upon the earth lifted up his hand to heaven, And sware by him that liveth for ever and ever, who created heaven, and the things that therein are, and the earth, and the things that therein are, and the sea, and the things which are therein, that there should be time no longer: But in the days of the voice of the seventh angel, when he shall begin to sound, the mystery of God should be finished, as he hath declared to his servants the prophets. (Revelation 10:5-7)

After the sixth angel has sounded his trumpet, but before the seventh angel blows his trumpet, a mighty angel will proclaim the world as we know it will come to an end. In the day when the seventh angel sounds his trumpet the mystery of God regarding the End Times will be accomplished.

The Seven Vials: The Seven Last Plagues

> And I saw another sign in heaven, great and marvellous, seven angels having the seven last plagues; for in them is filled up the wrath of God...And after that I looked, and, behold, the temple of the tabernacle of the testimony in heaven was opened: And the seven angels came out of the temple, having the seven plagues, clothed in pure and white linen, and having their breasts girded with golden girdles. And one of the four beasts gave unto the seven angels seven golden vials full of the wrath of God, who liveth for ever and ever. And the temple was filled with smoke from the glory of God, and from his power; and no man was able to enter into the temple, till the seven plagues of the seven angels were fulfilled. (Revelation 15:1, 5-8)

Seven angels in heaven will have the seven last plagues, which will be contained in seven golden vials. These are the final seven plagues, and in them the wrath of God is completed. When the seventh angel blows his trumpet, these final seven plagues, contained in the seven golden vials, are poured out, and the wrath of God is finished.

> And I heard a great voice out of the temple saying to the seven angels, Go your ways, and pour out the vials of the wrath of God upon the earth. And the first went, and poured out his vial upon the earth; and there fell a noisome and grievous sore upon the men which had the mark of the beast, and upon them which worshipped his image. (Revelation 16:1-2)

When the seventh angel sounds his trumpet, the first of seven golden vials will be poured upon the earth, and noisome (injurious, harmful) and grievous (hurtful, vicious) sores will fall upon those who have taken the mark of the Beast and worshipped his image. The events that accompany the pouring out of the second through sixth golden vials, which are described in Revelation 16:3-16, are just as devastating.

What will be the reaction of the unbelievers to this great devastation? Will they repent of their sins? Those who enter the Day of the Lord will be fully aware God is responsible for the events of the trumpets and vials (Revelation 6:15-17). Unfortunately, unbelievers do not repent of their sins, but instead curse God. In the midst of these terrible judgments, they will not fall on their faces before God and repent, they will shake their fists at God and blaspheme His name.

Under the sixth trumpet:

> And the rest of the men which were not killed by these plagues yet repented not of the works of their hands, that they should not worship devils, and idols of gold, and silver, and brass, and stone, and of wood: which neither can see, nor hear, nor walk: Neither repented they of their

> murders, nor of their sorceries, nor of their fornication, nor of their thefts. (Revelation 9:20-21)

Under the fourth vial:

> And men were scorched with great heat, and blasphemed the name of God, which hath power over these plagues: and they repented not to give him glory. (Revelation 16:9)

Under the fifth vial:

> And blasphemed the God of heaven because of their pains and their sores, and repented not of their deeds. (Revelation 16:11)

Under the seventh vial:

> And there fell upon men a great hail out of heaven, every stone about the weight of a talent: and men blasphemed God because of the plague of the hail; for the plague thereof was exceeding great. (Revelation 16:21)

Unbelievers, who will be on the earth during the Day of the Lord's wrath, will not repent of their sins. Their names are not written in the book of life, and their fate is the Great White Throne judgment – the second death – and the lake of fire.

> And the seventh angel poured out his vial into the air; and there came a great voice out of the temple of heaven, from the throne, saying, It is done. And there were voices, and thunders, and lightnings; and there was a great earthquake, such as was not since men were upon the earth, so mighty an earthquake, and so great. And the great city was divided into three parts, and the cities of the nations fell: and great Babylon came in remembrance before God, to give unto her the cup of the wine of the fierceness of his wrath. And every island fled away, and

> the mountains were not found. And there fell upon men a great hail out of heaven, every stone about the weight of a talent: and men blasphemed God because of the plague of the hail; for the plague thereof was exceeding great. (Revelation 16:17-21)

When the seventh angel pours out his vial into the air a great voice will come out of the temple in heaven saying, "it is done." There will be a massive earthquake, unlike any that has ever occurred. The shear magnitude of the earthquake will result in the destruction of every city on earth. The great city, Jerusalem (Revelation 11:8), will be divided into three parts.

Babylon, the great whore, is the false religion of the End Times, with whom the kings of the earth have committed spiritual fornication. This great whore has a golden cup full of abominations, and mankind is drunk with the wine of her spiritual fornications (Revelation 17:1-4). God in turn will give this great whore His cup. In His cup will be the, "wine of the fierceness of His wrath."

Every island will vanish into the depths of the sea and the mountains will crumble. Hailstones weighing approximately one hundred pounds will fall upon the earth, crushing anyone or anything they strike. It is important to mention this scene of complete devastation is not a fable. It will literally take place. With the pouring out of the seventh vial, the Day of the Lord is done; it is finished.

The following are the primary scriptures which describe the Day of the Lord.

A day that, "is great and very terrible" (Joel 2:11).

"A day of trouble and distress, a day of wasteness and desolation, a day of darkness and gloominess, a day of clouds and thick darkness" (Zephaniah 1:15).

A day that, "shall come as a destruction from the Almighty" (Isaiah 13:6),

A day, "the earth shall quake before them; the heavens shall tremble: the sun and the moon shall be dark, and the stars shall withdraw their shining" (Joel 2:10).

A day when God, "will shake the heavens, and the earth shall remove out of her place" (Isaiah 13:13).

A day when, "all the land shall be turned as a plain" (Zechariah 14:10).

A day when, "the fire hath devoured the pastures of the wilderness, and the flame hath burned all the trees of the field…the rivers of waters are dried up" (Joel 1:19-20).

A day when men, "shall go into the holes of the rocks, and into the caves of the earth, for fear of the Lord, and for the glory of his majesty, when he ariseth to shake terribly the earth" (Isaiah 2:19).

A day when, "every man's heart shall melt: And they shall be afraid: pangs and sorrows shall take hold of them" (Isaiah 13:7).

"A day of vengeance, that he may avenge him of his adversaries" (Jeremiah 46:10).

A day when God, "will punish the world for their evil, and the wicked for their iniquity" (Isaiah 13:11).

"A day of the trumpet and alarm" (Zephaniah 1:16).

A day when, "the Lord shall utter his voice before his army" (Joel 2:11).

A day when, "the Lord my God shall come, and all the saints with thee" (Zechariah 14:5).

A day when, "the Lord will smite all the people that have fought against Jerusalem; Their flesh shall consume away while they stand upon their feet, and their eyes shall consume away in their holes, and their tongue shall consume away in their mouth" (Zechariah 14:12).

A day when, "a great tumult from the Lord shall be among them; and they shall lay hold every one on the hand of his neighbour [brother], and his hand shall rise up against the hand of his neighbour" (Zechariah 14:13).

A day when the sinner's blood, "shall be poured out as dust, and their flesh as the dung" (Zephaniah 1:17),

A day when, "his feet shall stand in that day upon the mount of Olives" (Zechariah 14:4).

A day when, "the Lord alone shall be exalted" (Isaiah 2:17).

A day when, "the Lord shall be king over all the earth: in that day shall there be one Lord, and his name one" (Zechariah 14:9).

The Day of the Lord will be the culmination of God's dealings with Israel for their sin. In Daniel 9:24, the Lord said seventy weeks were determined upon the Jews. Daniel 12:7 says, at the end of the Day of the Lord, God will have succeeded in scattering the power of the holy people, Israel. God knows the strength of the Jews will need to be broken so they will accept Jesus Christ as their Messiah when He comes to rescue Israel at the end of the Seventieth Week of Daniel. Please continue to the next chapter, And So All Israel Shall Be Saved, for a discussion of the salvation of Israel.

CHAPTER 5

And So All Israel Shall Be Saved

> For I would not, brethren, that ye should be ignorant of this mystery, lest ye should be wise in your own conceits; that blindness in part is happened to Israel, until the fulness of the Gentiles be come in. And so all Israel shall be saved: as it is written, There shall come out of Sion the Deliverer, and shall turn away ungodliness from Jacob: For this is my covenant unto them, when I shall take away their sins. (Romans 11:25-27) (See also Romans 11:7-15; 2 Corinthians 3:13-16; Jeremiah 31:31-33; 39:27-29; Habakkuk 3:13; Zechariah 12:10)

Paul instructed the church at Rome not to be ignorant of a mystery of God. Spiritual blindness had come upon the nation of Israel. He said this blindness would continue until the full number of Gentiles who will be saved had been accomplished. These Gentiles are the wild olive branches that will be grafted into the natural olive tree, Israel (Romans 11:17-24). After the last Gentile comes into a saving relationship with Jesus Christ, then all Israel will be saved. They will be saved when Jesus Christ the Deliverer turns away wickedness from the nation of Israel. God said this is His covenant, or promise, with Israel – when He will take away their sins: "And so all Israel shall be saved." The mystery of Romans 11:25-27 is the salvation of the nation of Israel. There will come a day when the nation of Israel will turn to Jesus Christ as their Messiah, and they will be saved.

> Seventy weeks are determined upon thy people and upon thy holy city, to finish the transgression, and to make an end of sins, and to make reconciliation for iniquity, and to bring in everlasting righteousness, and to seal up the vision and prophecy, and to anoint the most Holy. (Daniel 9:24)

God determined seventy weeks of years upon Israel for their sins. Sixty-nine of these seventy weeks of years have already passed (Daniel 9:25). The Seventieth Week of Daniel, the last seven years, is suspended in time, waiting to be fulfilled. The Seventieth Week of Daniel is the time when God will finish his dealings with Israel. This means the *entire* seventy weeks are determined, including the seven years of Daniel's seventieth week. All Israel cannot be saved until the entire seventy weeks, including the seventieth week, have come to an end. Therefore, the nation of Israel will go through the final seven-year period, the Seventieth Week of Daniel. On the day Israel is saved, their transgressions will be finished, their sins will have come to an end, and their sins will have been atoned for, and Daniel 9:24 will have been fulfilled. That day, however, has not yet come.

The Great Tribulation is called Jacob's, or Israel's, trouble (Jeremiah 30:7). At the time of the Abomination of Desolation, those who are in Judaea, which includes Jerusalem, are told to flee into the mountains because, "then shall be great tribulation, such as was not since the beginning of the world to this time, no, nor ever shall be" (Matthew 24:21). Many Israelis will flee into the wilderness to a place provided by God where He will nourish and strengthen them for three and a half years (Revelation 12:6, 14). During the second half of the Seventieth Week of Daniel, the Beast will cause great suffering and distress for the Jews (Daniel 7:25).

> And they shall fall by the edge of the sword, and shall be led away captive into all nations: and Jerusalem shall

> be trodden down of the Gentiles, until the times of the Gentiles be fulfilled. (Luke 21:24)

> But the court which is without the temple leave out, and measure it not; for it is given unto the Gentiles: and the holy city shall they tread under foot forty and two months. (Revelation 11:2)

Jerusalem will be trampled by the Gentiles until their time is fulfilled, or completed. At the midpoint of the Seventieth Week of Daniel, when the Antichrist commits the Abomination of Desolation, a Gentile army under his direction will attack and occupy Jerusalem (Daniel 9:27). This occupation of the holy city, Jerusalem, by Gentile nations will continue, "until the times of the Gentiles be fulfilled." Revelation 11:2 says Gentiles will trample Jerusalem for forty-two months, or three and a half years. This three and a half year period is the second half of the seven years of Daniel's seventieth week.

Today, Israel is blind to the gospel. Their hearts are hardened and they are callous to the gospel message. God said Israel is, "stiffnecked and uncircumcised in heart and ears" (Acts 7:51a). Because of this spiritual condition they are not hearing or understanding the gospel. When will this blindness be removed? Israel will remain blind to the gospel until the full number of the Gentiles who are to be saved is complete. This moment – the "fulness of the Gentiles" – will occur at the Rapture. The last Gentile will be saved at the Rapture. Therefore, all Israel will be saved after the Rapture.

The Day of the Lord follows the Great Tribulation. Prior to the beginning of the Day of the Lord, during which God will pour out His wrath, the 144,000 Jews are sealed, or preserved by God (Revelation 7:1-8). These 144,000 Jews are the firstfruits, a beginning of sacrifice, of the multitude of Jews who will be saved (Revelation 14:1-5).

> But who may abide the day of his coming? and who shall stand when he appeareth? for he is like a refiner's fire, and like fullers' soap: And he shall sit as a refiner and

> purifier of silver: and he shall purify the sons of Levi, and purge them as gold and silver, that they may offer unto the LORD an offering in righteousness. (Malachi 3:2-3)

Before Israel is saved they will experience the events of the Day of the Lord. The Day of the Lord is a time of purifying for the nation of Israel prior to their acceptance of Jesus Christ as their Messiah. They will be refined by the Day of the Lord just as silver and gold are refined.

The Day of the Lord follows the Rapture. We know from Chapter 4 Israel will experience the events of the Day of the Lord. The Day of the Lord is the one year period of time during which God finishes his dealings with the nation of Israel for their sins. Therefore, all Israel cannot be saved until the end of the Day of the Lord. As the Day of the Lord comes to a close, the heavens will be opened, and Jesus Christ and his army of angels will come upon white horses to slay the wicked (Revelation 19:11-21).

Zechariah 12:10 says, "And I will pour upon the house of David, and upon the inhabitants of Jerusalem, the spirit of grace and of supplications: and they shall look upon me whom they have pierced, and they shall mourn for him, as one mourneth for his only son, and shall be in bitterness for him, as one that is in bitterness for his firstborn." Israel will accept Jesus Christ as their savior when they see the heavens opened and Jesus Christ coming on a white horse to slay the wicked. All Israel will be saved at the end of the Seventieth Week of Daniel, at the end of the Day of the Lord.

"There shall come out of Sion the Deliverer, and shall turn away ungodliness from Jacob: For this is my covenant unto them, when I shall take away their sins." Jesus Christ the Deliverer will come out of Zion and save the nation of Israel. The Bible clearly says when Jesus Christ comes He will stand upon the Mount of Olives (Zechariah 14:4). He will enter the rebuilt temple through the eastern gate, sit down upon His throne, and begin His glorious millennial reign (Ezekiel 43:1-5; Matthew 25:31).

How many Israelites will be saved at the end of the Seventieth Week of Daniel?

> And it shall come to pass in that day, *that* the remnant of Israel, and such as are escaped of the house of Jacob, shall no more again stay upon him that smote them; but shall stay upon the LORD, the Holy One of Israel, in truth. The remnant shall return, *even* the remnant of Jacob, unto the mighty God. For though thy people Israel be as the sand of the sea, *yet* a remnant of them shall return. (Isaiah 10:20-22)

A remnant of Israel will survive the Day of the Lord's wrath, and will no longer rely upon the Antichrist, with whom they signed the Covenant, but they will rely upon the Lord.

> And it shall come to pass, that in all the land, saith the LORD, two parts therein shall be cut off and die; but the third shall be left therein. And I will bring the third part through the fire, and will refine them as silver is refined, and will try them as gold is tried: they shall call on my name, and I will hear them: I will say, It is my people: and they shall say, The LORD is my God (Zechariah 13:8-9)

Two parts of Israel will be killed, but a third part will be left. The Lord will bring this third portion through the fire. The fire the Lord will bring them through will be the trying times of the Great Tribulation, after which they will be subjected to the Lord's wrath during the Day of the Lord. The remnant, the one third that will survive the Great Tribulation and the Day of the Lord, will accept Jesus Christ as their savior. God will use the Great Tribulation, and the Day of the Lord, to try and to purify the nation of Israel prior to their acceptance of Jesus Christ at the end of the Seventieth Week of Daniel.

At the end of the seventieth week, as the Lord is descending to the Mount of Olives, the Lord will say, "It is my people," and the nation of Israel will say, "The Lord is my God" (Zechariah 13:9). As the Lord is fighting against the nations of the world, Israel will look to the Lord, who they crucified, and will mourn for the Lord as one mourns for his only son (Zechariah 12:9-10). "So the house of Israel shall know that I am the Lord their God from that day and forward." (Ezekiel 39:22).

CHAPTER 6

The Battle of that Great Day of God Almighty, the Millennium, and the Final Battle

> And the sixth angel poured out his vial upon the great river Euphrates; and the water thereof was dried up, that the way of the kings of the east might be prepared. And I saw three unclean spirits like frogs come out of the mouth of the dragon, and out of the mouth of the beast, and out of the mouth of the false prophet. For they are the spirits of devils, working miracles, which go forth unto the kings of the earth and of the whole world, to gather them to the battle of that great day of God Almighty...And he gathered them together into a place called in the Hebrew tongue Armageddon. (Revelation 16:12-14, 16)

Sinful mankind never seems to get it right. In the warped recesses of their mind they think they can oppose God and still win. Of course, the Devil and his demons are always willing to help them conspire against God. This chapter will examine the two final battles of God – the Battle of that Great Day of God Almighty at the end of the Seventieth Week of Daniel, at the end of the Day of the Lord, and the Final Battle at the end of the

Millennium. They are actually the final battles of man against God. What could ever make men think they could fight against God? The very idea seems ludicrous. However, Satan will deceive men and, "God shall send them strong delusion, that they should believe a lie" (2 Thessalonians 2:11). Demonic spirits, operating through the Beast and the False Prophet, will deceive men and convince them they can fight against God. God will confuse the unrighteous because they have chosen not to believe the truth and have taken pleasure in unrighteousness. As you might have already surmised, mankind will lose both battles, miserably.

The events described in Revelation 16:12-16 take place under the sixth vial, during the Indignation, or wrath of God, the Day of the Lord. This is a description of sinful mankind being gathered together in a place in northern Israel called Armageddon. Demonic spirits will deceive the nations through false miracles into coming to battle against God.

The great river Euphrates will be dried up so the way of the kings of the east might be prepared for them to come to the Battle of that Great Day of God Almighty. These kings of the east will be gathered together in a place called Armageddon. When the kings of the east are gathered together at Armageddon it is almost universally understood that this battle will also take place at Armageddon. Let us see if we can determine where the Bible says this battle will take place.

> And I will turn thee back…and will cause thee to come up from the north parts, and will bring thee upon the mountains of Israel. Thou shalt fall upon the mountains of Israel, thou, and all thy bands, and the people that is with thee. (Ezekiel 39:2, 4a)

Armageddon is located in the Jezreel Valley in northern Israel, approximately 55 miles north of Jerusalem.[66] Ezekiel 39 says the armies that fight against God at the Battle of that Great Day of God Almighty will come up to the mountains of Israel from the "north parts." In this great battle, these

[66] This great army gathered at Armageddon will have an expansive plain in which to assemble, since the Jezreel Valley covers roughly 185 square miles.

armies will come up from the north and will fall, will be slain, upon the mountains of Israel.

> Behold, the day of the LORD cometh, and thy spoil shall be divided in the midst of thee. For I will gather all nations against Jerusalem to battle; and the city shall be taken, and the houses rifled, and the women ravished; and half of the city shall go forth into captivity, and the residue of the people shall not be cut off from the city. Then shall the LORD go forth, and fight against those nations, as when he fought in the day of battle. (Zechariah 14:1-3) (See also Zechariah 12:1-2, 9)

After the armies are gathered together at Armageddon, the Lord will bring them up to the mountains of Israel, to Jerusalem, where the Lord will fight against these nations.

> For, behold, in those days, and in that time, when I shall bring again the captivity of Judah and Jerusalem, I will also gather all nations, and will bring them down into the valley of Jehoshaphat, and will plead with them there for my people and for my heritage Israel, whom they have scattered among the nations, and parted my land. (Joel 3:1-2)

During the great and terrible Day of the Lord He will gather all nations and bring them into the Valley of Jehoshaphat. The Valley of Jehoshaphat, also known as the Kidron Valley, which is interpreted as the Valley of Judgment, lies between the Mount of Olives and the Temple Mount in Jerusalem.

> And this shall be the plague wherewith the LORD will smite all the people that have fought against Jerusalem; Their flesh shall consume away while they stand upon their feet, and their eyes shall consume away in their holes, and their tongue shall consume away in their mouth. (Zechariah 14:12)

During the Battle of that Great Day of God Almighty the Lord will smite with a plague all those who will fight against Him at Jerusalem.

God will dry up the Euphrates River, and spirits of devils will gather the kings of the east and their mighty army to a place in northern Israel, in the Jezreel Valley, to Armageddon. This great army that has been gathered together at Armageddon will then travel south to the mountains of Israel, to Jerusalem, possibly along the Way of the Patriarchs, an ancient north-south route traversing the land of Israel, where they will fight against God at the Battle of that Great Day of God Almighty.

> And I saw heaven opened, and behold a white horse; and he that sat upon him was called Faithful and True, and in righteousness he doth judge and make war. His eyes were as a flame of fire, and on his head were many crowns; and he had a name written, that no man knew, but he himself. And he was clothed with a vesture dipped in blood: and his name is called The Word of God. And the armies which were in heaven followed him upon white horses, clothed in fine linen, white and clean. And out of his mouth goeth a sharp sword, that with it he should smite the nations: and he shall rule them with a rod of iron: and he treadeth the winepress of the fierceness and wrath of Almighty God. And he hath on his vesture and on his thigh a name written, KING OF KINGS, AND LORD OF LORDS. And I saw an angel standing in the sun; and he cried with a loud voice, saying to all the fowls that fly in the midst of heaven, Come and gather yourselves together unto the supper of the great God; That ye may eat the flesh of kings, and the flesh of captains, and the flesh of mighty men, and the flesh of horses, and of them that sit on them, and the flesh of all men, both free and bond, both small and great. And I saw the beast, and the kings of the earth, and their armies, gathered together to make war against him that sat on the horse, and against his army. And the beast was taken, and with him the false prophet

> that wrought miracles before him, with which he deceived them that had received the mark of the beast, and them that worshipped his image. These both were cast alive into a lake of fire burning with brimstone. And the remnant were slain with the sword of him that sat upon the horse, which sword proceeded out of his mouth: and all the fowls were filled with their flesh. (Revelation 19:11-21)

Jesus Christ will come to this battle on a white horse at the end of the Seventieth Week of Daniel. There will be no doubt He is the Lord. He is called Faithful and True, The Word of God, the KING OF KINGS, AND LORD OF LORDS. He will come from heaven on a white horse with his armies, the angels of heaven, also on white horses. Unlike His first coming when He came not to judge the world but to save it, this time He will come to judge the world and make war. Jesus Christ will execute His righteous indignation on the ungodly. He will finally put all His enemies under His feet. The Antichrist, and the kings of the earth with their armies, will make war with Him who sits upon the white horse. Their fate is predictable. The Lord will smite them with a sharp sword that proceeds out of His mouth. The armies that oppose Him will become supper for the fowls of the air. At the end of this battle the Antichrist and the False Prophet will be cast alive into a lake of fire burning with brimstone.

> And another angel came out of the temple which is in heaven, he also having a sharp sickle. And another angel came out from the altar, which had power over fire; and cried with a loud cry to him that had the sharp sickle, saying, Thrust in thy sharp sickle, and gather the clusters of the vine of the earth; for her grapes are fully ripe. And the angel thrust in his sickle into the earth, and gathered the vine of the earth, and cast it into the great winepress of the wrath of God. And the winepress was trodden without the city, and blood came out of the winepress, even unto the horse bridles, by the space of a thousand and six hundred furlongs. (Revelation 14:17-20)

The reaping of the earth described in these scriptures is the slaying of the unjust at the Battle of that Great Day of God Almighty. This reaping will take place during the Day of the Lord because those who are reaped will be cast, "into the great winepress of the wrath of God." We are told an angel will come out of heaven with a sharp sickle and will thrust it into the earth to reap the vine of the earth. The unjust will be cast into the great winepress; their blood flowing as high as a horse's bridle for a thousand and six hundred furlongs. The blood of those slain will flow four feet deep for two hundred miles.

> Therefore, thou son of man, prophesy against Gog, and say, Thus saith the Lord GOD; Behold, I am against thee, O Gog, the chief prince of Meshech and Tubal: And I will turn thee back, and leave but the sixth part of thee, and will cause thee to come up from the north parts, and will bring thee upon the mountains of Israel: And I will smite thy bow out of thy left hand, and will cause thine arrows to fall out of thy right hand. Thou shalt fall upon the mountains of Israel, thou, and all thy bands, and the people that is with thee: I will give thee unto the ravenous birds of every sort, and to the beasts of the field to be devoured. Thou shalt fall upon the open field: for I have spoken it, saith the Lord GOD. And I will send a fire on Magog, and among them that dwell carelessly in the isles: and they shall know that I am the LORD. So will I make my holy name known in the midst of my people Israel; and I will not let them pollute my holy name any more: and the heathen shall know that I am the LORD, the Holy One in Israel...And, thou son of man, thus saith the Lord GOD; Speak unto every feathered fowl, and to every beast of the field, Assemble yourselves, and come; gather yourselves on every side to my sacrifice that I do sacrifice for you, even a great sacrifice upon the mountains of Israel, that ye may eat flesh, and drink blood. Ye shall eat the flesh of the mighty, and drink the blood of the princes of the earth, of rams, of lambs, and of goats, of

> bullocks, all of them fatlings of Bashan. And ye shall eat fat till ye be full, and drink blood till ye be drunken, of my sacrifice which I have sacrificed for you. Thus ye shall be filled at my table with horses and chariots, with mighty men, and with all men of war, saith the Lord GOD. And I will set my glory among the heathen, and all the heathen shall see my judgment that I have executed, and my hand that I have laid upon them. So the house of Israel shall know that I *am* the LORD their God from that day and forward. (Ezekiel 39:1-7, 17-22)

God will give these slain armies to the ravenous birds and beasts to be devoured. They will eat the flesh and drink the blood of these earthly princes and men of war. Five sixths of these armies will be slain, and only one sixth will be left. The heathen will see the judgment God has executed, and will know the Lord is God, the Holy One in Israel.

> Blow ye the trumpet in Zion, and sound an alarm in my holy mountain: let all the inhabitants of the land tremble: for the Day of the Lord cometh, for it is nigh at hand; A day of darkness and of gloominess, a day of clouds and of thick darkness, as the morning spread upon the mountains: a great people and a strong; there hath not been ever the like, neither shall be any more after it, even to the years of many generations. A fire devoureth before them; and behind them a flame burneth: the land is as the garden of Eden before them, and behind them a desolate wilderness; yea, and nothing shall escape them. The appearance of them is as the appearance of horses; and as horsemen, so shall they run. Like the noise of chariots on the tops of mountains shall they leap, like the noise of a flame of fire that devoureth the stubble, as a strong people set in battle array. Before their face the people shall be much pained: all faces shall gather blackness. They shall run like mighty men; they shall climb the wall like men of war; and they shall march every one on his ways, and

> they shall not break their ranks: Neither shall one thrust another; they shall walk every one in his path: and when they fall upon the sword, they shall not be wounded. They shall run to and fro in the city; they shall run upon the wall, they shall climb up upon the houses; they shall enter in at the windows like a thief. The earth shall quake before them; the heavens shall tremble: the sun and the moon shall be dark, and the stars shall withdraw their shining: And the LORD shall utter his voice before his army: for his camp is very great: for he is strong that executeth his word: for the Day of the Lord is great and very terrible; and who can abide it? (Joel 2:1-11)

This is a vivid description of the Lord's army – the ones who will fight against the Antichrist, the kings of the earth, and their armies at Jerusalem. The Lord will utter His voice before His army – a force unlike any that has ever been or ever will be. It is a great and strong people. The land is a Garden of Eden before them, and a desolate wilderness behind them. They will execute their duties with amazing skill and precision. The Battle of that Great Day of God Almighty will take place during the Day of the Lord because verse 11 says, "for the Day of the Lord is great and very terrible."

Pretribulationists contend that the army that accompanies Jesus Christ when he comes on a white horse to slay the wicked at the end of the Day of the Lord are the raptured Church. This description of that army most certainly is not of the raptured Church. They are clearly spiritual beings, the angels of God.

> Behold, it is come, and it is done, saith the Lord GOD; this is the day whereof I have spoken. And they that dwell in the cities of Israel shall go forth, and shall set on fire and burn the weapons, both the shields and the bucklers, the bows and the arrows, and the handstaves, and the spears, and they shall burn them with fire seven years: So that they shall take no wood out of the field, neither

> cut down any out of the forests; for they shall burn the weapons with fire: and they shall spoil those that spoiled them, and rob those that robbed them, saith the Lord GOD. And it shall come to pass in that day, that I will give unto Gog a place there of graves in Israel, the valley of the passengers on the east of the sea: and it shall stop the noses of the passengers: and there shall they bury Gog and all his multitude: and they shall call it The valley of Hamongog. And seven months shall the house of Israel be burying of them, that they may cleanse the land. Yea, all the people of the land shall bury them; and it shall be to them a renown the day that I shall be glorified, saith the Lord GOD. And they shall sever out men of continual employment, passing through the land to bury with the passengers those that remain upon the face of the earth, to cleanse it: after the end of seven months shall they search. And the passengers that pass through the land, when any seeth a man's bone, then shall he set up a sign by it, till the buriers have buried it in the valley of Hamongog. And also the name of the city shall be Hamonah. Thus shall they cleanse the land. (Ezekiel 39:8-16)

Israel will burn the weapons of the armies that will be defeated – a process that will take seven years. There will be so many weapons to burn Israel will not need to take wood out of the field, nor cut down any trees in the forest. There will be such a great multitude slain it will take seven months to bury the dead. God will be glorified in the day the wicked are slain.

> And his feet shall stand in that day upon the mount of Olives, which is before Jerusalem on the east, and the mount of Olives shall cleave in the midst thereof toward the east and toward the west, and there shall be a very great valley; and half of the mountain shall remove toward the north, and half of it toward the south. (Zechariah 14:4)

> Afterward he brought me to the gate, even the gate that looketh toward the east: And, behold, the glory of the God of Israel came from the way of the east: and his voice was like a noise of many waters: and the earth shined with his glory. And it was according to the appearance of the vision which I saw, even according to the vision that I saw when I came to destroy the city: and the visions were like the vision that I saw by the river Chebar; and I fell upon my face. And the glory of the LORD came into the house by the way of the gate whose prospect is toward the east. So the spirit took me up, and brought me into the inner court; and, behold, the glory of the LORD filled the house. (Ezekiel 43:1-5)

In that day, the Day of the Lord, after the defeat of the armies of the Antichrist at Jerusalem, Jesus Christ will stand upon the Mount of Olives, which is before Jerusalem on the east. Jesus Christ will return to earth in the same place He left (Acts 1:9-12). He departed from the Mount of Olives. He will return to it. The Mount of Olives will divide in the middle, and half of the mountain will move to the north, and half to the south.

The Mount of Olives is to the east of the Temple Mount. After Jesus Christ touches down, He will enter the Temple Mount through the eastern gate, the Golden Gate. Just as in Old Testament times when the glory of God departed from the temple through this gate, and then stood on the Mount of Olives (Ezekiel 10:4, 18-19, 11:23). the glory of the Lord will re-enter it through the same gate as Jesus Christ enters the temple. Today, the eastern gate is sealed. It will only be opened again at Jesus Christ's second coming. When Christ enters the temple the glory of the Lord will fill it again. The Lord will return to the temple and will rule and reign over Israel. Then He will sit on the throne of His glory (Matthew 25:31).

The Jews have been waiting for this Messiah. They have been waiting for Him to come and defeat their enemies. Jesus Christ did not come the first time as a conquering king; consequently, the Jews rejected Him as their Messiah. However, this time He will come on a white horse with the fierceness and wrath of Almighty God. He will return with His holy angels to smite the nations with the sharp sword that proceeds out of His mouth.

> And in the days of these kings shall the God of heaven set up a kingdom, which shall never be destroyed: and the kingdom shall not be left to other people, but it shall break in pieces and consume all these kingdoms, and it shall stand for ever. (Daniel 2:44)

God will destroy the ten kings or powers, the one-world government of the End Times, and will set up the millennial kingdom of Jesus Christ. His kingdom will never be destroyed; it will stand forever.

> And I saw thrones, and they sat upon them, and judgment was given unto them: and I saw the souls of them that were beheaded for the witness of Jesus, and for the word of God, and which had not worshipped the beast, neither his image, neither had received his mark upon their foreheads, or in their hands; and they lived and reigned with Christ a thousand years. But the rest of the dead lived not again until the thousand years were finished. This is the first resurrection. Blessed and holy is he that hath part in the first resurrection: on such the second death hath no power, but they shall be priests of God and of Christ, and shall reign with him a thousand years. (Revelation 20:4-6)

The resurrected Church, slain for the witness of Jesus and for the word of God, will not worshipped the Antichrist nor received his mark, and will live and reign with Christ on earth for a thousand years, His millennial reign. The Seventieth Week of Daniel will end with the Battle of that Great Day of God Almighty, and the millennial reign of Jesus Christ will begin.

> And I saw an angel come down from heaven, having the key of the bottomless pit and a great chain in his hand. And he laid hold on the dragon, that old serpent, which is the Devil, and Satan, and bound him a thousand years, And cast him into the bottomless pit, and shut him up,

> and set a seal upon him, that he should deceive the nations no more, till the thousand years should be fulfilled: and after that he must be loosed a little season. (Revelation 20:1-3)

That old serpent, the Devil, will be bound with a great chain for a thousand years, and cast into the bottomless pit. The Devil will be cast into the bottomless pit for the entirety of the Millennium, after which he will be loosed for a short time.

New Jerusalem

> And I John saw the holy city, new Jerusalem, coming down from God out of heaven, prepared as a bride adorned for her husband...And he carried me away in the spirit to a great and high mountain, and showed me that great city, the holy Jerusalem, descending out of heaven from God, Having the glory of God: and her light was like unto a stone most precious, even like a jasper stone, clear as crystal; And had a wall great and high, and had twelve gates, and at the gates twelve angels, and names written thereon, which are the names of the twelve tribes of the children of Israel: On the east three gates; on the north three gates; on the south three gates; and on the west three gates. And the wall of the city had twelve foundations, and in them the names of the twelve apostles of the Lamb. And he that talked with me had a golden reed to measure the city, and the gates thereof, and the wall thereof. And the city lieth foursquare, and the length is as large as the breadth: and he measured the city with the reed, twelve thousand furlongs. The length and the breadth and the height of it are equal. And he measured the wall thereof, an hundred and forty and four cubits, according to the measure of a man, that is, of the angel. And the building of the wall of it was of jasper: and the city was pure gold,

> like unto clear glass...And the twelve gates were twelve pearls: every several gate was of one pearl: and the street of the city was pure gold, as it were transparent glass. And I saw no temple therein: for the Lord God Almighty and the Lamb are the temple of it. And the city had no need of the sun, neither of the moon, to shine in it: for the glory of God did lighten it, and the Lamb is the light thereof. (Revelation 21:2, 10-18, 21-23)

One of the seven angels showed the apostle John the holy city – New Jerusalem. New Jerusalem had a great wall 216 feet thick (144 cubits, a cubit being 18 inches), with twelve gates, each gate made of a single pearl. The city was made of pure gold, clear as glass. The city was foursquare, having four corners. It was a cube measuring fifteen hundred miles (twelve thousand furlongs) on each side. The glory of God will be in the New Jerusalem. The city will come down out of heaven, and we will forever dwell there with God.

Some have questioned whether the New Jerusalem will be large enough to hold all who will be saved. A cube measuring fifteen hundred miles on each side is truly immense. The base of the New Jerusalem would occupy an area equivalent to the land mass from the Canadian border to the Mexican border, and from the Pacific Ocean to Chicago. Then, imagine that the distance from the base to the top will also be fifteen hundred miles. Unless some believers envision their mansion to be of gigantic proportions, there should be plenty of elbowroom in the New Jerusalem. Considering that there are approximately ten million people living in Los Angeles county, which occupies only a small corner of these expansive western states, it appears the New Jerusalem will be a fairly spacious living environment for the redeemed.

> And he showed me a pure river of water of life, clear as crystal, proceeding out of the throne of God and of the Lamb. In the midst of the street of it, and on either side of the river, was there the tree of life, which bare twelve manner of fruits, and yielded her fruit every month: and

> the leaves of the tree were for the healing of the nations. And there shall be no more curse: but the throne of God and of the Lamb shall be in it; and his servants shall serve him: And they shall see his face; and his name shall be in their foreheads. And there shall be no night there; and they need no candle, neither light of the sun; for the Lord God giveth them light: and they shall reign for ever and ever. (Revelation 22:1-5)

A pure river of living water will flow out of the throne of God in the New Jerusalem. On each side of that river will grow the tree of life. We will dwell with God in the New Jerusalem for eternity. We will enjoy the blessings of God forever and ever.

The Millenium: The Lord's Day

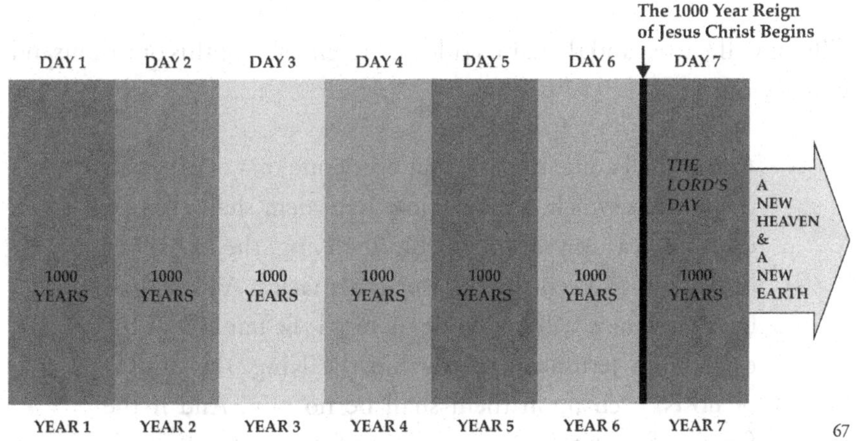

[67]

The Millennium: The Lord's Day

> But, beloved, be not ignorant of this one thing, that one day is with the Lord as a thousand years, and a thousand years as one day. (2 Peter 3:8)

---

[67] Wood, *Six Days to the Rapture*, Page 6.

If we follow the pattern that God retains the seventh period of time for Himself, the final one thousand years of earth history, the Millennium, will be the seventh part that God retains for Himself – the Lord's day.

> Do ye not know that the saints shall judge the world? and if the world shall be judged by you, are ye unworthy to judge the smallest matters? (1 Corinthians 6:2)

> And he that overcometh, and keepeth my works unto the end, to him will I give power over the nations. (Revelation 2:26)

During the millennial reign of Jesus Christ, God's saints will participate with Christ in judging the world. For those saints who remain faithful to the Lord to the end, He will give them power over the nations during the Millennium.

Whom will Christ and the saints rule and reign over for this one thousand year period?

> And it shall come to pass, that every one that is left of all the nations which came against Jerusalem shall even go up from year to year to worship the King, the LORD of hosts, and to keep the feast of tabernacles. And it shall be, that whoso will not come up of all the families of the earth unto Jerusalem to worship the King, the LORD of hosts, even upon them shall be no rain. And if the family of Egypt go not up, and come not, that have no rain; there shall be the plague, wherewith the LORD will smite the heathen that come not up to keep the feast of tabernacles. This shall be the punishment of Egypt, and the punishment of all nations that come not up to keep the feast of tabernacles. In that day shall there be upon the bells of the horses, HOLINESS UNTO THE LORD; and the pots in the LORD'S house shall be like the bowls before the altar. Yea, every pot in Jerusalem and in Judah shall be holiness unto the LORD of hosts: and

> all they that sacrifice shall come and take of them, and seethe therein: and in that day there shall be no more the Canaanite in the house of the LORD of hosts. (Zechariah 14:16-21)
>
> So shall ye know that I am the LORD your God dwelling in Zion, my holy mountain: then shall Jerusalem be holy, and there shall no strangers pass through her any more. (Joel 3:17)

Christ and the saints will rule and reign over, "every one that is left of all the nations that came against Jerusalem," the one sixth of those who survived the Battle of that Great Day of God Almighty. Zechariah describes everyone who is left as heathen. Jesus Christ will rule and reign with the saints from Jerusalem over the heathen that will be on the earth at that time. The heathen will be required to observe the feasts and to go up to Jerusalem to worship the Lord. If they do not go up to Jerusalem to observe the feasts and worship the King, no rain will fall on them. If they persist in not coming up to the feasts to worship the King after no rain has fallen, the Lord will smite them with plagues. However, none of these heathen will be allowed in the house of the Lord in Jerusalem. Jesus Christ will live in Zion (Jerusalem), which will be holy. No stranger or profane person will be able to pass through the city.

> Blessed are they that do his commandments, that they may have right to the tree of life, and may enter in through the gates into the city. For without are dogs, and sorcerers, and whoremongers, and murderers, and idolaters, and whosoever loveth and maketh a lie. (Revelation 22:14-15)

Only the saints, those who have a right to the tree of life, will be able to enter through the gates of the city of Jerusalem. Who will be outside of the city? The heathen whom Jesus Christ and the saints will rule and reign over with a rod of iron. "For without (the city of Jerusalem) are dogs, and sorcerers, and whoremongers, (fornicators) and murderers, and idolaters, (image worshippers) and whosoever loveth and maketh a lie."

The Final Battle

The Final Battle will take place at the end of the Millennium, the one thousand year reign of Jesus Christ. This will be Satan's, and mankinds, final rebellion against God.

> And when the thousand years are expired, Satan shall be loosed out of his prison, And shall go out to deceive the nations which are in the four quarters of the earth, Gog and Magog, to gather them together to battle: the number of whom is as the sand of the sea. And they went up on the breadth of the earth, and compassed the camp of the saints about, and the beloved city: and fire came down from God out of heaven, and devoured them. (Revelation 20:7-9)

When the thousand years have expired, Satan will be loosed from his prison, and will go out upon the earth and deceive the nations for the last time. He will gather the nations to battle, "the number of whom is as the sand of the sea." The armies that are deceived will surround Jerusalem, and fire will come down from God out of heaven and devour them.

> And the devil that deceived them was cast into the lake of fire and brimstone, where the beast and the false prophet are, and shall be tormented day and night for ever and ever. (Revelation 20:10)

After the Final Battle, the Devil that deceived the world will be cast into the lake of fire and brimstone where the Beast and the False Prophet are, and they will be tormented day and night forever and ever.

> And I saw a great white throne, and him that sat on it, from whose face the earth and the heaven fled away; and there was found no place for them. And I saw the dead, small and great, stand before God; and the books were opened: and another book was opened, which is the book of life: and the dead were judged out of those things which

> were written in the books, according to their works. And the sea gave up the dead which were in it; and death and hell delivered up the dead which were in them: and they were judged every man according to their works. And death and hell were cast into the lake of fire. This is the second death. And whosoever was not found written in the book of life was cast into the lake of fire. (Revelation 20:11-15)

After the Devil is cast into this lake of fire, the Great White Throne judgment of God will take place. This is the second resurrection, the second death – the resurrection of those who are damned for eternity. This is the resurrection of the unjust. The dead, small and great, will stand before God. Books will be opened in which every man's works are recorded. These works will provide the basis for the judgment of every man. The book of life will prove to those who have been resurrected in this second resurrection that they are not worthy of the first resurrection – the Rapture of the Church. The wicked will then be cast into the lake of fire, which is the second death.

CHAPTER 7

THE 144,000 JEWS

> And after these things I saw four angels standing on the four corners of the earth, holding the four winds of the earth, that the wind should not blow on the earth, nor on the sea, nor on any tree. And I saw another angel ascending from the east, having the seal of the living God: and he cried with a loud voice to the four angels, to whom it was given to hurt the earth and the sea, Saying, Hurt not the earth, neither the sea, nor the trees, till we have sealed the servants of our God in their foreheads. And I heard the number of them which were sealed: and there were sealed an hundred and forty and four thousand of all the tribes of the children of Israel. (Revelation 7:1-4)

The 144,000 of the book of Revelation are Jews. The Bible is very clear they are Jews, and they will be redeemed or purchased by God just prior to the beginning of the Day of the Lord. They are the firstfruits of a multitude of the nation of Israel who will be saved at the end of the Seventieth Week of Daniel.

Some have said they are not Jews, but the Church. When they claim the 144,000 are the Church they are taking a promise made by God to Israel, and applying it to the Church. Others have said the way to salvation is narrow; therefore, only 144,000 will be saved – the 144,000 of the book of Revelation. Still others say the 144,000 will come exclusively from their denomination, since their denomination is the only one that holds to all spiritual truth. The 144,000 Jews of the book of Revelation can clearly be identified as the redeemed of Israel if the Bible is interpreted literally.

These scriptures are quite clear in identifying the 144,000 as being Jews, "of all the tribes of the children of Israel." Specifically, these 144,000 of Israel will come equally from each of the twelve tribes of the children of Israel – 12,000 from each tribe. They are sealed, as a sign of possession, and are protected from God's wrath during the Day of the Lord, which will take place after their sealing. They will be a remnant of Israel, maintained by the covenant between God and Abraham (Genesis 17:6-8), who will have survived the Great Tribulation. They will go through the Day of the Lord sealed, or protected, from God's wrath.

The sealing of the 144,000 Jews will take place after the cosmic disturbances of the sixth seal (Revelation 6:12-17), but before the Rapture of the Church (Revelation 7:9-17). In verse 1, four angels are preparing for the Day of the Lord – the Indignation of God – which takes place under the seventh seal (Revelation 8). These four angels are told that the wrath of God, the plagues of the trumpets and vials, should not be poured out upon the earth until after the 144,000 are sealed in their foreheads.

Why are the angels told not to hurt the earth until after the 144,000 Jews have been sealed?

> And the fifth angel sounded, and I saw a star fall from heaven unto the earth: and to him was given the key of the bottomless pit. And he opened the bottomless pit; and there arose a smoke out of the pit, as the smoke of a great furnace; and the sun and the air were darkened by reason of the smoke of the pit. And there came out of the smoke locusts upon the earth: and unto them was given power, as the scorpions of the earth have power. And it was commanded them that they should not hurt the grass

> of the earth, neither any green thing, neither any tree; but only those men which have not the seal of God in their foreheads. (Revelation 9:1-4)

The seal of God will protect the 144,000 from the plagues of the trumpets and vials – the Indignation of God under the seventh seal. Locusts from hell will torment all of mankind – a plague of the fifth trumpet – except those who have the seal of God in their foreheads. Therefore, the 144,000 Jews must be sealed before the Indignation begins so they will be protected from the judgment of God during the Day of the Lord.

What is the significance of the 144,000 Jews being sealed? Rosenthal explains the meaning of sealing.

> Sealing has two basic concepts associated with it. In the Roman world, things were sealed to indicate ownership and to guarantee protection. Commenting on the sealing of believers in Ephesians 1:13, Ryrie wrote, "A seal indicates possession and security." Here in Revelation 7 the 144,000 are sealed in their foreheads as an indication that they belong to God (possession) and will experience His security (protection). Their sealing will be for the purpose of exempting them from God's wrath, which had just been announced and then delayed until they were sealed.[68]

> And I looked, and, lo, a Lamb stood on the mount Sion, and with him an hundred forty and four thousand, having his Father's name written in their foreheads. And I heard a voice from heaven, as the voice of many waters, and as the voice of a great thunder: and I heard the voice of harpers harping with their harps: And they sung as it were a new song before the throne, and before the four beasts, and the elders: and no man could learn that song but the hundred and forty and four thousand, which were redeemed from

[68] Rosenthal, *The Pre-Wrath Rapture of the Church*, p. 171.

> the earth. These are they which were not defiled with women; for they are virgins. These are they which follow the Lamb whithersoever he goeth. These were redeemed from among men, being the firstfruits unto God and to the Lamb. And in their mouth was found no guile: for they are without fault before the throne of God. (Revelation 14:1-5)

These verses give us a wealth of information about the 144,000. They are purchased by God, and are the firstfruits or a beginning of sacrifice – the first of many Jews who will be redeemed at the end of the Seventieth Week of Daniel. They are men, and they are virgins. Some have said the designation as virgins is a spiritual reference, that they do not prostitute themselves spiritually and worship the Antichrist. This is certainly true; however, this verse specifically says they, "were not defiled with women." They follow Jesus Christ; they are servants of God (Revelation 7:3). They are without guile or deceit and are faultless, or unblemished, before God.

Many have questioned whether these 144,000 Jews come into a saving relationship with Jesus Christ at the moment they are sealed. Revelation chapter 14 says they follow the Lamb, Jesus Christ, wherever He goes, and they are firstfruits unto God. However, it does not appear they are saved at that time. The 144,000 are sealed prior to the Rapture of the Church, which takes place in Revelation 7:9-17. If they became Christians at the time they were sealed, they would be raptured with the rest of the Church, since all Christians are raptured, whether they are Jews or Gentiles.

Some, including pretribulationists, have said the 144,000 Jews will function as evangelists during the End Times. LaHaye said, "During the Tribulation…the gospel will be entrusted into the hands of the 144,000 Jewish evangelists."[69] However, there is no scriptural basis for this position. There is not one passage in the Bible that specifically mentions, or even infers, the 144,000 Jews function as evangelists during the End Times.

---

[69] LaHaye, *The Rapture*, p. 55.

Pretribulationists claim the Holy Spirit will be removed from the earth during the Rapture, and some of those left behind will be saved during the tribulation period, the work of the 144,000 Jewish evangelists. Since someone must be responsible for assisting with the salvation of those who are left behind, pretribulationists say the 144,000 are the most logical candidates. Designating the 144,000 Jews as evangelists during the End Times is one of the best examples of pretribulationists inventing a concept in order to justify a theory that has no biblical foundation whatsoever.

These 144,000 Jews, the redeemed of Israel, will be sealed, protected by God, and will not experience the wrath of God that will be poured out during the Day of the Lord. They are the firstfruits of the nation of Israel that will be redeemed at the end of the Day of the Lord. They will be sealed by God, protected from the wrath of God, until they enter the kingdom at the end of the Day of the Lord.

CHAPTER 8

THE TWO WITNESSES: THE TWO PROPHETS

These *are* the two anointed ones, that stand by the Lord of the whole earth. (Zechariah 4:14)

Christians are familiar with two prophets who will prophesy during the End Times. Their role has been portrayed in movies and mentioned in books that deal with the End Times. The Bible refers to these two prophets in several ways: as the two olive trees, the two anointed ones, the two witnesses, and the two prophets. They will be sent by God to warn the world of the deceptions of the Antichrist and his False Prophet, and to persuade mankind to worship and serve God. They will be used by God to speak the plagues of God into existence during the Day of the Lord. The Church, and the entire world, will see these two witnesses prophesy in the streets of Jerusalem during the second half of the Seventieth Week of Daniel. They will be very active during the time of the end. They will preach to the Jews, and to the world, for three and a half years. During the Day of the Lord, the Indignation of God, these two prophets will torment unbelievers who have taken the mark of the Beast with the plagues of the trumpets and vials.

And the angel that talked with me came again, and waked me, as a man that is wakened out of his sleep, And said unto me, What seest thou? And I said, I have looked, and

> behold a candlestick all of gold, with a bowl upon the top of it, and his seven lamps thereon, and seven pipes to the seven lamps, which are upon the top thereof: And two olive trees by it, one upon the right side of the bowl, and the other upon the left side thereof. So I answered and spake to the angel that talked with me, saying, What are these, my lord? Then the angel that talked with me answered and said unto me, Knowest thou not what these be? And I said, No, my lord...Then answered I, and said unto him, What are these two olive trees upon the right side of the candlestick and upon the left side thereof? And I answered again, and said unto him, What be these two olive branches which through the two golden pipes empty the golden oil out of themselves? And he answered me and said, Knowest thou not what these be? And I said, No, my lord. Then said he, These are the two anointed ones, that stand by the Lord of the whole earth. (Zechariah 4:1-5, 11-14)

An angel woke Zechariah the prophet and asked him what he saw. Zechariah said he saw a golden candlestick with a bowl on top, and the golden candlestick had seven lamps with seven pipes to the seven lamps. He also saw two olive trees, one on the left side and one on the right side of the golden candlestick. Zechariah asked the angel the identity of these two olive trees. The angel answered, "These are the two anointed ones, that stand by the Lord of the whole earth."

> And I will give power unto my two witnesses, and they shall prophesy a thousand two hundred and threescore days, clothed in sackcloth. These are the two olive trees, and the two candlesticks standing before the God of the earth. And if any man will hurt them, fire proceedeth out of their mouth, and devoureth their enemies: and if any man will hurt them, he must in this manner be killed. These have power to shut heaven, that it rain not in the days of their prophecy: and have power over waters to turn

> them to blood, and to smite the earth with all plagues, as often as they will. (Revelation 11:3-6)

Revelation chapter 11 identifies the two olive trees of Zechariah chapter 4. These two olive trees are God's two witnesses. These are the, "two anointed ones, that stand by the Lord of the whole earth." They will prophesy the word of the Lord, and their ministry will last 1260 days, or three and a half years. If any man harms them they will be killed, and these two witnesses will punish mankind with plagues – the plagues of the trumpets and vials under the seventh seal. If we compare the acts of the two witnesses in Revelation 11:6 with the plagues of the trumpets and vials, the Indignation of God, we will see they are the same. (See Trumpet 2 and Vials 2, 3 and 6) The two witnesses are responsible for speaking the plagues of the trumpets and vials into existence.

It is interesting to note that both Zechariah and Revelation mention that these two witnesses stand by God. They stand by God, or often appear near to God. We will see from the following scriptures these two witnesses do indeed appear often with the Lord.[70]

Revelation 11:3 says their ministry will last for 1,260 days, which is three and a half years, based upon a Jewish month of thirty days. Since the Seventieth Week of Daniel is divided into two periods of three and a half years, it would seem reasonable their ministry would either take place during the first, or the second, half of the Seventieth Week of Daniel. Revelation chapter 11 also says the two witnesses are responsible for smiting the earth with plagues. The plagues they speak into existence include breathing fire out of their mouths, causing the rain to stop, and turning water into blood. If we compare the plagues of the trumpets and vials with the plagues the two witnesses speak into existence during their earthly ministry, we find they are the same. The plagues of the trumpets and vials take place during the second half of the Seventieth Week of Daniel. Therefore, the ministry of the two witnesses also takes place during the second half of the Seventieth Week of Daniel. The ministry of the two witnesses begins the day the Antichrist desecrates the temple – the Abomination of Desolation.

[70] Wood, *Six Days to the Rapture*, Tape 10.

Their ministry is provided by God as a counter to the signs and wonders of the Antichrist and his False Prophet. The ministry of the two prophets ends 1,260 days later, at the end of the Day of the Lord.

> But thou, O Daniel, shut up the words, and seal the book, even to the time of the end: many shall run to and fro, and knowledge shall be increased. Then I Daniel looked, and, behold, there stood other two, the one on this side of the bank of the river, and the other on that side of the bank of the river. And one said to the man clothed in linen, which was upon the waters of the river, How long shall it be to the end of these wonders? And I heard the man clothed in linen, which was upon the waters of the river, when he held up his right hand and his left hand unto heaven, and sware by him that liveth for ever that it shall be for a time, times, and an half; and when he shall have accomplished to scatter the power of the holy people, all these things shall be finished. And I heard, but I understood not: then said I, O my Lord, what shall be the end of these things? And he said, Go thy way, Daniel: for the words are closed up and sealed till the time of the end. (Daniel 12:4-9)

In this vision, Daniel sees two men standing on opposite banks of a river. There is also a man, clothed in linen, standing upon the waters of the river. This man is Jesus Christ (Daniel 8:16), and the two men on opposite sides of the river are the two witnesses. One of the witnesses asks the Lord how long will it be from the Abomination of Desolation – the beginning of the Great Tribulation (Daniel 11:45; 12:1), to the end of the wonders of the book of Daniel. The Lord answers that it will be for a time, times, and an half, or three and a half years, then all these things will have finished. Revelation 11:3-6 says the two witnesses will minister on the earth for three and a half years - the same period of time mentioned here in the book of Daniel, which is the time from the Abomination of Desolation to the end of the Seventieth Week of Daniel.

> And when he had spoken these things, while they beheld, he was taken up; and a cloud received him out of their sight. And while they looked stedfastly toward heaven as he went up, behold, two men stood by them in white apparel; Which also said, Ye men of Galilee, why stand ye gazing up into heaven? this same Jesus, which is taken up from you into heaven, shall so come in like manner as ye have seen him go into heaven. (Acts 1:9-11)

After Jesus Christ was resurrected, he spent forty days with the apostles (Acts 1:3). On the day He was taken from them into heaven in a cloud, two men stood with the apostles and told them Jesus would come again in the same manner. These two men are the two witnesses.

Moses & Elijah

The Church has often speculated as to the identity of these two prophets. Let us see if we can identify who the two witnesses will be.

> Behold, I will send you Elijah the prophet before the coming of the great and dreadful day of the LORD: And he shall turn the heart of the fathers to the children, and the heart of the children to their fathers, lest I come and smite the earth with a curse. (Malachi 4:5-6)

The great and dreadful Day of the Lord is the wrath of God, which will immediately follow the Rapture of the Church. God said He would send Elijah the prophet before the great and dreadful day of the Lord, before the Indignation of God. Therefore, Elijah will return to the earth to minister before the Day of the Lord, before the Rapture of the Church.

> And his disciples asked him, saying, Why then say the scribes that Elias must first come? And Jesus answered and said unto them, Elias truly shall first come, and restore all things. But I say unto you, That Elias is come already, and they knew him not, but have done unto him whatsoever

> they listed. Likewise shall also the Son of man suffer of them. Then the disciples understood that he spake unto them of John the Baptist. (Matthew 17:10-13)

Some have said Elijah the prophet has already returned. These scriptures have been interpreted to say Elijah returned as John the Baptist.

> But the angel said unto him, Fear not, Zacharias: for thy prayer is heard; and thy wife Elisabeth shall bear thee a son, and thou shalt call his name John...And he shall go before him in the spirit and power of Elias, to turn the hearts of the fathers to the children, and the disobedient to the wisdom of the just; to make ready a people prepared for the Lord. (Luke 1:13, 17)

Elijah did not come back to the earth as John the Baptist. Luke clearly says John the Baptist came, "in the spirit and power of Elias (Elijah)." In John 1:21, the Jews ask John, "Art thou Elias? And he saith, I am not." John the Baptist was a type of Elijah, but not Elijah. Elijah will return before the Day of the Lord, before the Rapture of the Church.

> And after six days Jesus taketh Peter, James, and John his brother, and bringeth them up into an high mountain apart, And was transfigured before them: and his face did shine as the sun, and his raiment was white as the light. And, behold, there appeared unto them Moses and Elias talking with him. Then answered Peter, and said unto Jesus, Lord, it is good for us to be here: if thou wilt, let us make here three tabernacles; one for thee, and one for Moses, and one for Elias. (Matthew 17:1-4)

In the transfiguration, Moses and Elijah appeared with Jesus. The transfiguration is a preview of Jesus Christ's glory that will be manifested at the time of his His second coming.

> And they that dwell upon the earth shall rejoice over them, and make merry, and shall send gifts one to another; because these two prophets tormented them that dwelt on the earth. (Revelation 11:10)

The two witnesses are prophets. Moses was a prophet (Deuteronomy 34:10), as was Elijah (Malachi 4:5).

Let us compare the plagues of the trumpets and vials, which the two witnesses will speak into existence, with the acts of Moses and Elijah when they walked upon the earth.[71]

The Plagues of the Trumpets and Vials

Trumpet One – "The first angel sounded, and there followed hail and fire mingled with blood" (Revelation 8:7a).

Trumpet Two – "And the second angel sounded…and the third part of the sea became blood" (Revelation 8:8).

Vial Two – "And the second angel poured out his vial upon the sea; and it became as the blood of a dead man" (Revelation 16:3a).

Vial Three – "And the third angel poured out his vial upon the rivers and fountains of waters; and they became blood" (Revelation 16:4).

Vial Six – "And the sixth angel poured out his vial upon the great river Euphrates; and the water thereof was dried up that the way of the kings of the east might be prepared" (Revelation 16:12).

Trumpet Six – "And the six angel sounded…And thus I saw the horses… and out of their mouths issued fire and smoke and brimstone. By these three was the third part of men killed" (Revelation 9:13a, 17-18a).

---

[71] Ibid., Tape 10.

The Acts of Moses and Elijah

"And Moses stretched forth his rod toward heaven: and the Lord sent thunder and hail...Son there was hail, and fire mingled with the hail" (Exodus 9:23a,-24a).

"And it came to pass at the time of the offering of the evening sacrifice, that Elijah the prophet came near, and said...Hear me, O Lord, hear me, that this people may know that thou are the Lord God, and that thou hast turned their heart back again. Then the fire of the Lord fell, and consumed the burnt sacrifice, and the wood, and the stones, and the dust, and licked up the water that was in the trench" (1 Kings 18:36-38).

"And Moses...lifted up the rod, and smote the waters that were in the river...and all the waters that were in the river were turned to blood" (Exodus 7:20).

"And Elijah the Tishbite, who was of the inhabitants of Gilead, said unto Ahab, As the Lord God of Israel liveth, before whom I stand, there shall not be dew nor rain these years, but according to my word...And it came to pass after a while, that the brook dried up, because there had been no rain in the land" (1 Kings 17:1, 7).

"And Moses said, Thus saith the Lord, About midnight will I go out into the midst of Egypt; And all the firstborn in the land of Egypt shall die... And it came to pass, that at midnight the Lord smote all the firstborn in the land of Egypt" (Exodus 11:4-5a, 12:29a).

It appears the plagues of the trumpets and vials closely resemble the acts of Moses and Elijah. This is a further confirmation the two witnesses are probably Moses and Elijah.

> And when they shall have finished their testimony, the beast that ascendeth out of the bottomless pit shall make war against them, and shall overcome them, and kill them. And their dead bodies shall lie in the street of the great city, which spiritually is called Sodom and Egypt,

> where also our Lord was crucified. And they of the people and kindreds and tongues and nations shall see their dead bodies three days and an half, and shall not suffer their dead bodies to be put in graves. And they that dwell upon the earth shall rejoice over them, and make merry, and shall send gifts one to another; because these two prophets tormented them that dwelt on the earth. And after three days and an half the Spirit of life from God entered into them, and they stood upon their feet; and great fear fell upon them which saw them. And they heard a great voice from heaven saying unto them, Come up hither. And they ascended up to heaven in a cloud; and their enemies beheld them. (Revelation 11:7-12)

After the two witnesses, the two prophets from heaven, have completed their ministry they will be killed by the Antichrist, and their dead bodies will be left in the streets of Jerusalem for three and a half days. The people on earth during the Day of the Lord's wrath will rejoice that the two witnesses are dead because they have been tormenting them with the plagues of the trumpets and vials for almost a year. These unbelievers will send gifts to one another in celebration of the death of these two witnesses. After their dead bodies lay in the streets for three and a half days, the Spirit of God will enter into them and they will come back to life. Then a great voice from heaven will summon them, and their enemies will see them ascend into heaven in a cloud.

In conclusion, Moses and Elijah appear to be the two witnesses. It would be appropriate for the Jews that Moses, representing the law, and Elijah, representing the prophets, would come back to witness to them before the coming of the Lord. What more appropriate witness could God send than Moses who would bring conviction on Israel for their sins? They have held to what Moses taught. They have declared they are Moses' disciples (John 9:28). Let Moses convict them for what they have said and done.[72]

---

[72] Ibid., Tape 10.

CHAPTER 9

ANCIENT BABYLON

> And they said, Go to, let us build us a city and a tower, whose top *may reach* unto heaven; and let us make us a name, lest we be scattered abroad upon the face of the whole earth. (Genesis 11:4)

There was an ancient Babylon that was both a city and a religion. There is also a modern Babylon that is both a city and a religion. This chapter will examine ancient Babylon. Chapter 10 will address modern Babylon. The purpose of studying the teachings and practices of ancient Babylon is to compare them with modern Babylon. As we shall see, the teachings and practices of modern Babylon are very similar to those of ancient Babylon; in fact, they mirror those of ancient Babylon.

Many associate the name Babylon with an undesirable or objectionable place or group of people. The name Babylon has been used to describe very unpleasant or even scary civilizations. Babylon's identity is very important to the study of the Seventieth Week of Daniel. She plays a very important role in the End Times. Babylon has a very specific biblical identity. Unfortunately, Babylon's biblical identity is not well understood by the Church. Babylon's true identity is important and scripture is very clear in identifying Babylon.

> And Cush begat Nimrod: he began to be a mighty one in the earth. He was a mighty hunter before the LORD:

> wherefore it is said, Even as Nimrod the mighty hunter before the LORD. And the beginning of his kingdom was Babel, and Erech, and Accad, and Calneh, in the land of Shinar. Out of that land went forth Asshur, and builded Nineveh, and the city Rehoboth, and Calah, And Resen between Nineveh and Calah: the same is a great city. (Genesis 10:8-12)

Nimrod was a descendent of Noah. Noah had three sons; Shem, Japheth, and Ham. Ham had a son named Cush. Cush married Semiramis. Cush and Semiramis had a son named Nimrod. In these scriptures Nimrod is referred to as a mighty hunter before the Lord. These scriptures are not referring to Nimrod as a hunter of animals, but as a hunter of men's souls. Nimrod was also a builder of cities. The first city he built was Babylon.

When the waters of the flood had receded, and the ark came to rest, Noah and his sons settled in the area of Babylonia. Hundreds of years latter the descendents of Noah had increased in number and were still living in Babylonia. While in the area of Babylonia, they built a city and a tower that would reach to heaven. Why would they build a great tower that would reach heaven? Did they want to get closer to God Almighty in heaven? Unfortunately, the purpose of the tower was not to get closer to God. The tower that would reach to heaven was built for the purpose of worshipping the sun, moon, and stars. These descendents of Noah were practicing astrology.[73]

> And the LORD came down to see the city and the tower, which the children of men builded. And the LORD said, Behold, the people is one, and they have all one language; and this they begin to do: and now nothing will be restrained from them, which they have imagined to do. Go to, let us go down, and there confound their language, that they may not understand one another's speech. So the LORD scattered them abroad from thence upon the face of all the earth: and they left off to build the

[73] Ibid., Tape 3.

> city. Therefore is the name of it called Babel; because the LORD did there confound the language of all the earth: and from thence did the LORD scatter them abroad upon the face of all the earth. (Genesis 11:5-9)

The Lord looked down to earth to see what Noah's descendents were doing. He saw they had built a city and a tower. God said, "this they begin to do: and now nothing will be restrained from them, which they have imagined to do." What they had began to do, and what they had imagined to do, was to use the city and the tower to worship the sun, moon, and stars. In their imaginations they were plotting against the will of God. Astrology is a vain imagination of man's mind. God knew nothing would restrain them from their evil ways, so he confused their language and scattered them across the earth.

It is interesting to note that God scattered them because of the evil they had committed in practicing astrology, as well as other vile endeavors. There is a teaching in the Church that God confounded their language because they failed to obey God's command to leave Babylon and spread over the earth. Genesis 9:1 is the key verse used to support their teaching, "And God blessed Noah and his sons, and said unto them, Be fruitful, and multiply, and replenish the earth." This verse is not a command from God to spread throughout the earth. God said they were to replenish the earth. The flood had destroyed all of its inhabitants, other than those in the ark. Therefore, this was God's command to repopulate the earth. It is clearly not a natural interpretation of scripture to contend that God was commanding Noah and his descendents to spread throughout the earth. He only scattered them once they rebelled and practiced astrology.

It is important to know what kind of cities Nimrod built. They were wicked cities. Babylon practiced astrology. Nineveh was known for immorality and the worship of the queen of heaven. Jonah was sent to Nineveh to bring judgment against that wicked city. Calah was known for statuary and images of winged lions and bulls of half men and half animals. Erech is where the first tower or ziggurat was built which was similar to the tower of Babel. Through the ages towers, pyramids, and other structures have been constructed for the purpose of practicing astrology.[74]

When Cush died, his wife Semiramis married their son, Nimrod. When Nimrod married his mother Semiramis his name was changed to Ninus, which means husband-son. After Ninus married his mother, he was killed by Shem, who was very displeased with Ninus' actions. He divided Ninus' body into fourteen parts and sent them into the various provinces of Babylon. This was a sign from Shem that anyone who committed the same deplorable acts as Ninus' would suffer the same fate. After Ninus was killed, and his body parts were dispersed throughout Babylon, Semiramis sent men to collect the body parts of Ninus. They were collected, entombed, and worshipped. Semiramis claimed when Ninus died he became a god. This was the origin of relic worship – the worship of body parts.[75]

Like her son Ninus, when Semiramis died she was deified and worshipped as a god. The logic was, if Ninus was god, then she was the mother of god. Therefore, in death, she was worshipped as the mother of god – the queen of heaven and the mediator to god. Babylonians prayed to her, and believed she would intercede for them to Ninus. She was worshipped as a virgin, even though she had a son. Babylonians taught that Semiramis did not die, but was translated into heaven. The Babylonian trinity is the father, mother, and son. The mother was given the position of preeminence, followed by the son, while the father is relegated to a relatively unimportant role. Israel worshipped the queen of heaven in the days of Jeremiah (Jeremiah 7:18, 44:17-19, 25).

Ancient Babylonians celebrated the birth of Ninus on Yule (infant, child) Day. Yule log means man branch. Ninus was the man branch of Semiramis. She was the trunk of the tree, and Ninus was a branch, or offshoot, of that trunk. In ancient Babylon fir trees were cut down, and the base of the trees were cut off – which was the Yule log. This log was then burned in hopes of bringing good luck and to ward off evil spirits. The following day the

---

[74] Dr. David Whitehouse, Ancient Builders Followed Stars, http://news.bbc.co.uk/2/hi/science/nature/3592631.stm, April 2, 2004.

[75] Wood, Six Days to the Rapture, Tape 3.

remainder of the fir tree was erected, symbolizing their god, Nimrod, had died and had sprouted as a tree, or was living again. This same ritual is being practiced today during the Christmas holiday when the Yule log is burned and the Christmas tree is erected. Christmas clearly has it roots in paganism, being observed near the winter solstice, the time when the sun renews its course, an obvious reference to the birth of their sun-god.

Notice the progression. Ninus died and his mother-wife promoted him to the status of a god. Then Semiramis died and she was deified as a god. She was worshipped as the trunk and Ninus was a branch of that trunk. She became the principal figure of worship.

The Madonna originated in ancient Babylon. A Madonna is a representation of a mother and an infant. Semiramis was the mother figure and Ninus was the infant. The Madonna appeared later in other false religions.

> From Babylon, this worship of the Mother and the Child spread to the ends of the earth. In Egypt, the Mother and the Child were worshipped under the names of Isis and Osiris. In India, even to this day, as Isi and Iswara; in Asis, as Cybele and Deoius; in Pagan Rome, as Fortuna and Jupiter-puer, or Jupiter, the boy; in Greece, as Ceres, the Great Mother, with the babe at her breast, or as Irene, the goddess of Peace, with the boy Plutus in her arms.[76]

Babylonians sacrificed their children to their god – a ritual called passing through the fire. They killed their children in a furnace as an offering to their god. The children of Israel committed these same deplorable acts (2 Kings 17:17, 21:6, 23:10; 2 Chronicles 33:6; Jeremiah 32:35; Ezekiel 16:21, 20:26, 31). This practice of sacrificing their children in the fire was eventually discontinued. Instead, they instituted a ceremony where they would bake bread and drink wine in a covenant meal with their god. Babylonians baked cakes and carved a cross on them. They ate the cakes as a form of worship supporting a covenant between themselves and Semiramis. This later practice was referred to as the unbloody sacrifice.

[76] Alexander Hislop, *The Two Babylons* (Neptune, New Jersey, 1959) p. 20.

The book of Jeremiah notes that the women of Judah observed this same practice by baking cakes and worshipping the queen of heaven[77] (Jeremiah 44:15-19).

Semiramis was celebrated as Astarte in the pagan holiday of Easter, an event which took place after the vernal equinox. Babylonians would fast for forty days. At the end of the fast they would hold a feast, which included painting eggs. They would celebrate the end of the fast by baking a special bread and would carve the symbol of a cross on the bread. Please note that this practice was taking place long before the crucifixion of Jesus Christ on a cross. Christians are celebrating Easter today much like it was celebrated in ancient Babylon. Just as it was centuries ago, Easter is celebrated on the first Sunday following the first full moon after the vernal equinox.[78]

The cross was a very important symbol in the ancient Babylonian religion. The Babylonian cross is called the Tau, which refers to their sun god. It was worshipped as a symbol of their sun god, and was thought to have magic powers which could protect the devotee from evil. When a circle was placed on top of the cross, or the cross was placed within a circle, the circle represented the sun.

Ancient Babylonians practiced sun worship. They worshipped a representation of the sun in the form of a sunburst, which had a human face. The sunburst represented the sun god, and the face was that god in the flesh. This image was traditionally erected on a pole and worshipped. The Bible notes that Israel practiced this same pagan ritual of sun worship in the days of Ezekiel[79] (Ezekiel 8:15-16).

Diana of the Ephesians was a later representation of Semiramis. Diana of the Ephesians wore a rosary or prayer beads. Prayer beads were part of ancient pagan religious practices. Long repetitious prayers were said while counting the prayer beads.

---

[77] Wood, *Six Days to the Rapture*, Tape 3.

[78] Ibid., Tape 3.

[79] Ibid., Tape 3.

Babylonians prayed for the dead. Purgatory was a place of punishment where one was perfected for entrance into heaven. Babylonians paid money to priests who would then pray loved ones out of purgatory.

Babylonian priests were given the title of Cardinal. The term Cardinal means to turn on the hinge. Cardinals had the power of turning the hinge, or opening the door to deeper understanding. The Chaldean mysteries could not be understood by mere men, but only by those who could open the door on the hinge. Cardinals could open the door of understanding to the mysteries. Ordinary men were not able to understand the deep things, or mysteries, of god.[80]

These are but a few of the facts concerning ancient Babylon and its religious practices. The purpose of examining these rituals and practices is to compare ancient Babylon with modern Babylon. In Chapter 10, we will see that modern Babylon is, in fact, a mirror image of ancient Babylon.

---

80 Ibid., Tape 3.

CHAPTER 10

MODERN BABYLON

> MYSTERY, BABYLON THE GREAT, THE MOTHER OF HARLOTS AND ABOMINATIONS OF THE EARTH. (Revelation 17:5)

There was an ancient Babylon that was both a city and a religion. There is a modern Babylon that is both a city and a religion. The teachings and practices of modern Babylon are very similar to the teachings and practices of ancient Babylon. In fact, modern Babylon is simply a mirror image of ancient Babylon. Is there a religious organization, active today, that mirrors ancient Babylon? As you may have already concluded from reading Chapter 9, Roman Catholicism is modern Babylon.

Rome is Babylon

> The church that is at Babylon, elected together with you, saluteth you; and so doth Marcus my son. (1 Peter 5:13)

Biblical scholars agree that Peter wrote his first epistle from Rome. It was commonly accepted during the Apostle Peter's day that Rome was Babylon. Up until very recent times the Church almost universally acknowledged that Rome was Babylon. The Catholic Church, with headquarters at the Vatican in Rome, is modern Babylon.

Dave Hunt, in his book, *A Woman Rides the Beast*, notes that Karl Keating, a defender of Catholicism, acknowledges that Rome is Babylon.

> Even Catholic apologist Karl Keating admits that Rome has long been known as Babylon. Keating claims that Peter's statement "The church here in Babylon...sends you her greeting" (from 1 Peter 5:13) proves that Peter was writing from Rome. He explains further: Babylon is a code word for Rome. It is used that way six times in the last book of the Bible [four of the six are in chapters 17 and 18] and in extrabiblical works such as *Sibylling Oracles* (5, 159f.), the *Apocalypse of Baruch* (ii,1), and 4 *Esdras* (3:1). Eusebius Pamphilius, writing about 303, noted that "it is said that Peter's first epistle...was composed at Rome itself: and that he himself indicates this, referring to the city figuratively as Babylon."[81]

Revelation chapter 17 clearly identifies Rome, and Roman Catholicism, as modern Babylon.

> So he carried me away in the spirit into the wilderness: and I saw a woman sit upon a scarlet coloured beast, full of names of blasphemy, having seven heads and ten horns... And here is the mind which hath wisdom. The seven heads are seven mountains, on which the woman sitteth... And the woman which thou sawest is that great city, which reigneth over the kings of the earth. (Revelation 17:3, 9, 18)

Modern Babylon is both a city and a religion. The city is Rome and the religion is Roman Catholicism. The woman sitting on the scarlet colored beast is the apostate religion of Roman Catholicism. This woman is identified as that great city which has seven mountains, she "is that great city." Rome is recognized the world over as the city of seven hills.

---

[81] Dave Hunt, *A Woman Rides the Beast* (Eugene, Oregon, 1994) p. 68.

> No other city in the world has ever been celebrated, as the city of Rome has, for its situation on seven hills. Pagan poets and orators, who had no thought of elucidating prophecy, have alike characterized it as 'the seven hilled city.'[82]

The city of Rome and the apostate religion of Roman Catholicism are one and the same.

At this point it is extremely important to say that the identification of Roman Catholicism as modern Babylon is not a personal attack on Catholics–it is not Catholic bashing. A strong indictment is indeed being brought against the system of Catholicism, but not against individuals in the Catholic Church. It is unfortunate there are multitudes being led astray by the false religion of Roman Catholicism. Catholics are in desperate need of the truth of the gospel of Jesus Christ, which will free them from the bondage of the teachings of Catholicism. There are born again Christians in the Catholic Church in spite of the teachings of Rome. We know this because God says, in Revelation 18:4, referring to Babylon, "Come out of her, my people, that ye be not partaker of her sins, and that ye receive not of her plagues." God will lovingly persuade believers, my people, to come out of Catholicism before His judgment falls on Babylon.

Roman Catholicism: The Great Whore

Modern Babylon - Roman Catholicism - is the great whore of Revelation chapter 17.

> And there came one of the seven angels which had the seven vials, and talked with me, saying unto me, Come hither; I will show unto thee the judgment of the great whore that sitteth upon many waters: With whom the kings of the earth have committed fornication, and the inhabitants of the earth have been made drunk with the

[82] Hislop, *The Two Babylons*, p. 2.

> wine of her fornication. So he carried me away in the spirit into the wilderness: and I saw a woman sit upon a scarlet coloured beast, full of names of blasphemy, having seven heads and ten horns. And the woman was arrayed in purple and scarlet colour, and decked with gold and precious stones and pearls, having a golden cup in her hand full of abominations and filthiness of her fornication: And upon her forehead was a name written, MYSTERY, BABYLON THE GREAT, THE MOTHER OF HARLOTS AND ABOMINATIONS OF THE EARTH. And I saw the woman drunken with the blood of the saints, and with the blood of the martyrs of Jesus: and when I saw her, I wondered with great admiration. And the angel said unto me, Wherefore didst thou marvel? I will tell thee the mystery of the woman, and of the beast that carrieth her, which hath the seven heads and ten horns...And here is the mind which hath wisdom. The seven heads are seven mountains, on which the woman sitteth...And he saith unto me, The waters which thou sawest, where the whore sitteth, are peoples, and multitudes, and nations, and tongues...And the woman which thou sawest is that great city, which reigneth over the kings of the earth. (Revelation 17:1-7, 9, 15, 18)

The Apostle John is shown a woman sitting upon a scarlet colored beast. John describes this woman as a great whore who has committed fornication. The fornication she has committed is not physical fornication, but spiritual fornication. She is a spiritual fornicator and as such she is involved in forbidden spiritual relationships. The forbidden spiritual relationship in which she is involved is the worship of God combined with idolatry. Modern Babylon – Roman Catholicism – practices spiritual fornication by mixing Christianity with idolatry, mixing truth with error.

John says the kings of the earth have committed spiritual fornication with this great whore, and the inhabitants of the earth are made drunk with her fornications. World rulers and the inhabitants of the earth have become intoxicated with her idolatry. This great whore is holding a golden cup which is full of abominations and the filthiness, or impurity, of her spiritual fornications. Kings and inhabitants of the earth have drunk from her golden cup, which means they have been partakers of her idolatry. Men have become intoxicated with the spiritual fornications of modern Babylon, and are no longer able to discern truth from error, as they mix Christianity with idolatry.

Mixing Christianity with idolatry is not the only misuse of the Christian faith by the Catholic Church. The Catholic Church rejects the gift of grace through faith alone in Jesus Christ, and replaces it with the legalism and bondage of fulfilling the law of the Old Testament. No man can be justified by the works of the law (Galatians 2:16), but by faith in Jesus Christ, who alone was able to fulfill the works of the law (Matthew 5:17). The Catholic Church is leading their faithful away from the commandments of Christ – and placing them back under the law. They are rejecting the sacrifice of Jesus Christ on the cross, and replacing it with works of the flesh, by which no man can be justified. Catholics believe they can work their way into heaven through penance – a voluntary act of reparation, or self punishment, for their sins.

"MYSTERY, BABYLON THE GREAT, THE MOTHER OF HARLOTS AND ABOMINATIONS OF THE EARTH." Ancient Babylon is the mother of harlots. She has mothered or has given birth to harlot children. Her harlot children are other false religions. She is a false religion and is the mother of false religions; in fact, she is the mother of *all* false religions. Ancient Babylon was the original false religion. Modern Babylon is a copy of ancient Babylon. All other false religions, including Buddhism, Hinduism, Mormonism, Jehovah's Witnesses, and the new age movement were all mothered by ancient Babylon.

This great whore sits upon many waters. These many waters are peoples, and tongues, and nations. Therefore, this woman resides, or dwells, throughout the earth. Roman Catholicism is practiced by more than one billion people from diverse ethnic backgrounds throughout the nations of the world.

She is drunk with the blood of the saints, and with the blood of the martyrs of Jesus Christ. This false religion has been responsible for the killing of countless Christians, many of whom were unwilling to profess the Catholic Church as the only means of salvation. For example, multitudes of Christians were killed by Catholic Inquisitors during the Spanish Inquisition for refusing to confess their faith, not in Jesus Christ, but in the Catholic Church.

This woman is exceedingly rich. She is decked with gold, precious stones, and pearls. The wealth of the Catholic Church is incredible.

Hunt describes the great wealth of the Catholic Church, as documented by a journalist familiar with its riches.

> Nino Lo Bello, former Rome correspondent for *Business Week*, calls the Vatican 'the tycoon on the Tiber' because of its incredible wealth and worldwide enterprises. His research indicates that it [Roman Catholic Church] owns fully one-third of Rome's real estate and is probably the largest holder of stocks and bonds in the world, to say nothing of its ownership of industries from electronics and plastics to airlines and chemical and engineering firms.[83]

The Scarlet Colored Beast: The Antichrist

This great whore sits on a scarlet colored beast – the man beast – the Antichrist. The Beast has seven heads. These seven heads represent the seven hills of the city where the woman resides. In fact, we are told in verse 18 the woman *is* that great city, the city of seven hills. This great whore, which is Roman Catholicism, sits upon the Antichrist who carries her, or is her driving force. The Antichrist is the power that propels this false religion. The woman is arrayed in purple and scarlet. The Beast wears scarlet, which indicates an association between the woman and the Beast.

[83] Hunt, *A Woman Rides the Beast*, p. 241.

> And I stood upon the sand of the sea, and saw a beast rise up out of the sea, having seven heads and ten horns, and upon his horns ten crowns, and upon his heads the name of blasphemy. (Revelation 13:1)

This verse describes a beast having seven heads and ten horns. The Beast is the Antichrist. The seven heads are the apostate religion of the End Times, the Roman Catholic Church. Upon these seven heads is the name of blasphemy, which is evil speaking against God. The Catholic Church is guilty of blasphemy against God. It blasphemes God by teaching its faithful that the only way to the Father is not by grace through faith alone in Jesus Christ, but by works of the flesh and faith in the Catholic Church. We will examine the scarlet colored beast, the Antichrist, in more detail in Chapter 11.

The Mystery of Iniquity: The Doctrines of Catholicism

> For the mystery of iniquity doth already work. (2 Thessalonians 2:7a)

The mystery of iniquity—the secret of wickedness, the power of sin—was at work in biblical times through the false religion of Babylon. The word "mystery" is associated with Babylon in Revelation 17:5, "MYSTERY, BABYLON THE GREAT." In ancient Babylon the Chaldean secrets were called the Chaldean mysteries. The Babylonian power, the power of sin, the mystery, was at work in biblical times, and is still at work today.

> And it came to pass, as he spake these things, a certain woman of the company lifted up her voice, and said unto him, Blessed is the womb that bare thee, and the paps which thou hast sucked. But he said, Yea rather, blessed are they that hear the word of God, and keep it. (Luke 11:27-28)

These verses tell us that Babylonian religious practices were prevalent in biblical times. "Blessed is the womb that bare thee, and the paps which thou hast sucked." This is a blessing that would have been common in the Babylonian religion. The woman was speaking a blessing for Mary, the mother of Jesus. Jesus instead countered with, "Yea rather, blessed are they that hear the word of God, and keep it." Jesus was saying, yes rather, blessed are they that hear the Son of God and keep His words than those who worship the earthly mother of the Messiah.

The teachings and practices of ancient Babylon were an abomination before God. In Isaiah 47:1-5, God promises He will take vengeance on Babylon for the multitude of her sins. The Old Testament records that the Jews were guilty of Babylonian idolatry by practicing sun worship, and by worshipping the queen of heaven (Ezekiel 8:15-16; Jeremiah 44:17-19). These same teachings and practices have been passed down through the ages. The rites and rituals of modern Babylon – Roman Catholicism – directly contradict the Bible. That is why she is called the great whore, a spiritual fornicator.

It is important to examine the many teachings and practices of modern Babylon. These teachings and practices imitate those of ancient Babylon, and are an abomination before the Lord. They were introduced in the modern Babylonian church, over a period of time, and they form the mystery religion of Catholicism.

Alexander Hislop, in *The Two Babylons*, outlines the gradual formation of the doctrines of Roman Catholicism.

> Therefore it was brought in secretly, and by little and little, one corruption being introduced after another, as apostacy proceeded, and the backsliding Church became prepared to tolerate it, till it has reached the gigantic height we now see, when in almost every particular the system of the Papacy is the very antipodes of the system of the primitive Church...Craftily and gradually did Rome lay the foundation of its system of priest-craft, on which it was afterwards to rear so vast a superstructure.[84]

[84] Hislop, *The Two Babylons*, pp. 8-9.

The Roman Catholic Church has proclaimed there is but one Church – the Catholic (universal) Church. Salvation can only be obtained through faith in the Holy Roman Catholic Church. It considers itself the only way of salvation offered by God to man. The Catholic Church believes it alone is the true religion, that God has commanded all men to join the Church. It has declared that competing bodies of believers, including Protestants, are misleading and pernicious. They consider anyone who is not obedient to the Church to be a heathen, and not a part of the kingdom of God.

> We teach, moreover, and declare that, by the disposition of God, the Roman Church possesses supreme ordinary authority over all Churches.[85]

> Basing itself on scripture and tradition, it teaches that the Church, a pilgrim now on earth, is necessary for salvation…Hence, they could not be saved who knowing that the Catholic Church was founded as necessary by God through Christ, would refuse either to enter it, or to remain in it.[86]

> …only by entering the Church can we participate in the redemption wrought for us by Christ…The Church alone dispenses the sacraments. It alone makes known the light of revealed truth. Outside the Church these gifts cannot be obtained. From all this there is but one conclusion: Union with the Church is not merely one out of various means by which salvation may be obtained: it is the only means.[87]

To be saved, one must confess faith, not in Jesus Christ, but in the Catholic Church. During the inquisition, men were required to confess the Roman Catholic Church as the only means of salvation. The head of the Inquisition was the grand inquisitor, and he was confirmed by

---

[85] The Catholic Encyclopedia, Volume XII, October, 2005.

[86] Flannery, O.P., general editor, *Vatican Council II,* Volume 1, pp. 365-366.

[87] The Catholic Encyclopedia, Volume III, Robert Appleton Company, Online Edition by Kevin Knight, http://www.newadvent.org/cathen, October, 2005.

the pope. Inquisitors demanded everyone – Catholics and non-Catholics alike – make a confession of faith in the Catholic Church. The court of the Inquisition held public ceremonies, called the *auto-da-fe'*, or act of faith, where judgment was proclaimed upon heretics. The punishment for failure to confess the Catholic Church as the only way to heaven was death. Revelation 17:6 says, "And I saw the woman drunken with the blood of the saints, and with the blood of the martyrs of Jesus."

> Now the Spirit speaketh expressly, that in the latter times some shall depart from the faith, giving heed to seducing spirits, and doctrines of devils; Speaking lies in hypocrisy; having their conscience seared with a hot iron; Forbidding to marry, and commanding to abstain from meats, which God hath created to be received with thanksgiving of them which believe and know the truth. (1 Timothy 4:1-3)

Paul said in the End Times two false doctrines will be taught in the Church. These teachings will originate from, "seducing spirits, and doctrines of devils." Those who teach these doctrines will have had, "their conscience seared (cauterized, rendered insensitive) with a hot iron." First, the Church will teach celibacy. Priests of Rome are required to be celibate. Vatican Council II says through virginity, or celibacy, priests are set apart for their ministry to Christ. Thus, they are more likely to execute their responsibility as spiritual fathers. Without having an obligation as a husband, or father, they can better serve the Church in this capacity. However, God said it is not good that man should be alone (Genesis 2:18).[88]

Vatican Council II confirms that priests must be celibate.

> But at the same time the [Second Vatican] Council did not hesitate to confirm solemnly the ancient, sacred and providential present law of priestly celibacy.[89]

---

[88] Wood, *Six Days to the Rapture*, Tape 4.

[89] Austin Flannery, O.P., general editor, *Vatican Council II*, (Northport, New York, 1982) Volume 2, p. 290.

Secondly, the Church will teach abstention from eating as a form of righteousness. Priests of Rome are required to fast as an act of godliness. The Roman fast is called Lent, which comes from the word Lenten, which describes the longest days of the sun. This fast has its origin in sun worship. The Lenten or Easter fast lasts forty days.[90]

Just as Semiramis, the mother of Nimrod, was worshipped in ancient Babylon, Mary, the mother of Jesus, is worshipped in modern Babylon. The trinity in ancient Babylon consisted of the father, the mother and the son. As Hislop notes, the Catholic Church has proclaimed the same. "Is there one, who fears God, and who reads these lines, who would not admit that Paganism alone could ever have inspired such a doctrine as that avowed by the Melchites at the Nicene Council, that the Holy Trinity consisted of 'the Father, the Virgin Mary, and the Messiah their Son'?"[91]

Catholics say they do not worship Mary, they say they offer her veneration. Veneration is special worship, called Dulia, which Mary deserves because she shares in the honor given to Jesus Christ. Therefore, veneration is worship. In other words, they believe Mary has a part in our salvation, along with Jesus Christ; she receives honor and glory that we are to give to Christ alone.[92]

The Catholic Church worships Mary in the Madonna. The Madonna is a characterization of the mother Mary and the baby Jesus. It is only a Madonna when the principal figure is the virgin Mary, and Jesus is represented as a child. In the ancient Babylonian religion Semiramis was worshipped as the mother of God. She became the principal figure of worship, and her son Ninus was depicted in a secondary role, as a child. Instead of praying to Ninus, Babylonians were to pray to Semiramis, and she would then intercede on their behalf to Ninus; she was his mediator. The Catholic Church claims Mary is the mediator between God and man. This nullifies Jesus Christ's position as the only mediator between God and man, which was given to Him alone by the Father. According to 1

---

90 Wood, *Six Days to the Rapture*, Tape 4.

91 Hislop, *The Two Babylons*, p. 89.

92 Wood, *Six Days to the Rapture*, Tape 4.

Timothy 2:5, Jesus Christ is the only mediator between God and man. For Catholics, Christ is now sharing this title with flesh and blood.

The Catholic Church has given Mary multiple titles. All of these titles are an abomination because they raise Mary up to a position equal to or greater than Jesus Christ. Through these many titles Mary's stature is increased, while Jesus Christ's stature is diminished. Mary is worshipped as Regina Coeli. Regina Coeli means queen of heaven. Catholics venerate Mary as the queen of heaven. Keep in mind, this is the same title given to Semiramis in ancient Babylon. God made the land of Israel a desolation because of their worship of her (Jeremiah 44:22). Mary is worshipped as the Co-Redemptrix. Co-Redemptrix means Co-Redeemer. This means Mary and Jesus Christ are our redeemers. In other words, Mary and Jesus Christ have equal status before God in redeeming us from our sins. According to Titus 2:14, Jesus Christ is the only one who has redeemed us from our sins. Mary is also worshipped as the mediatrix of all graces – the blessed mother. Mary now pleads in heaven for the application of graces, and then distributes them to the believer. This means all the blessings that God gives to the believer must come through Mary, just as Semiramis was worshipped as the mediator between God and man. Mary has been given the title of Mary, Mylitta or mediatrix of God. Mary is the mediator between God and man. Even though Semiramis had a son, it was taught she was undefiled, she was a virgin. Mary is worshipped as a virgin, even though the Bible clearly says Jesus had siblings (Matthew 6:3).[93]

Vatican Council II proclaims Mary's virginity and her position in the Catholic Church as mediator and redeemer:

> Finally the Immaculate Virgin preserved free from all stain of original sin, was taken up body and soul into heavenly glory, when her earthly life was over, and exalted by the Lord as Queen over all things.[94]

---

[93] Ibid., Tape 4.

[94] Austin Flannery, O.P., general editor, *Vatican Council II*, (Northport, New York, 1984), Volume 1, pp. 417-418.

> Taken up to heaven she [Mary] did not lay aside this saving office but by her manifold intercession continues to bring us gifts of eternal salvation.[95]

Revelation chapter 17 speaks of the whore of Babylon, which is the Roman Catholic Church. This whore is depicted as a woman – the mother of harlots. Just as Semiramis was worshipped as the queen of heaven in ancient Babylon, Mary is the visible expression of the Catholic Church, modern Babylon. She is worshipped and adored by the church. She is the queen of the Church. Revelation 18:7 speaks of this queen saying, "How much she hath glorified herself, and lived deliciously, so much torment and sorrow give her: for she saith in her heart, I sit a queen, and am no widow, and shall see no sorrow." Mary's importance in the Catholic Church will increase as the second coming of the Lord draws near. Apparitions of Mary dramatically increased in number during the 20th century, and continue to increase at an alarming rate today.[96] Through these apparitions Mary has declared to all that her importance to the Catholic Church, and to the world at large, will increase. Miracles such as physical healings and supernatural phenomena supposedly take place when Mary makes her appearances. Observers say she has proclaimed she will perform greater signs and wonders in the future. These apparitions are not just taking place in areas with large Catholic populations, but in nations around the world, regardless of their religious composition. Shrines commemorating apparitions of Mary attract millions every year. Tens of millions visit the shrine at Guadalupe, Mexico each year. Fatima, Medjugorje, Lourdes, Sabena Grande, and other shrines similarly attract millions. 1 Timothy 4:1 warns, "that in the latter times some shall depart from the faith, giving heed to seducing spirits." Mary as worshiped by the Catholic Church is an imposter, and the Church should not be seduced by these demonic apparitions.

The Catholic Church has adopted the practice of praying through patron saints. Certain dead saints are designated as intercessors. These are patron saints. Catholics are instructed to pray to these dead saints, and they

95 Ibid., p. 419.

96 Queen of All, http://www.harpazo.net/Queen.html, March, 2006.

in turn will pray to Mary, or to Jesus. Again, this is not what the Bible instructs; Jesus Christ is our only mediator or intercessor.[97]

Catholics pray the rosary. The rosary is both a prayer and the beads used to count the number of times the devotion is prayed. This prayer is directed toward the virgin Mary. Catholics who pray the rosary repetitively are offered an indulgence. According to Matthew 6:7, we are not to pray repetitious prayers.

The Catholic Encyclopedia instructs the faithful in the proper method of reciting the rosary.

> The Rosary is a certain form of prayer wherein we say fifteen decades or tens of Hail Marys with an Our Father between each ten, while at each of these fifteen decades we recall successively in pious meditation one of the mysteries of our Redemption.[98]

Purgatory is the place where Catholics must reside after death until they are perfected, and are then ready for entrance into heaven.

Catholics believe when they die they are not free from their sins. They have not paid the full price for their sins until they first suffer punishment in purgatory. In other words, Jesus Christ's death on the cross for the sin of the world is not sufficient for Catholics. Ephesians 2:8-9 says, "For by grace are ye saved through faith; and that not of yourselves: it is the gift of God: Not of works, lest any man should boast." We are either free of our sins through faith in Jesus Christ at the time of our death, or our fate is the second death and the lake of fire. There is no biblical justification for belief in a cleansing of ones sins after death.

The only way for a Catholic to be freed from purgatory is to be granted an indulgence, which is only granted after a required payment is made. An indulgence is a remission of the punishment a person endures as a result

---

[97] Wood, *Six Days to the Rapture*, Tape 4.

[98] The Catholic Encyclopedia, Volume XII, Robert Appleton Company, Online Edition by Kevin Knight, http://www.newadvent.org/cathen, October, 2005.

of sins committed. Since the Catholic Church believes Christ gave the Church the power to forgive sins, they believe they also have the power of granting indulgences. This forgiveness of sin extends both to the guilt and to the punishment; therefore, the Church can free the sinner from the penalty of sin.

Vatican Council II explains the use of indulgences in the Church.

> An indulgence is a remission before God of the temporal punishment due to sins whose guilt has already been forgiven, which the faithful Christian who is duly disposed gains under certain defined conditions through the Church's help when, as minister of Redemption, she dispenses and applies with authority the treasury of the satisfaction won by Christ and the saints.
>
> An indulgence is partial or plenary according as it removes either part or all of the temporal punishment due to sin.[99]

The Catholic Encyclopedia also endorses the use of indulgences.

> Since the power of granting indulgences has been given to the Church by Christ, and since the Church from the earliest times has made use of this Divinely given power, the holy synod teaches and ordains that the use of indulgences, as most salutary to Christians and as approved by the authority of the councils, shall be retained in the Church; and it further pronounces anathema against those who either declare that indulgences are useless or deny that the Church has the power to grant them (Enchridion, 989).[100]

The Catholic Church has declared an anathema against anyone who says indulgences are useless or denies the Church has the power to

[99] Flannery, O.P., general editor, *Vatican Council II*, Volume 1, p. 75.

[100] The Catholic Encyclopedia, Volume VII, Robert Appleton Company, Online Edition by Kevin Knight, http://www.newadvent.org/cathen, October, 2005.

grant them. An anathema is, "A ban or curse solemnly pronounced by ecclesiastical authority and accompanied by excommunication."[101] The Catholic Church has pronounced a ban or curse on all, be they Catholics or non-Catholics, who do not accept their teaching on indulgences. This curse is accompanied by excommunication from the Church. Since they teach there is no salvation apart from the Catholic Church, they are, through excommunication, committing to hell those who do not accept indulgences as being useful to the Church.

The Catholic Church has pronounced more than one hundred anathemas regarding doctrines such as indulgences, which seems very severe, especially considering their expressed desire not to be criticized by non-Catholics, and to be accepted in the Christian community. These numerous anathemas fly in the face of the mission of Evangelicals and Catholics Together, an organization diligently working to bridge the considerable doctrinal differences separating evangelicals and Catholics.

T.A. McMahon notes the intentions of Evangelicals and Catholics Together.

> Highly influential Catholic clergy and evangelical leaders had participated in ECT in the hope of developing closer ties and greater collaboration in activities of common interest to both traditions, especially working together for the moral good of society and winning souls to Christ...the most significant declaration in the original ECT document had been 'the simple statement that we [Catholics and evangelicals] recognize one another as brothers and sisters in Christ.[102]

Catholics say they want to be recognized as brothers and sisters in Christ. They say they are weary of Catholic bashing. What then can be said of the more than one hundred anathemas of the Catholic Church?

---

[101] Webster's Seventh New Collegiate Dictionary, (Springfield, MA, G. & C. Merriam Company, 1971), p. 33.

[102] T.A. McMahon, "The Berean Call," July, 2002.

Salvation through faith alone is not sufficient for the Catholic Church, as was affirmed in The Canons and the Decrees of the Council of Trent.

> If anyone says that after the reception of the grace of justification the guilt is so remitted and the debt of eternal punishment so blotted out to every repentant sinner, that no debt of temporal punishment remains to be discharged either in this world or in purgatory before the gates of heaven can be opened, let him be anathema.[103]

In ancient Babylon, when a covenant was made, blood was required; in the form of human sacrifices. However, these sacrifices were eventually eliminated and the ceremonies evolved into unbloody sacrifices. The Catholic Mass is an unbloody sacrifice. The celebration of the bread and wine in the Catholic Church is very different from a Protestant communion where the bread and the wine are a *representation* of the body and blood of Christ. The Eucharist, the consecrated bread and wine in the Catholic Holy Communion, is believed to be literally and physically changed, through a concept called transubstantiation, into the actual body and blood of Jesus Christ. The Catholic priest alone has the power to change the sacraments into the body and blood of Jesus Christ. The Catholic Church teaches that these sacraments are necessary for the salvation of the believer. Herein lies much of the control the Church exerts over Catholics. Because only a Catholic priest has the power to transform the wafer and the wine into the body and blood of Jesus Christ, and only Catholics in good standing in the Church are allowed to take Holy Communion, the believer has no choice but to join and remain a faithful member. The alternative is to be pronounced a heretic, to be excluded from taking Holy Communion, and to be subject to an anathema that commits them to the flames of hell forever. Is it any wonder Catholics cling so tightly to their Church and will defend it vehemently, but are constantly fearful of the possibility of losing their salvation?

Hunt provides a clear explanation of the importance of the sacrifice of the Mass to Catholics.

---

[103] Hunt, *A Woman Rides the Beast*, p. 352.

> We have come to the very heart of Roman Catholicism, that unique element which separates it from all other religions and especially from evangelical Christianity: the sacrifice of the Mass. In it 'the sacrifice of the cross is perpetuated. [It is] the source and the summit of the whole of the Church's worship and of the Christian life.' Declared present on the altar through the miracle of transubstantiation (which only the Catholic priest can perform) is the 'true body and blood of Jesus Christ, who is really and substantially present under the appearance of bread and wine in order to offer himself in the sacrifice of the Mass and to be received as spiritual food in Holy Communion.
>
> Christ said from the cross just as he died, 'It is finished' (John 19:30). But to the Catholic it isn't finished. Christ's sacrifice continues to this day, being endlessly repeated on Catholic altars: 'Each time Mass is offered, the Sacrifice of Christ is repeated. A new sacrifice is not offered, but by divine power, one and the same sacrifice is repeated...In the Mass Christ continues to offer Himself to the Father as He did on the Cross' but in an 'unbloody manner under the appearance of bread and wine.[104]

The host, or wafer, in the Catholic communion must be round or it is rejected. However, there is no biblical admonition to make the representation of the body of our Lord in communion round. The Catholic wafer must be round because it is fashioned to represent the sun. The host is placed in a sunburst, called the monstrance, and is then worshipped. This is the same sunburst used by ancient Babylonians, who worshipped it as a representation of Ninus their sun god, who nourished the souls of men. When Catholics worship the sunburst, or monstrance, they are imitating ancient Babylonian practices.

---

[104] Ibid., p. 369.

The Canons and the Decrees of the Council of Trent, and Vatican Council II, confirm the necessity of the sacraments to the life of a Catholic.

> If anyone says that the sacraments of the New Law are not necessary for salvation but are superfluous, and that without them or without the desire of them men obtain from God through faith alone the grace of justification, though all are not necessary for each one, let him be anathema.[105]
>
> The celebration of the Eucharist which takes place at Mass is the action not only of Christ, but also of the Church. For in it Christ perpetuates in an unbloody manner the sacrifice offered on the cross, offering himself to the Father for the world's salvation through the ministry of priests.[106]
>
> We believe that the mass which is celebrated by the priest in the person of Christ in virtue of the power he receives in the Sacrament of Order, and which is offered by him in the name of Christ and of the members of his Mystical Body, is indeed the Sacrifice of Calvary sacramentally realized on our altars. We believe that, as the bread and wine consecrated by the Lord at the Last Supper were changed into his Body and Blood which were to be offered for us on the Cross, so likewise are the bread and wine consecrated by the priest changed into the Body and Blood of Christ now enthroned in glory in heaven.[107]
>
> If anyone says that in the sacred and holy sacrament of the Eucharist the substance of the bread and wine remains conjointly with the body and blood of our Lord Jesus Christ, and denies that wonderful and singular change of the whole substance of the bread into the body and the whole substance of the wine into the blood, the appearances

[105] H.J. Schroeder, O.P., *The Canons And Decrees Of The Council Of Trent*, (1978) p. 52.

[106] Flannery, O.P., general editor, *Vatican Council II*, Volume 1, p. 103.

[107] Flannery, O.P., general editor, *Vatican Council II*, Volume 2, p. 393.

> only of bread and wine remaining, which change the Catholic Church most aptly calls transubstantiation, let him be anathema.[108]

The Catholic Church gives veneration or worship to images, idols, and art.

> From the very earliest days of the Church there has been a tradition whereby images of our Lord, his holy Mother, and of saints are displayed in churches for the veneration of the faithful.[109]

The second commandment of Exodus 20:4 says, "Thou shalt not make unto thee any graven image (carved resemblance, idol), or any likeness of any thing that is in heaven above, or that is in the earth beneath, or that is in the water under the earth." God said we are not to make images or idols of anything in heaven or in earth. We are not to bow down to them or serve them.

The Catholic Church practices relic worship. A relic is a body part remaining as a memorial of a departed Catholic saint. The Catholic Church worships thousands of relics of dead patron saints, which they believe are sacred. In ancient Babylon, after Ninus was killed, his body was dismembered, and was scattered throughout the region. After Semiramis collected the body parts of Ninus they were placed in a container and worshipped. Relics are placed in a container called a reliquary. Catholics believe relics sanctify the building in which they are placed. Miracles have been attributed to relics.

It is a custom in Catholic Churches to possess a relic of a more important saint. Pope John Paul II, on a trip to Bulgaria, donated a piece of the body of his predecessor, Pope John XXIII, to a new cathedral in Sofia.

> According to the Rome daily La Repubblica the relic, wrapped in a medieval cloth, will be kept in the cathedral as an object of veneration. It was removed from John's

[108] Schroeder, O.P., *The Canons And Decrees Of The Council Of Trent*, p. 79.
[109] Hunt, *A Woman Rides the Beast*, p. 178.

> exhumed and restored corpse last July after he was put in a glass coffin and displayed in St. Peter's square to thousands of pilgrims...Sofia's new cathedral, built to replace one destroyed by bombing in 1944, was expecting a relic in order to make a shrine, but had no inkling it would receive such a spectacular present from the Vatican... The basilica in Padua displays St Anthony's tongue, jawbone and vocal cords. Other churches and cathedrals boast hanks of hair, bits of bone, heads, fingers and toes. This practice of venerating relics has been criticized as a medieval hangover. In a 1520 pamphlet Martin Luther mocked the collection of the archbishop of Mainz, Germany, for including 'three flames of the bush of Moses on Mount Sinai' and 'two feathers and an egg from the Holy Ghost.' John Paul is a traditionalist whose reverence for relics has reinvigorated the tradition.[110]

It would be appropriate to take a moment to consider the rather unusual practice of worshiping a relic of a dead patron saint. The thought of an intelligent, reasoning, twenty-first century person praying to a patron saint, a special dead Church member, who in turn prays to Mary, the dead mother of Jesus, who then prays to God, seems rather bizarre. The Bible does not distribute any such abilities, or give any such authority, to special dead Church members, or the mother of Jesus. Relic worship is clearly a pagan practice that has no biblical foundation.

"And call no man your father upon the earth" (Matthew 23:9). We are not, in a spiritual sense, to call any man our father. This scripture is not referring to our biological fathers. In ancient Babylon priests were spiritual fathers. The Catholic Church adopted the term father from ancient Babylon. The Catholic confession involves admitting sins to a Catholic priest, or father. The priest, acting as a judge, can grant the remission of sin. The Catholic Church has given the priest the authority to say, "I absolve you of your sins in the name of God." 1 John 1:9 and Acts 10:43 say that Christ alone can

---

[110] Rory Carroll, Pope Donates a Fragment of Forerunner, http://www.guardian.co.uk/international/story/0,,722706,00.html, May 27, 2002.

forgive our sin. There is only one mediator between God and man – Christ Jesus (1 Timothy 2:5). It is clear from scriptures the Catholic Church does not have this authority; it cannot give absolution, or remission of sins. However, Vatican Council II, and The Canons and the Decrees of the Council of Trent, command Catholics to practice confession.[111]

> Confession of sins is part of the sacrament of penance. It issues from true self-knowledge and sorrow for sin. Such interior heart-searching and external accusation ought to be done in the awareness of God's mercy. Confession presupposes in the penitent the willingness to open his heart to God's minister. It presupposes in the minister spiritual judgment, for it is he who, acting for Christ and having the power of the keys, the power to forgive and to retain sins, pronounces judgment.[112]

> If anyone denies that sacramental confession was instituted by divine law or is necessary to salvation; or says that the manner of confessing secretly to a priest alone, which the Catholic Church has always observed from the beginning and still observes, is at variance with the institution and command of Christ and is a human contrivance, let him be anathema.[113]

Within the Catholic Church, the office immediately below the pope is that of Cardinal. Cardinals are dignitaries of the Catholic Church and counselors of the pope. There is no biblical reference for the office or title of Cardinal; it is of ancient Babylonian origin. Cardinals in ancient Babylon opened the Chaldean mysteries that could not be understood by mere men. Cardinals had the power to turn the hinge, or open the door, to deeper understanding – to discern the doctrines that the common man could not understand. The College of Cardinals opens the numerous mysteries of the Catholic Church. It is the Church alone that claims the ability to

[111] Wood, *Six Days to the Rapture*, Tape 4.

[112] Flannery, O.P., general editor, *Vatican Council II*, Volume 2, p. 38.

[113] Schroeder, O.P., *The Canons And Decrees Of The Council Of Trent*, pp. 102-103.

understand the deep things of God. The mysteries are understood by the Cardinals, who then communicate them to the members of the Church. Revelation 17:5 says, "Upon her forehead was a name written, MYSTERY, BABYLON THE GREAT."

The Catholic Church has declared Christ's death and resurrection will be observed according to the full moon, just as it was observed in ancient Babylon. Easter is now celebrated on the first Sunday following the first full moon after the vernal equinox. Celebrating Easter according to the stages of the moon is clearly a direct carryover from the practice of astrology in ancient Babylon.

Roman Catholicism functions as a bridge between Christianity and paganism. The Catholic Church plays both sides of the spiritual fence. To Christians, it claims to be Christian in an attempt to bring them under the covering of the Catholic Church. Christians who dialogue with the Catholic Church should be aware of its motives. It has no intention of compromising even one article of its faith in order to come together with evangelicals, or be accepted into the Christian community. To the Catholic Church there is only one way – its way; it is the evangelicals who need to amend their ways. Christians should know that the Catholic Church views them as sheep who have lost their way. The Catholic Church believes it is reaching out in an attempt to bring lost souls back under the covering of the Mother Church, who alone possesses the means of salvation. To pagans, it claims to be pagan in an attempt to bring them under the covering of the Catholic Church. It has reached out to people of all religions – Muslims, Hindus, voodoo worshippers and snake charmers – and has told them there is a place for them under the covering of the Catholic Church.

As the End Times approach, the Christian Church will be to a great degree a compromising Church; it will be more interested in a spirit of unity than in a unity of the Spirit. Rome will offer the unity the Church is seeking. For those who are caught up in a desire to reconcile with all those who call themselves people of faith, movements like Evangelicals and Catholics Together will offer the religious togetherness they are seeking.

As Hunt makes quite clear, the declaration of, "Evangelicals and Catholics Together: The Christian Mission in the 3rd Millennium," basically overturned the reformation.

> The key element behind this historic joint declaration is the previously unthinkable admission on the part of leading evangelicals that active participation in the Catholic Church makes one a Christian. If that is indeed the case, then the Reformation was a tragic mistake. The millions who were martyred (during a thousand years before the Reformation and since then to the present time) for rejecting Catholicism as a false gospel have all died in vain. If, however, the Reformers were right, then this new agreement between Catholics and evangelicals could well be the cleverest and deadliest blow struck against the gospel in the entire history of the church.[114]

The editor of Alexander Hislop's work, *The Two Babylons,* provides insight as to why men promote the idolatrous religion of Catholicism.

> But it is deplorable to think that, notwithstanding all the revelations made from time to time of the true character and origin of Popery, Ritualism still makes progress in the Churches, and that men of the highest influence in the State are so infatuated as to seek to strengthen their political position by giving countenance to a system of idolatry.[115]

God made it quite clear how He feels about idolatry. The second commandment says, "Thou shalt not make unto thee any graven image, or any likeness of any thing that is in heaven above, or that is in the earth beneath, or that is in the water under the earth: Thou shalt not bow down thyself to them, nor serve them: for I the Lord thy God am a jealous God, visiting the iniquity of the fathers upon the children unto the third and

---

[114] Hunt, *A Woman Rides the Beast,* p. 6.

[115] Hislop, *The Two Babylons,* p. vii.

fourth generation of them that hate me" (Exodus 20:4-5). What other commandment carries such a weighty consequence? It would be advisable for those who consider too lightly the sin of idolatry to also consider the judgment of God that will be visited upon those who participate in it.

The Roman Catholic Church – modern Babylon – is the great whore of the book of Revelation. It preaches another gospel, one that has no saving power, which leads astray those who follow it.

Hunt provides clever insight into Acts 16:31.

> Paul didn't tell the desperate jailer in Acts 16:31: "Believe on Christ and that will get you started on a long road of good deeds, Church membership, sacraments, prayers to saints, etc. If you stick with it, eventually, after excruciating suffering in the flames of purgatory and if enough Masses and Rosaries are said for you, heaven's gates will at last open." But that is the gospel of Rome. These ideas are all later inventions, which give Rome incredible power over those who look to her for salvation. That hundreds of millions are still being led astray concerns us deeply.[116]

The following summary demonstrates that Roman Catholicism, modern Babylon—a mirror image of ancient Babylon, the original false religion—is the woman who rides the Beast.

- The Roman Catholic Church has proclaimed there is one Church, the Roman Catholic Church, and salvation can only come through faith in the Church.
- The Roman Catholic Church worships the Madonna.
- The Roman Catholic Church worships the queen of heaven.
- The Roman Catholic Church teaches Mary is our redeemer.
- The Roman Catholic Church worships the earthly mother of God as the mediator between God and man.

[116] Hunt, *A Woman Rides the Beast,* p. 362.

- The Roman Catholic Church teaches Mary was a virgin, did not die, and was assumed into heaven.
- The Roman Catholic Church uses the rosary.
- The Roman Catholic Church believes in indulgences.
- The Roman Catholic Church celebrates the unbloody sacrifice.
- The Roman Catholic Church uses the monstrance as a symbol in worship.
- The Roman Catholic Church worships relics.
- The Roman Catholic Church uses the term father for their priests.
- The Roman Catholic Church teaches the church alone, through the office of the cardinal, can open understanding to the mysteries of God.
- The Roman Catholic Church is decked in gold and precious stones.
- The Roman Catholic Church celebrates the resurrection of Jesus Christ on the first Sunday following the first full moon after the vernal equinox.
- The Roman Catholic Church worships images, idols, and art.

CHAPTER 11

THE BEAST: THE ANTICHRIST

> So he carried me away in the spirit into the wilderness: and I saw a woman sit upon a scarlet coloured beast, full of names of blasphemy, having seven heads and ten horns. (Revelation 17:3)

Revelation 17:3 describes the Beast, the son of perdition, the man of sin, the Antichrist. This is the man who will confirm a covenant between Israel and many nations for seven years. In the middle of this seven-year period – the Seventieth Week of Daniel – he will break the Covenant with Israel. He will enter the temple in Jerusalem, sit down on the Mercy Seat, and declare he is God on earth. This is the Abomination of Desolation. The Abomination of Desolation is the event that begins the Great Tribulation, Jacob's trouble. The Antichrist will then begin an all out assault on Israel in hopes of annihilating the Jews. He will eventually subdue every nation on earth, and will demand the world bow down and worship him.

The entire world is looking for a messiah. Christians are waiting for the return of Jesus Christ the Messiah. The Jews are anxiously awaiting the coming of the Messiah. The nations of the world are looking for a messiah, or deliverer, to bring peace to the Middle East. Unfortunately, many will accept a counterfeit messiah – the Antichrist. Those who are not looking for the return of Jesus Christ will be deceived. When the

Antichrist brings peace to the Middle East, and produces mighty signs and wonders, multitudes will fall down and worship him.

Dave Hunt, in his book, *How Close Are We?*, provides insight into the identity of the Antichrist.

> The ultimate purpose of the Messiah's coming is clearly stated in Scripture: to establish a Kingdom of everlasting peace. Jesus didn't do that. It is therefore reasoned that He couldn't have been the Messiah. Whoever establishes peace in the Middle East and throughout the world—and it will be established temporarily—will be hailed as the long-awaited Messiah, both by Israel and the world. That man, for whom the entire world waits, will, in fact, be the Antichrist. "Him ye will receive," said Christ (John 5:43), and all for a lack of understanding what the prophets have said![117]

The word Antichrist comes from the Greek, *Antichristos*, which means an opponent of the Messiah. He is opposed to, or is against Christ; he is a substitute for, or in the place of Him. The spirit of Antichrist declares that Jesus Christ is not the Son of God. This spirit denies Jesus Christ came in the flesh and that He is God. This is what the Antichrist will do when he sits down in the temple. He will declare he is God, and will demand the world bow down and worship him.

Through satanically induced charisma, and false signs and lying spirits, the Antichrist will deceive the world, Israel, and many in the Church. This individual will be an extremely popular figure. He will be worshipped by the world. Yet, he will not deceive those who will recognize him from scripture and from a witness of the Holy Spirit.

> Little children, it is the last time: and as ye have heard that Antichrist shall come, even now are there many Antichrists; whereby we know that it is the last time.

[117] Hunt, *How Close Are We?*, pp. 10-11.

> They went out from us, but they were not of us; for if they had been of us, they would no doubt have continued with us: but they went out, that they might be made manifest that they were not all of us. But ye have an unction from the Holy One, and ye know all things. I have not written unto you because ye know not the truth, but because ye know it, and that no lie is of the truth. Who is a liar but he that denieth that Jesus is the Christ? He is Antichrist, that denieth the Father and the Son. Whosoever denieth the Son, the same hath not the Father: (but) he that acknowledgeth the Son hath the Father also. (1 John 2:18-23)

> And every spirit that confesseth not that Jesus Christ is come in the flesh is not of God: and this is that spirit of Antichrist, whereof ye have heard that it should come; and even now already is it in the world. (1 John 4:3)

> For many deceivers are entered into the world, who confess not that Jesus Christ is come in the flesh. This is a deceiver and an Antichrist. (2 John 1:7)

Many are waiting for the identity of the Antichrist to be revealed. Christians have an unction, an endowment or anointing, from the Holy Spirit to know all things. The Holy Spirit can reveal all things to us. We can know the identity of the Antichrist through a witness of the Spirit of God, and the word of God. It will not be difficult to identify the Antichrist because he will be empowered by Satan, will deny the Father and the Son, and will enter the temple and demand to be worshipped as God.

> Now we beseech you, brethren, by the coming of our Lord Jesus Christ, and by our gathering together unto him, That ye be not soon shaken in mind, or be troubled, neither by spirit, nor by word, nor by letter as from us, as that the day of Christ is at hand. Let no man deceive you by any means: for that day shall not come, except there

> come a falling away first, and that man of sin be revealed, the son of perdition. Who opposeth and exalteth himself above all that is called God, or that is worshipped; so that he as God sitteth in the temple of God, showing himself that he is God. (2 Thessalonians 2:1-4)

Paul told the Thessalonian church not to be shaken by reports the day of Christ, the Rapture of the Church, had already taken place. He told them not to be deceived because that day, the gathering together, cannot occur until two events have taken place. First, there will be a falling away (apostasy, defection from the truth). The falling away mentioned in 2 Thessalonians does not refer to a general apostasy that would begin in biblical times and continue until the End Times. Instead, it is a very specific falling away, one that will take place during the Seventieth Week of Daniel. The second event that must take place is the revealing (uncovering, disclosing) of the Antichrist. The revealing of the Antichrist will take place at the Abomination of Desolation, when he will enter the temple and declare he is God on earth.

Daniel's Visions

Daniel was a prophet (Matthew 24:15) and his prophetic dreams and visions provide us with a tremendous amount of information regarding the End Times. These visions contain a wealth of information regarding the identity of the Antichrist, as well as an account of the succession of world powers, and other significant events in world history.

The first of Daniel's visions is described in Daniel chapter 2. Nebuchadnezzar, king of Babylon, had a dream and saw a vision that troubled him. The king called his magicians, astrologers, sorcerers, and Chaldeans, and told them he had a dream, but that he could not remember the dream – it was, "gone from me." The king commanded them to reveal to him both the dream and the interpretation. They responded by saying there is no man who could tell the king both the dream and its interpretation. In essence, they were admitting the gods they worshipped were powerless to help them. They could have fabricated an interpretation if the king had told them his dream. The king was very displeased and he ordered all of the wise men of Babylon slain.

Unfortunately, the king's decree meant Daniel and his friends would also be slain, since they were included in the company of the wise men of Babylon. Daniel and his friends were part of the captives of Judah who were carried away into Babylon after Nebuchadnezzar had defeated Israel. They were the best and the brightest of the children of Israel, and the king had taken them into his palace to learn the ways of the Chaldeans. As an indication of Daniel's abiding relationship with the Father, he fell on his face before God and asked for mercy. God revealed to Daniel both Nebuchadnezzar's dream and its interpretation. Daniel blessed the God of heaven, went before the king, and revealed the dream and the interpretation.

> Thou, O king, sawest, and behold a great image. This great image, whose brightness was excellent, stood before thee; and the form thereof was terrible. This image's head was of fine gold, his breast and his arms of silver, his belly and his thighs of brass, His legs of iron, his feet part of iron and part of clay. Thou sawest till that a stone was cut out without hands, which smote the image upon his feet that were of iron and clay, and brake them to pieces. Then was the iron, the clay, the brass, the silver, and the gold, broken to pieces together, and became like the chaff of the summer threshingfloors; and the wind carried them away, that no place was found for them: and the stone that smote the image became a great mountain, and filled the whole earth. This is the dream; and we will tell the interpretation thereof before the king. Thou, O king, art a king of kings: for the God of heaven hath given thee a kingdom, power, and strength, and glory. And wheresoever the children of men dwell, the beasts of the field and the fowls of the heaven hath he given into thine hand, and hath made thee ruler over them all. Thou art this head of gold. And

> after thee shall arise another kingdom inferior to thee, and another third kingdom of brass, which shall bear rule over all the earth. And the fourth kingdom shall be strong as iron: forasmuch as iron breaketh in pieces and subdueth all things: and as iron that breaketh all these, shall it break in pieces and bruise. And whereas thou sawest the feet and toes, part of potters' clay, and part of iron, the kingdom shall be divided; but there shall be in it of the strength of the iron, forasmuch as thou sawest the iron mixed with miry clay. And as the toes of the feet were part of iron, and part of clay, so the kingdom shall be partly strong, and partly broken. And whereas thou sawest iron mixed with miry clay, they shall mingle themselves with the seed of men: but they shall not cleave one to another, even as iron is not mixed with clay. And in the days of these kings shall the God of heaven set up a kingdom, which shall never be destroyed: and the kingdom shall not be left to other people, but it shall break in pieces and consume all these kingdoms, and it shall stand for ever. Forasmuch as thou sawest that the stone was cut out of the mountain without hands, and that it brake in pieces the iron, the brass, the clay, the silver, and the gold; the great God hath made known to the king what shall come to pass hereafter: and the dream is certain, and the interpretation thereof sure. (Daniel 2:31-45)

There is tremendous significance to Nebuchadnezzar's dream. Contained in it are descriptions of dramatic world events that would take place thousands of years in the future. It provides an account of the rise and fall of kings and kingdoms, contrasted with the kingdom of Jesus Christ that will never end. It predicts the succession of every world kingdom that would have a significant impact on the Jews, from Daniel's time, until the second coming of Jesus Christ.

Daniel was shown a great image, whose brightness was excellent, and whose form was terrible. The image had a head of gold, breast and arms of silver, belly and thighs of brass, legs of iron, and feet of part iron and part clay.

Daniel told the king, "Thou art this head of gold." Nebuchadnezzar was the king of Babylon and he ruled over the greatest kingdom upon the earth. He was ruler over the third great kingdom upon the earth; two great kingdoms had preceded him – Egypt and Assyria.

"And after thee shall arise another kingdom inferior to thee." The kingdom of the Medes and Persians succeeded the kingdom of Babylon. They are the breast and arms of silver. The two arms of silver represent the two separate nations, the Medes and the Persians, which comprise this kingdom.

"And another third kingdom of brass, which shall bear rule over all the earth." The third kingdom of Nebuchadnezzar's dream is Greece. It is the belly and thighs of brass.

"And the fourth kingdom shall be strong as iron: forasmuch as iron breaketh in pieces and subdueth all things: and as iron that breaketh all these, shall it break in pieces and bruise." The fourth kingdom is the Roman Empire. It is the legs of iron. Verse 41 says, "The kingdom shall be divided." The legs of iron indicated a split or division in power. Just as the two arms of silver depict the two nations of the Medes and Persians, the two legs of iron represent the two divisions of the Roman Empire – Roman Catholicism and Eastern Orthodoxy.

Hunt explains the division of the Roman Empire.

> The two legs in the image foretold the division of the fourth empire, the Roman, into East and West, and so it occurred. In AD 330 Constantine established Constantinople (today's Istanbul) as his new imperial capital, leaving the Bishop of Rome in charge in the West and setting the stage for the later political and religious division of the empire. The final break came religiously in 1054 when the Orthodox Church in the East broke off from the Roman Catholic Church in the West and

> Pope Leo IX excommunicated Michael Cerularius, Patriarch of Constantinople. That division between Roman Catholicism and Eastern Orthodoxy remains to this day.[118]

"And whereas thou sawest the feet and toes, part of potters' clay, and part of iron, the kingdom shall be divided; but there shall be in it of the strength of the iron, forasmuch as thou sawest the iron mixed with miry clay. And as the toes of the feet were part of iron, and part of clay, so the kingdom shall be partly strong, and partly broken (fragile)." The fifth kingdom will consist of ten kings or powers. They are the ten toes that are part iron and part clay. This fifth kingdom, which will proceed from the Roman Empire, the iron kingdom, will not possess the strength of the Roman Empire. Unlike the Roman Empire, which was composed entirely of iron, meaning it was strong or mighty, this fifth kingdom will be a mixture of iron and clay. Unlike iron, clay is fragile or weak, and can easily be broken. Therefore, this kingdom consisting of ten powers will be partly strong and partly fragile.

The kings that are part iron will not cleave to or stick to those that are part clay; they will not mix well together. "The kingdom shall be divided." Divided could mean that the iron kings and the clay kings will not be in agreement; they may not agree on how to rule. Divided could also mean these ten kings or powers will separate into two ruling factions, the iron kings and the clay kings.

Daniel tells Nebuchadnezzar God is making known to him, "what shall be in the latter days." The latter days are the End Times. In the days when God sets up His kingdom that will, "stand forever," which will occur at the end of the Seventieth Week of Daniel. They will be the reigning one-world government of the End Times. The Beast, the Antichrist, will come out from these ten toes, these ten kings or powers, and he will rule over them.

Nebuchadnezzar saw a stone that was cut out without hands; this stone is Jesus Christ. This is, "The stone which the builders rejected, the same

---

[118] Ibid., p. 38.

is become the head of the corner" (Matthew 21:42). This stone will strike these ten powers and will destroy them at the end of the Seventieth Week of Daniel. After these ten nations are defeated, Jesus Christ will rule and reign forever and ever.

> After this I saw in the night visions, and behold a fourth beast, dreadful and terrible, and strong exceedingly; and it had great iron teeth: it devoured and brake in pieces, and stamped the residue with the feet of it: and it was diverse from all the beasts that were before it; and it had ten horns. I considered the horns, and, behold, there came up among them another little horn, before whom there were three of the first horns plucked up by the roots: and, behold, in this horn were eyes like the eyes of man, and a mouth speaking great things…Then I would know the truth of the fourth beast, which was diverse from all the others, exceeding dreadful, whose teeth were of iron, and his nails of brass; which devoured, brake in pieces, and stamped the residue with his feet; And of the ten horns that were in his head, and of the other which came up, and before whom three fell; even of that horn that had eyes, and a mouth that spake very great things, whose look was more stout than his fellows. I beheld, and the same horn made war with the saints, and prevailed against them; Until the Ancient of days came, and judgment was given to the saints of the most High; and the time came that the saints possessed the kingdom. Thus he said, The fourth beast shall be the fourth kingdom upon earth, which shall be diverse from all kingdoms, and shall devour the whole earth, and shall tread it down, and break it in pieces. And the ten horns out of this kingdom are ten kings that shall arise: and another shall rise after them; and he shall be diverse from the first, and he shall subdue three kings. And he shall speak great words against the most High, and shall wear out the saints of the most High, and think to change times and laws: and they shall be given into

> his hand until a time and times and the dividing of time. (Daniel 7:7-8, 19-25)

In this vision, Daniel sees a fourth beast that is dreadful and terrible. This fourth beast, which has great iron teeth, is the Roman Empire; it is the fourth kingdom, the kingdom of iron, of Daniel chapter 2. This fourth beast had ten horns. These ten horns are ten kings or powers that will come out of this fourth kingdom. These ten horns are the ten kings that will arise in the last days and will rule the whole earth; they are the one-world government of the End Times.

Daniel considered the ten horns, and saw a little horn come out from among the ten horns. This little horn with, "eyes like a man and a mouth speaking great things…whose look was more stout than his fellows," is the Antichrist. This ten king confederacy will come into power first, and then the Antichrist will surface from among its members. Following his rise to power, he will, "subdue three kings," they will be, "plucked up by the roots," which means the Antichrist will defeat three of these powers, politically, and or militarily.

The Antichrist will make war with the saints – Israel – during the Great Tribulation, and will prevail against them. He will blaspheme God, and will, "wear out the saints of the most high." Israel will be given into the hands of the Antichrist, "until a time and times and the dividing of time," which is three and a half years – the second half of the Seventieth Week of Daniel. The Antichrist will break the Covenant with Israel at the Abomination of Desolation, and Israel will be given into the hands of the Antichrist until the Lord defeats the armies of the world at the end of the Seventieth Week of Daniel.

> And in the latter time of their kingdom, when the transgressors are come to the full, a king of fierce countenance, and understanding dark sentences, shall stand up. And his power shall be mighty, but not by his own power: and he shall destroy wonderfully, and shall prosper, and practice, and shall destroy the mighty and

> the holy people. And through his policy also he shall cause craft to prosper in his hand; and he shall magnify himself in his heart, and by peace shall destroy many: he shall also stand up against the Prince of princes; but he shall be broken without hand. (Daniel 8:23-25)

> For when they shall say, Peace and safety; then sudden destruction cometh upon them, as travail upon a woman with child; and they shall not escape. (1 Thessalonians 5:3)

Daniel understands from a vision that in the latter times, the End Times, a king of fierce countenance, and understanding dark sentences (puzzles, riddles), will stand up. This fierce king is the Antichrist. His will have tremendous power, but it will not be his power; he will simply be a conduit for Satan (Revelation13:2). When the Antichrist signs the Covenant he will be seen as a messiah, a man of peace. After the Covenant is signed, his influence will increase dramatically. Prior to the mid-point of the Seventieth Week of Daniel he will have gained the power necessary to exercise absolute rule over the ten kings; over the entire world. When the world is saying peace and safety (1 Thessalonians 5:3) the Antichrist will use his power to break the Covenant and attack Israel, and will subdue the entire world. At the end of the Seventieth Week of Daniel he will stand up against the Prince of princes (Revelation 19:19), at which time he will be utterly defeated.

> And arms shall stand on his part, and they shall pollute the sanctuary of strength, and shall take away the daily sacrifice, and they shall place the abomination that maketh desolate. And such as do wickedly against the covenant shall he corrupt by flatteries: but the people that do know their God shall be strong, and do exploits. And they that understand among the people shall instruct many: yet they shall fall by the sword, and by flame, by captivity, and by spoil, many days. Now when they shall fall, they shall be helped with a little help: but many shall cleave to them with flatteries. And some of them

> of understanding shall fall, to try them, and to purge, and to make them white, even to the time of the end: because it is yet for a time appointed. And the king shall do according to his will; and he shall exalt himself, and magnify himself above every god, and shall speak marvellous things against the God of gods, and shall prosper till the Indignation be accomplished: for that that is determined shall be done. Neither shall he regard the God of his fathers, nor the desire of women, nor regard any god: for he shall magnify himself above all. But in his estate shall he honour the God of forces: and a god whom his fathers knew not shall he honour with gold, and silver, and with precious stones, and pleasant things. Thus shall he do in the most strong holds with a strange god, whom he shall acknowledge and increase with glory: and he shall cause them to rule over many, and shall divide the land for gain. (Daniel 11:31-39)

The Antichrist will desolate the, "sanctuary of strength," – the Jewish temple – and will take away the daily sacrifices. This is a description of the Abomination of Desolation, the event that begins the Great Tribulation. The Antichrist will surround Jerusalem and the temple with his armies (Luke 21:20), and will enter the temple and sit down and declare himself to be God. The Antichrist is revealed to the world when he breaks the Covenant and commits the most abominable act imaginable to the Jews. The rule of the Beast will continue, "til the Indignation be accomplished." The Beast will prosper until the end of the Indignation of God – until the end of the Seventieth Week of Daniel (Revelation 13:5). He will, "divide the land (of Israel) for gain." He will give the Palestinians a homeland in Israel and will receive great approval when he does. The gain or worth he will acquire from giving away a portion of the nation of Israel to her enemies is political influence, which he will use to solidify his position as the reigning world power of the End Times. Verse 37 describes two very distinct characteristics of the Beast. First, he will not regard the God of his fathers. His ancestors must have had a faith in the God of heaven. Second, he will not have a desire for women. He will be celibate.

> So he carried me away in the spirit into the wilderness: and I saw a woman sit upon a scarlet coloured beast, full of names of blasphemy, having seven heads and ten horns...And the angel said unto me, Wherefore didst thou marvel? I will tell thee the mystery of the woman, and of the beast that carrieth her, which hath the seven heads and ten horns...And here is the mind which hath wisdom. The seven heads are seven mountains, on which the woman sitteth...And the ten horns which thou sawest are ten kings, which have received no kingdom as yet; but receive power as kings one hour with the beast. These have one mind, and shall give their power and strength unto the beast. These shall make war with the Lamb, and the Lamb shall overcome them: for he is Lord of lords, and King of kings: and they that are with him are called, and chosen, and faithful...For God hath put in their hearts to fulfil his will, and to agree, and give their kingdom unto the beast, until the words of God shall be fulfilled. And the woman which thou sawest is that great city, which reigneth over the kings of the earth. (Revelation 17:3, 7, 9, 12-14, 17-18)

This woman, who is the false religion of the End Times—modern Babylon, Roman Catholicism—sits upon a scarlet colored beast – the Antichrist. This great whore sits upon the Antichrist, who carries her – gives her power or drives Catholicism. The Antichrist is the power that propels this false religion of the End Times. The woman is arrayed in purple and scarlet. The Beast is scarlet, indicating an association between the woman and the Beast. The Beast has seven heads and ten horns. The seven heads of the Beast represent the seven hills of the city upon which the woman sits. We are told in verse 18 the woman *is* that great city, the city of seven hills. The great whore is the city of seven hills, Rome, and the false religion of Catholicism which resides there. The Beast has seven heads, therefore, he is part of or connected to Roman Catholicism. The Beast has ten horns. A horn represents a king, kingdom, nation, or great power. These ten horns are the one-world government of the End Times. These ten horns indicate he is part of, or connected to, this one-world government. In fact, the Antichrist will rule over this ten king or ten power confederacy of the End Times.

The Eighth Beast: The Antichrist

Revelation 17:8, 10, 11

The Beast that Was, And is Not, And Yet Is

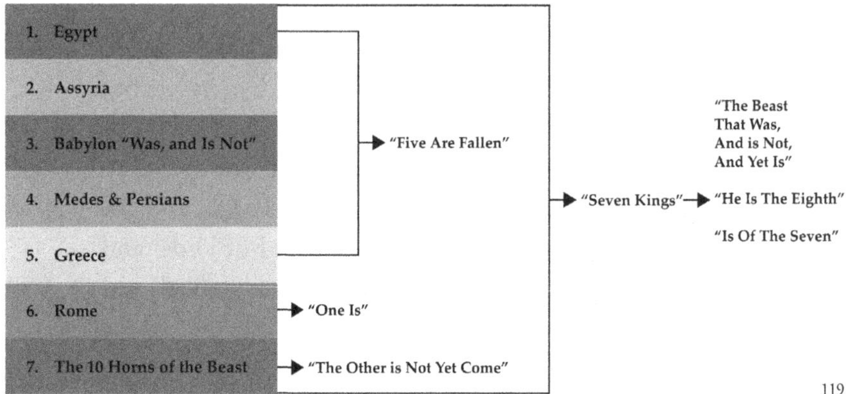

[119]

The Riddle of the Eighth Beast: The Antichrist

> The beast that thou sawest was, and is not; and shall ascend out of the bottomless pit, and go into perdition: and they that dwell on the earth shall wonder, whose names were not written in the book of life from the foundation of the world, when they behold the beast that was, and is not, and yet is…And there are seven kings: five are fallen, and one is, and the other is not yet come; and when he cometh, he must continue a short space. And the beast that was, and is not, even he is the eighth, and is of the seven, and goeth into perdition. And the ten horns which thou sawest are ten kings, which have received no kingdom as yet; but receive power as kings one hour with the beast. (Revelation 17:8, 10-12)

[119] Ibid., Page 27.

This is a riddle that will help to identify the Antichrist. It may appear at first to be difficult to understand, but it can be understood. The Bible contains many riddles which the Church, with the help of the Holy Spirit, has been able to unravel. For example, Revelation 4:8 says, speaking of the Lord Jesus Christ, "Holy, holy, holy, Lord God Almighty, which was, and is, and is to come". Jesus Christ existed before He walked upon this earth – "which was." Jesus Christ came as the savior of the world – "and is." Jesus Christ's second coming is yet in the future – "and is to come." We can understand this riddle about the Lord. We can also understand this riddle about the Antichrist.[120]

"The beast that thou sawest was, and is not…and yet is." The Beast in this riddle is the Antichrist.

The apostle John says the Beast "was" – that it existed before he wrote the book of Revelation. Then John says the Beast "is not" – that it did not exist at the time of the writing of the book of Revelation. Finally, John says the Beast "and yet is" – that it did exist at the time of the writing of the book of Revelation. John is saying that the Beast did exist at one time, that it does not exist now, but that it does exist now. How could the Beast once exist, not exist and yet exist?

The Beast "was." There were five kingdoms or powers that had ruled the world before the writing of the book of Revelation. These five kingdoms or powers were Egypt, Assyria, Babylon, the Medes and Persians, and Greece. This means the Beast will proceed from, or will come out of, one of these five former kingdoms or powers, because John says the Beast "was." Babylon is the world power that "was."

The Beast "is not." John says the Beast no longer exists; that it did not exist at the time of the writing of the book of Revelation. The Roman Empire, the sixth world power, ruled the world at the time Revelation was written. Babylon, as a world power, did not exist at the time. The Medes and Persians destroyed it. Babylon is the world power that "is not."

[120] Wood, *Six Days to the Rapture*, Tape 5.

The Beast "and yet is." John says the Beast does exist, that it was in existence during the time of the writing of the book of Revelation. Babylon, the world power, did not exist at the time of the writing of the book of Revelation; it "is not." However, Babylon did exist as a religion. The Babylonian religion was being practiced at that time (2 Thessalonians 2:7a; Luke 11:27). Babylon the religion "and yet is." Babylon the world power did not exist, but Babylon the religious power did exist. It does not exist, and yet it does exist.

The Beast "was." Babylon the world power had existed at one time in the past. The Beast "is not." Babylon as a world power did not exist at the time of the writing of the book of Revelation. The Beast "and yet is." Babylon the false religion did exist at the time of the writing of the book of Revelation. Therefore, the Antichrist will come out of modern Babylon, the mirror image of ancient Babylon, the false religion of Roman Catholicism.

"And there are seven kings." These seven kings are the seven world powers that will precede the Antichrist. "Five are fallen." The five kings or world powers that have fallen are: Egypt, Assyria, Babylon, the Medes and Persians, and Greece. "And one is." The one king or world power; the one that "is" - the Roman Empire. At time of the writing of the book of Revelation the Roman Empire was the reigning world power. The Roman Empire was the sixth great world power. "And the other is not yet come; and when he cometh, he must continue a short space." The king or world power that has not yet come is the ten horns of the Beast – the one-world government of the End Times. These ten kings will receive their power for one hour (a short season) and will give their power and strength to the Beast. The one-world government of the End Times will be the seventh great world power.

"He is the eight, and is of the seven." The Antichrist is the eighth king or world power. The seven world powers that will precede him are Egypt, Assyria, Babylon, the Medes and Persians, Greece, Rome, and the one-world government of the End Times. That the Beast "is of the seven" means it will come out of, or descend from, the prior seven world powers.

There clearly is an association between ancient Babylon, modern Babylon, and the Antichrist. The Beast will come out of modern Babylon.

These former world powers have had one thing in common – they have been zealous in persecuting Israel. Satan has used these former world powers as his tool to destroy God's people. It will be no different with the future world powers. They will persecute Israel with the same intensity.

> And I stood upon the sand of the sea, and saw a beast rise up out of the sea, having seven heads and ten horns, and upon his horns ten crowns, and upon his heads the name of blasphemy. And the beast which I saw was like unto a leopard, and his feet were as the feet of a bear, and his mouth as the mouth of a lion: and the dragon gave him his power, and his seat, and great authority. And I saw one of his heads as it were wounded to death; and his deadly wound was healed: and all the world wondered after the beast. And they worshipped the dragon which gave power unto the beast: and they worshipped the beast, saying, Who is like unto the beast? who is able to make war with him? And there was given unto him a mouth speaking great things and blasphemies; and power was given unto him to continue forty and two months. And he opened his mouth in blasphemy against God, to blaspheme his name, and his tabernacle, and them that dwell in heaven. And it was given unto him to make war with the saints, and to overcome them: and power was given him over all kindreds, and tongues, and nations. (Revelation 13:1-7)

The Antichrist is a political power. He has ten horns; a horn represents mighty power. The Antichrist will rule over ten kings or powers in the End Times. Upon these ten horns are ten crowns, each crown representing authority. The one-world government of the End Times will consist of these ten horns that are ten kings or powers.

The Antichrist is also a religious power. He has seven heads. The seven heads represent the seven hills of the city upon which the woman, the great whore, sits. That city is Rome, the city of seven hills (Revelation 17:9, 18). The Vatican, located in Rome, is the seat of the false religious system of Catholicism. Verse 18 says the woman *is* that great city. Therefore, the city and the false religious system are one and are inseparable.

One of the Antichrist's heads will be "wounded to death" and this "deadly wound" will heal. Does this mean the Antichrist will die and then come back to life? Verse 3 clearly says that only *one* of his heads is wounded to death. Does this mean he has more than one head? The Antichrist will have the physical body of a man; therefore, he will have only one head. Despite this, verse 1 clearly says the Beast has seven heads. Since the Antichrist's physical body does not have seven heads, or ten horns, this is a reference to the religious and political power of the Antichrist. It is not the Antichrist, the physical individual, who recovers from the deadly wound - it is one of the seven heads that is wounded to death and then heals. The seven heads are the seven hills of the city of Rome, and the religion of Roman Catholicism. Therefore, the wounding of one of the heads could refer either to the physical destruction of a portion of the city of Rome, or to an event that would lead to a partial loss of power of Roman Catholicism. In either case, the deadly wound will be healed and, either Rome, "that great city which reigneth over the kings of the earth," or the power and influence of the apostate religion of Roman Catholicism, will be healed.

The world will worship the Antichrist and the Devil that gives the Antichrist his power. He will be given power to rule for forty-two months, or three and a half years. This period will begin with the Abomination of Desolation, in the middle of the Seventieth Week of Daniel, and will conclude at the end of the Day of the Lord. The Antichrist will make war with the saints and will overcome them. The Beast will be responsible for killing multitudes of Christians. He will have power over all the earth, "over all kindreds, and tongues, and nations." The Antichrist will subdue the entire world. Every nation and geographic area will be subject to his rule.

Another Beast: The False Prophet

The False Prophet will be a satanic imitation of the Holy Spirit. Like the Antichrist, he will be empowered by Satan. The diabolical mission of the False Prophet will be to promote the Antichrist. Instead of directing worship to Jesus Christ, the False Prophet will deceive the world into worshipping the Antichrist through signs and lying wonders.

> And I beheld another beast coming up out of the earth; and he had two horns like a lamb, and he spake as a dragon. And he exerciseth all the power of the first beast before him, and causeth the earth and them which dwell therein to worship the first beast, whose deadly wound was healed. And he doeth great wonders, so that he maketh fire come down from heaven on the earth in the sight of men, And deceiveth them that dwell on the earth by the means of those miracles which he had power to do in the sight of the beast; saying to them that dwell on the earth, that they should make an image to the beast, which had the wound by a sword, and did live. And he had power to give life unto the image of the beast, that the image of the beast should both speak, and cause that as many as would not worship the image of the beast should be killed. And he causeth all, both small and great, rich and poor, free and bond, to receive a mark in their right hand, or in their foreheads: And that no man might buy or sell, save he that had the mark, or the name of the beast, or the number of his name. Here is wisdom. Let him that hath understanding count the number of the beast: for it is the number of a man; and his number is Six hundred threescore and six. (Revelation 13:11-18)

The Antichrist is a beast. The False Prophet is another beast. He will be given satanic power like the Antichrist, and will speak like the dragon, Satan. He will promote the Antichrist rather than himself. The False

Prophet will cause the world to worship the Antichrist. He will deceive the world by performing great wonders and miracles in the sight of the Antichrist, even causing fire to come down from heaven. The False Prophet will convince men to create an image of the Antichrist, and will cause that image to come to life and to speak. He will kill those who refuse to worship the Beast, and will cause men to receive the mark of the Beast, his name, or his number. No man will be able to buy or sell without his mark, his name, or his number, which is 666.

The Mark of the Beast

The Greek word for mark is *charagma*.

> *Charagma* - a scratch or etching, stamp (as a badge of servitude), or sculptured figure (statue): graven, mark.[121]

The mark of the Beast could be:

> A scratch - To mark, break, or cut the surface of slightly with something pointed or sharp.[122]
>
> An etching – To make (a drawing, design, etc.) on metal, glass, etc. by the action of an acid.[123]
>
> A stamp – To impress, mark, or imprint with some design, characters, etc., as to decorate or to show authenticity, ownership, sanction, or the like.[124]
>
> A sculptured figure: graven – To shape by carving; carve out; sculpture.[125]

---

[121] Strong, *Dictionary of the Greek Testament*, p. 77.

[122] Webster's Seventh New Collegiate Dictionary, p. 1279.

[123] Ibid., pp. 480-481.

[124] Ibid., p. 619.

[125] Ibid., p. 1387.

Since the mark of the Beast has not been instituted, any attempt to determine its form is purely speculation. It could be a computer chip, placed under the skin, which will transmit data unique to each individual. Technology is currently in place to inject humans with a biochip that can be tracked by the global positioning system.[126] It could be a bar code that is placed on the right hand or forehead. It could be a tattoo similar to the one given to the Jews in German concentration camps during World War II. No matter what form the mark of the Beast takes during the Great Tribulation we should avoid taking any scratch, etching, stamp or sculptured figure in our right hand or forehead that is associated with the Antichrist, his name, or his number.

> And the third angel followed them, saying with a loud voice, If any man worship the beast and his image, and receive his mark in his forehead, or in his hand, The same shall drink of the wine of the wrath of God, which is poured out without mixture into the cup of his indignation; and he shall be tormented with fire and brimstone in the presence of the holy angels, and in the presence of the Lamb: And the smoke of their torment ascendeth up for ever and ever: and they have no rest day nor night, who worship the beast and his image, and whosoever receiveth the mark of his name. Here is the patience of the saints: here are they that keep the commandments of God, and the faith of Jesus. (Revelation 14:9-12)

God says that anyone who worships the Beast and his image, or receives his mark, will be subject to His indignation and wrath, and will spend eternity in the lake of fire. The meaning of the word *receive* is to accept, or to take. God will punish those who have chosen to accept the mark of the Beast. Christians need to be watchful and aware, and avoid taking a mark that is in any way associated with the Antichrist.

There are some who have wondered if it is possible they might mistakenly accept some mark without knowing it is the mark of the Beast, and suffer

---

[126] Sherrie Gossett, Implantable-Chip Company Attacks WND http://www.worldnetdaily.com/news/article.asp?ARTICLE_ID=27047, April 2, 2002.

the consequences. The mark of the Beast will be accepted, will be chosen, when a person has made the decision to submit to the rule of the Antichrist.

> And I saw heaven opened, and behold a white horse; and he that sat upon him was called Faithful and True, and in righteousness he doth judge and make war. His eyes were as a flame of fire, and on his head were many crowns; and he had a name written, that no man knew, but he himself. And he was clothed with a vesture dipped in blood: and his name is called The Word of God. And the armies which were in heaven followed him upon white horses, clothed in fine linen, white and clean. And out of his mouth goeth a sharp sword, that with it he should smite the nations: and he shall rule them with a rod of iron: and he treadeth the winepress of the fierceness and wrath of Almighty God. And he hath on his vesture and on his thigh a name written, KING OF KINGS, AND LORD OF LORDS. And I saw an angel standing in the sun; and he cried with a loud voice, saying to all the fowls that fly in the midst of heaven, Come and gather yourselves together unto the supper of the great God; That ye may eat the flesh of kings, and the flesh of captains, and the flesh of mighty men, and the flesh of horses, and of them that sit on them, and the flesh of all men, both free and bond, both small and great. And I saw the beast, and the kings of the earth, and their armies, gathered together to make war against him that sat on the horse, and against his army. And the beast was taken, and with him the false prophet that wrought miracles before him, with which he deceived them that had received the mark of the beast, and them that worshipped his image. These both were cast alive into a lake of fire burning with brimstone. And the remnant were slain with the sword of him that sat upon the horse, which sword proceeded out of his mouth: and all the fowls were filled with their flesh. (Revelation 19:11-21)

These scriptures are describing the defeat of the Antichrist, the False Prophet, and the kings of the earth and their armies by Jesus Christ and his armies. Jesus Christ rides upon a white horse. The armies that follow him on white horses are the angels of heaven (Matthew 25:31). The Lord will come in fierceness and wrath to make war, and He will smite the kings of the earth and their armies with the sharp sword that proceeds out of His mouth. The Lord will utterly defeat those assembled to fight against him. The Antichrist and the False Prophet will be cast alive into the lake of fire at the end of the Day of the Lord.

Identity of the Antichrist

Who will be the Antichrist? A more important question is, from what position will the Antichrist proceed? Which individual, holding what position, could claim he was God on earth, and then demand his image be created and worshipped? A Roman Catholic pope will fulfill the prophecies which predict a religious man, associated with Babylon, will enter the Jewish temple during the Seventieth Week of Daniel, and declare himself God.

The pope has already been proclaimed God on earth by the Catholic Church. The pope is hailed by the Catholic Church, modern Babylon, as the Vicar of Christ. Vicar of Christ means to live vicariously as Christ, or in the place of Christ. The title of Vicar of Christ declares that the pope is the fleshly representative of Christ on earth, and the visible head of the church. In the eyes of Roman Catholics worldwide, the pope already holds the position of Christ on earth, even though Christians know there is only one head of the church, Jesus Christ (Colossians 1:18).[127]

> The Latin equivalent of the Greek 'anti' is 'vicarious,' from which comes 'vicar.' Thus 'vicar of Christ' literally means Antichrist.[128]

---

[127] Wood, *Six Days to the Rapture,* Tape 4.

[128] Hunt, *A Woman Rides the Beast,* p. 45.

The pope of Roman Catholicism is the eighth beast of Revelation chapter 17. He will be the reigning world power of the End Times. He will be the religious and political power that will subdue the entire world, and will cause the world to bow down and worship him. He will rule over the ten horns of the Beast, the ten kings or powers that will form the one-world government of the End Times. These ten rulers will give their power and strength to the Antichrist. Whoever is the pope when the Covenant is signed will be the Antichrist.

Today, more than one billion people claim the pope of Roman Catholicism is God on earth. He carries the titles of Sovereign of the State of Vatican City, Bishop of Rome, Primate of Italy, The Prince of the Apostles, and Supreme Pontiff. The Roman pontiff, by divine law, has supreme jurisdiction over the Catholic Church. Within that church, he is considered to be the foundation of the faithful, the chief pastor of the whole church, and Christ on earth.

The Catholic Church teaches that the pope is infallible. When, in his capacity as the supreme Apostolic authority, he teaches doctrine of faith and morals, he is considered infallible. His teachings do not have to be ratified by the church. Papal infallibility is personal and incommunicable, and cannot be shared by any church body. The Catholic Church asserts that papal infallibility was promised directly to Peter, and to each of Peter's successors, and it cannot be delegated to others. Infallibility would certainly have to be one of the attributes of the Antichrist, since he will claim he is God on earth.

> The Vatican Council has defined as "a divinely revealed dogma" that "the Roman pontiff, when he speaks ex cathedra-- that is, when in the exercise of his office as pastor and teacher of all Christians he defines, by virtue of his supreme Apostolic authority, a doctrine of faith or morals to be held by the whole Church-- is, by reason of the Divine assistance promised to him in blessed Peter, possessed of that infallibility with which the Divine Redeemer wished His Church to be endowed in defining

> doctrines of faith and morals; and consequently that such definitions of the Roman Pontiff are irreformable of their own nature (ex sese) and not by reason of the Church's consent.[129]

The Catholic Church contends that Matthew 16:18 is proof of the pope's infallibility.

> And I say also unto thee, That thou art Peter, and upon this rock I will build my church; and the gates of hell shall not prevail against it. (Matthew 16:18)

The Catholic Church professes that Peter is the foundation of the Church. It is his person, and his office upon which the Church is built, and his successors are heirs of that promise. The pope is to the Church what the foundation is to a house. As the supreme head of that body, he alone is responsible for its stability, unity, and increase.

The Catholic Church asserts that Christ conferred the supreme pastorate upon Peter to govern the Church, and the permanence of that office is essential to its very being. Since the Church is universal, extending to all members, and possesses supreme authority over all churches, the pope has jurisdiction over all believers. Since Christ told Peter to feed His sheep, Peter – the chief shepherd – and his successors have authority over all the sheep of the flock. The Catholic Church asserts that Christ made Peter the chief apostle over the other eleven apostles, and as such, was designated the undisputed single supreme head of the Church – a position they claim is perpetual. The pope is the vicegerent to rule in Christ's place. He alone has been given the keys to the kingdom of heaven, and the power to bind and loose. The pope has the judicial authority to make laws and to cancel them, and to judge offenses against his laws. He has the power to pardon sin because sin is a violation of the laws he has instituted. As the supreme teacher of the Church, the pope determines what is to be believed by all its members. He even has the right to interpret natural law. He can say what is lawful or unlawful in regard to social and

[129] The Catholic Encyclopedia, Volume VII, October, 2005.

family life. The pope gives stability to the Church; he is the foundation, the rock of the Church.

> Above all, they acknowledge the authority of the successor of Blessed Peter, the key bearer of heaven. To them the Savior himself entrusted the task of feeding his flock and ruling his Church.[130]

> If anyone shall say that Blessed Peter the Apostle was not constituted by Christ our Lord as chief of all the Apostles and the visible head of the whole Church militant: or that he did not receive directly and immediately from the same Lord Jesus Christ a primacy of true and proper jurisdiction, but one of honour only: let him be anathema.[131]

It is quite clear from Matthew 16:18; however, that the Lord will build His Church upon the rock which is Christ Himself, and upon Peter's confession of faith in Jesus Christ.

> So he carried me away in the spirit into the wilderness: and I saw a woman sit upon a scarlet coloured beast, full of names of blasphemy, having seven heads and ten horns...And the angel said unto me, Wherefore didst thou marvel? I will tell thee the mystery of the woman, and of the beast that carrieth her, which hath the seven heads and ten horns. (Revelation 17:3, 7)

The woman in Revelation chapter 17 is modern Babylon, Roman Catholicism. The Beast is the Antichrist, the pope of Roman Catholicism. Roman Catholicism sits upon the pope and he carries her. The Catholic Church asserts it is the pope who is the foundation that gives stability to the Church, the foundation upon which the Church is built. The pope is the power behind the Catholic Church. It is the woman who rides the Beast, not the Beast who rides the woman. Therefore, the concept that the

---

[130] The Catholic Encyclopedia, Volume V, Robert Appleton Company, Online Edition by Kevin Knight, http://www.newadvent.org/cathen, October, 2005.

[131] Flannery, O.P., general editor, *Vatican Council II*, Volume 1, p. 72.

Beast, the pope, carries the woman, Roman Catholicism, makes perfect sense.

Through the ages, the Church of Jesus Christ has acknowledged that the pope of Roman Catholicism would be the Antichrist.

> This teaching shows forcefully that the Pope is the very Antichrist, who has exalted himself above, and opposed himself against Christ because he will not permit Christians to be saved without his power, which, nevertheless, is nothing, and is neither ordained nor commanded by God. This is, properly speaking to exalt himself above all that is called God as Paul says, 2 Thess. 2,4.[132] Martin Luther
>
> It is the bounden duty of every Christian to pray against Antichrist, and as to what Antichrist is no sane man ought to raise a question. If it be not the Popery in the Church of Rome there is nothing in the world that can be called by that name.
>
> It wounds Christ, robs Christ of His glory, puts sacramental efficacy in the place of His atonement, and lifts a piece of bread in the place of the Saviour.
>
> If we pray against it, because it is against Him, we shall love the persons though we hate their errors; we shall love their souls though we loathe and detest their dogmas.[133] Charles Haddon Spurgeon - Nineteenth century English preacher
>
> Nay, at this very hour, there resides a man in the city of Rome, whom one-half of Christendom itself hails, honors and adores as the vicar of Jesus Christ, the vicegerent of

[132] Project Wittenberg, The Smalcald Articles, by Martin Luther (1537). Translated by F. Bente and W.H.T. Dau. Published in: Triglot Concordia: The Symbolical Books of the Ev. Lutheran Church. (St. Louis: Concordia Publishing House, 1921), pp. 453-529.

[133] Hunt, *A Woman Rides the Beast*, p. 412.

> God upon earth, infallible, the sole possessor of the keys of heaven, - a man whom the greater festivals exhibit as a divinity, borne along in solemn procession on the shoulders of consecrated priests, while sacred incense fumes before him.[134] William R. Newell – Pastor & Educator

The pope is the man the world will turn to when peace in the Middle East appears to be hopeless. He will be the religious and political figure world leaders believe will be able to bring Israel and her enemies together one last time for peace negotiations. As the End Times approach, the pope's status as a political force will be unequaled. World leaders will acknowledge the Vatican has been instrumental in determining the outcome of major world events, such as the fall of the Soviet Union and the Berlin Wall. The pope even offered to mediate peace talks between Russia and Ukraine. They will be hopeful the Vatican might prevail in the monumental feat of bringing peace to the Middle East.

The pope will be the preeminent religious figure of his time. He will be very active in efforts to unify all religions under the umbrella of Roman Catholicism, including Muslims, Jews, and Christians. The Catholic Church will try and convince Christians to come under the umbrella of Catholicism by feigning true Christianity. The majority of Christians will fail to recognize the wide gulf that exists between Catholicism and Christianity. Roman Catholicism's masterful blend of Christian and pagan doctrines and rituals will no longer alienate many Christians. During the End Times, Christians will be more eager to overlook any differences between Catholics and Christians in an attempt to be loving and tolerant. They will unite spiritually with Catholics, even if it means compromising the word of God. Prominent evangelical and Catholic leaders will work together to convince Christians to willingly embrace the pope and Roman Catholicism. The Catholic Church will convince pagans to come under the umbrella of Catholicism by practicing the same abominable acts, such as idol worship.

---

[134] Newell, *The Book of the Revelation*, p. 188.

Today, religious leaders are asking the pope of Rome to be their pope. Robert Schuller said, "It's time for Protestants to go to the shepherd (the pope) and say, 'What do we have to do to come home?'"[135] It is rather interesting that the Crystal Cathedral, which he was responsible for building in 1980, went bankrupt in 2010, and the Catholic Church bought it in 2012. Catholic World News reported that Lord Carey of Clifton, former Archbishop of Canterbury, "has suggested that all Christian leaders—including non-Catholics—should make regular ad limina[136] visits to consult with the Pope."[137] In the End Times, all religions will come under the covering of the pope and Roman Catholicism. This will be the one-world religion of the End Times. Marian apparitions will become almost epidemic, and will be widely accepted by Muslims, Jews, and Christians as being of divine inspiration. These apparitions will direct the world to come together in peace and unity under the direction of the pope and Roman Catholicism.

The pope, who will be the most charismatic and influential world figure, will be successful in convincing Israel and her enemies to sign a temporary peace treaty that will last for only seven years. Israel will get the peace they have so desperately longed for, and the opportunity to rebuild the temple on Temple Mount in Jerusalem. Israel will give up a portion of her land for a Palestinian state. The world will hail the pope as a messiah.

The temporary peace that will follow the signing of the Covenant will allow the pope time to solidify his power over all religious and political affairs. Prior to the end of the first half of the seven-year peace treaty he will have assumed leadership of the one-world government. From his headquarters in the Vatican in Rome, the pope will rule over the one-world religion and the one-world government of the End Times. He will be the

---

[135] Hunt, *A Woman Rides the Beast*, p. 412.

[136] Obligation of visiting the "thresholds of the Apostles", and of presenting themselves before the pope, to show the proper reverence for the Successor of St. Peter, to acknowledge his universal jurisdiction, to receive his admonitions and counsels, and thus to bind more closely to its Divinely appointed head, http://ww.newadvent.org.

[137] Bold ecumenical suggestion from Anglican leader, http://www.cwnews.com/news/viewstory.cfm?recnum=22317, May 12, 2003.

undisputed world ruler. The Covenant will cause Israel to feel that peace and safety has finally come to their beleaguered land. Israel will relax her defenses, and begin to settle into a more normal way of life.

Three and a half years after the pope has negotiated peace in the Middle East, he will break the Covenant. The Antichrist's ultimate hour will have finally arrived. He will muster the military forces under his control, and will direct them to surround Jerusalem, and take control of the temple. The pope will enter the temple, sit down on the Mercy Seat of the Ark of the Covenant in the Holy of Holies, and declare that he is God on earth. He will blaspheme God and proclaim that he alone is worthy to be worshipped. The Jews will be totally surprised and shocked by the pope's actions. Even though the pope is the most revered religious man on the face of the earth, he is still a gentile, and as a gentile, his entrance into the Jewish temple will be an abominable act. The Jewish temple will then be desolate to worship. To many outside of the nation of Israel, the pope's declaration that he is to be worshipped as God on earth will not be at all shocking. More than one billion faithful Roman Catholics worldwide already proclaim him to be the Vicar of Christ, God on earth. When the Covenant was signed, adoring multitudes hailed him as a messiah. Some even said he was *the* Messiah. Following the desecration of the temple, the pope will direct his military forces to attach the Jews. Half of the city of Jerusalem will flee into the wilderness from the attacking armies; the other half will be captured. Following his attack on the Jews, the pope will use his military forces to subdue the entire world.

The pope will appoint a man to be his prophet. This False Prophet will use signs and lying wonders to convince the world to follow the directives of the pope. The pope's prophet will inform every inhabitant on earth they will be required to take a mark in order to make financial transactions. This mark will indicate their acceptance of the pope as the undisputed ruler of every facet of their daily lives, whether religious or political. Using his immense power, the pope will take control of all worldly commodities and will artificially inflate the price of all goods. The world will groan and chafe under these strict controls. Men will complain that a day's wage will not buy enough food to feed themselves, let alone their family. Multitudes will starve in a worldwide famine. This famine will continue unabated, and ultimately, billions will die of starvation.

Many in the Church will be confused and frightened by these unexpected developments. They will ask their pastors and church leaders why they are still on earth and not in heaven, why they have not been raptured before all of these horrible events have taken place. They will also be dismayed at the pope's blatant hostility toward them. Many Christians will have placed their hope and trust in the pope and his message of togetherness between evangelicals and Catholics. He will have called for unity and peace between Catholics and Christians, as well as other people of faith. Instead of togetherness and peace, the pope will now actively and diligently persecute Christians, as well as any others who oppose him. He will vehemently deny that Jesus Christ is the coming Messiah who will rescue Christians from this great tribulation. Instead, he will claim he is the Messiah, and as such, he alone must be worshipped.

The Antichrist's prophet will create an image of the pope. This image will miraculously come to life, and the False Prophet will command the entire world worship the pope's image or be killed. Christians will be severely persecuted for their faith. Many who stand fast in their faith, and refuse to worship the Antichrist, will be martyred. However, Christians should not despair. God said He would protect the Church while in this time of danger and give eventual safe deliverance out of this troublous time. He will never leave us or forsake us, and the Holy Spirit will be there to provide comfort. The Church will overcome this great testing of their faith, and will stand before the Lord as His completed bride.

In summary, the following are the characteristics of the Antichrist, the pope of Roman Catholicism.

- The Antichrist will come out from one of the first five world powers, Babylon (Revelation 17:8).
- The Antichrist will give power to the whore of Babylon, the Roman Catholic Church. She sits upon him as the rider and he carries her (Revelation 17:3, 7).

- The Antichrist has seven heads. The seven heads are the seven hills of the city on which the whore of Babylon sits, which is the city of Rome (Revelation 17:9).
- The Antichrist has ten horns, which represent the ten kings or powers over whom he will rule. He will rule over this one-world government of the End Times (Revelation 13:1).
- The Antichrist is a political figure. He will change times and laws (Daniel 7:25).
- The Antichrist is a religious figure. He will sit down in the temple and declare he is God (2 Thessalonians 2:4).
- The Antichrist is a blasphemer. He is full of names of blasphemy (Revelation 13:1, 5, 17:3).
- The Antichrist will cause craft (deceit, fraud, treachery) to prosper (Daniel 8:25).
- The Antichrist will not regard the god of his fathers (Daniel 11:37).
- The Antichrist will not have the desire of women. He will be celibate (Daniel 11:37).
- The Antichrist will confirm a covenant, or peace treaty, between Israel and many nations or powers for seven years (Daniel 9:27).
- The Antichrist will use peace to destroy many (Daniel 8:25).
- The Antichrist will divide the holy land of Israel for his benefit (Daniel 11:39).
- The Antichrist will be revealed before the Great Tribulation, at the Abomination of Desolation (2 Thessalonians 2:3).
- The Antichrist will be given power to continue three and a half years – the second half of the Seventieth Week of Daniel (Revelation 13:5).
- The Antichrist will kill many Jews, and will take many captive (Luke 21:20-24).
- The Antichrist will make war with the saints, and overcome them – a prediction of the death of a multitude of Christians (Revelation 13:7).
- The Antichrist will have tremendous economic success (Daniel 11:36). He will control the world economy, and will decide who can buy and sell.

- The Antichrist's number is the number of a man, 666 (Revelation 13:18).
- The Antichrist's dominion or empire will be consumed and destroyed (Daniel 7:26).
- The Antichrist will be cast alive into a lake of fire burning with brimstone (Revelation 19:21).

CHAPTER 12

THE TEN HORNS OF THE BEAST: THE ONE-WORLD GOVERNMENT OF THE END TIMES

> And the ten horns which thou sawest are ten kings, which have received no kingdom as yet; but receive power as kings one hour with the beast. These have one mind, and shall give their power and strength unto the beast. These shall make war with the Lamb, and the Lamb shall overcome them: for he is Lord of lords, and King of kings: and they that are with him are called, and chosen, and faithful. (Revelation 17:12-14)

There will be a future one-world government, and it will be a tool in the hands of Satan. He will use it to subdue and control the entire world for his purposes. The Bible says ten kings will rule the world in the End Times. These ten powers are the ten horns and the ten toes of the book of Daniel (Daniel 2:41- 43, 7:7, 20, 24), and the ten horns of the book of Revelation (Revelation 12:3, 13:1, 17:3, 7, 12-14, 16-17). These ten powers comprise the future one-world government of the End Times.

What will the geopolitical structure of this government look like? Will there be ten nations that rule the entire world, or will the world's populace be divided into ten kingdoms? Many have attempted to identify this one-world government. Some have mentioned the European Union as a possible candidate, since it represents, to some extent, a revival of the Roman Empire. It would only be speculation to mention the European Union as a possible candidate. However, it is interesting to note that France, Italy, Germany, Belgium, the Netherlands, and Luxembourg met in Rome in 1957, and agreed to form this union, which at the time was called the European Common Market. Collectively, they signed the Treaty of Rome, whose goal was European economic unity. The European Union has certainly made a considerable contribution to the effort of centralizing power in Europe. The Treaty of Rome was a huge step in the direction of a global union.

There have been many other advances toward a one-world government. Thirty-two African nations formed the Organization of African Unity in Addis Ababa, Ethiopia, in May of 1963. At that time the OAU, which eventually expanded to fifty-three African nations, was largely a ceremonial body and did not have sufficient power to impose its will upon African nations. That changed in July of 2002 when the member nations of the OAU met in Durban, South Africa, to form the African Union. The AU has the potential to exercise far greater control over African nations than the OAU.

In October of 2003, the Association of Southeast Asian Nations (ASEAN) signed the Bali Concord II. The aim of this concord was to create an ASEAN Economic Community, modeled after the European Union.

The North American Free Trade Agreement, or NAFTA, was signed by the United States, Canada, and Mexico in January of 1994. In August of 2005, the United States agreed to the Central American Free Trade Agreement, or CAFTA. U.S. Trade Representative Robert Zoellick called CAFTA, "a milestone along the way to the administration's big prize of a 34-nation Free Trade Agreement of the Americas, or FTAA, covering all countries in the Western Hemisphere, except Cuba."[138]

[138] United States Agrees to Another Free Trade Pact, The Associated Press, December 18, 2003.

Now that the European Union and African Union are a reality, and ASEAN is forming a Southeast Asian Economic Community, can an American Union, Asian Union, or other similar unions be far behind?

We should expect to see future developments that will move the world closer to the final form of a one-world government. For a world government to exercise control over every nation a lot would have to change. A one-world government would require a single worldwide currency. Members of the European Union have already abandoned their respective currencies – the Drachma, Escudo, Franc, Gulden, Lira, Mark, Markka, Punt, and Schilling – for the Euro. Trade barriers would need to be eliminated. The World Trade Organization has made great strides in reducing or eliminating tariffs and initiating unhindered trade between all nations. Military power would need to be centralized. Today, world leaders and governments are rushing headlong toward a one-world government.

The United Nations

If we look at current world events, it does not appear a stretch of the imagination would be required to envision the formation of a world government, consisting of ten kings or powers, in the not too distant future. In reality, the United Nations already functions as a world government. With the addition of Switzerland in 2002, every nation on the face of the earth is now a member of the United Nations. This body already wields tremendous political, economic, and military power. It has consistently used this power to impose its will upon the nations of the world.

The United Nations has not been a champion of national sovereignty. Instead, it has clearly promoted a socialist agenda. Alger Hiss, an American diplomat under U.S. President Franklin Roosevelt, was one of the leaders promoting the concept of the United Nations. In 1945, he became Secretary General of the San Francisco Conference that organized the United Nations. In 1948, he was exposed as a communist spy and was sent to prison. The United Nations has not only promoted a socialist agenda, but every one of its Secretaries General has been a socialist.[139]

The constitution of the United Nations allows for mediation between nations; however, it is prohibited from intervening in the affairs of its member states. Despite this prohibition, the United Nations has consistently ignored its own constitution, and has repeatedly interfered in the affairs of the nations of the world. In 1999, a civil war was raging in Yugoslavia. Kosovar Muslims were fighting for independence from a predominately Orthodox Yugoslavia. The United Nations threatened Yugoslavia with a military invasion if the country did not allow UN forces to enter their country and resolve the conflict. It refused, and the United Nations invaded the country. This invasion was a direct interference in the internal affairs of a sovereign nation, and a contravention of the UN's own rules. This invasion was not the only example of an illegal intervention on the part of the UN. The United Nations intervened in the civil war in Somalia in 1993, as was portrayed in the movie *Black Hawk Down*. It also intervened in an internal conflict in Haiti in 1994. The Aristide government in Haiti was a Marxist regime that was overthrown in a military coup. The United Nations determined it was not in the best interest of the Haitian people that the Haitian military had overthrown a Marxist regime. Therefore, it placed the communist Aristide government back in power using political and military force. Clearly, the United Nations has determined that sovereign nations cannot be relied upon to properly manage their own internal affairs.

The International Criminal Court

For a global government to rule effectively, it must exercise control in every arena, including the world's judicial affairs. The United Nations has added a permanent judicial body called the International Criminal Court. The Rome Statute of the International Criminal Court was adopted at a United Nations treaty conference in Rome in July of 1998. In April of 2002, the

[139] Irvin Baxter, What the UN Doesn't Want You to Know, http://www.endtime.com/past_article.asp?ID=7, March/April 1995.

ICC was formally established when the required sixty nations ratified the Rome Statute.

> On 1 July 2002, the Rome Statute of the International Criminal Court (ICC) will enter into force, triggering the jurisdiction of the first permanent court capable of investigating and bringing to justice individuals who commit the most serious violations of international humanitarian law, namely war crimes, crimes against humanity, genocide, and once defined, aggression. Unlike the International Court of Justice in The Hague, whose jurisdiction is restricted to States, the ICC will have the capacity to indict individuals.[140]

Grave concerns have been raised regarding the extensive powers of this court. The ICC has jurisdiction over every individual, from every nation, regardless of whether a nation has ratified the Rome Statute. The court can prosecute individuals – whether civilian or military – without the consent of their nation, when it determines a given nation's court has not been willing to prosecute its own offenders. The United States has not ratified the Rome Statute. Former US President Bill Clinton signed the accord, but due to overwhelming opposition in Congress, he never submitted it for ratification. President George W. Bush officially withdrew Clinton's signature, and notified the United Nations the United States did not consider itself bound in any way to the actions of the court. However, United States citizens will still be denied the protections laid out in the US Constitution because the ICC asserts its power supersedes the laws of individual nations. The US Constitution provides checks and balances to protect the liberties of every citizen. The ICC has completely unchecked powers, and is not accountable to any elected body.

> The ICC does not provide for trial by jury, guaranteed by the Sixth Amendment. The ICC does not provide the Fourth Amendment's protection against unreasonable

---

[140] International Criminal Court, http://www.icc-cpi.int, July, 1998.

> searches and seizures. It lacks the right against self-incrimination offered by the Fifth Amendment. The experience of other international tribunals shows that other Sixth Amendment rights such as choosing appointed counsel, speedy trials, and confrontation of witnesses will also be ignored. America provides the greatest degree of ordered liberty in the history of the planet for precisely these reasons. National sovereignty, a written Constitution, checked and balanced government power, guaranteed rights, and accountable government officials are all critical to the liberty we enjoy. The ICC undermines, ignores, or contradicts them all.[141]

Prior to the formation of the ICC, the United Nations could already exert formidable political, economic, and military power. With the ratification of the Rome Statute, the United Nations now has the ability to subject every nation to its will. The ICC essentially makes the concept of national sovereignty obsolete.

The ICC was presented to the world as a court that would bring to justice individuals who commit the most serious offenses, such as genocide, or war crimes. Proponents of the court have repeatedly claimed the court would focus on aggressively pursuing despots like Pol Pot of Cambodia and Idi Amin of Uganda. Article 7 of the Rome Statute; however, deals with crimes against humanity. The ICC's definition of genocide and war crimes are relatively straightforward, but its vague description of crimes against humanity has been left deliberately broad, which allows it maximum latitude to prosecute whomever it sees fit. How will the court define religious persecution? How will it determine if inhumane acts have been committed against the mental health of an individual? Bear in mind this court, not held accountable to anyone, will be prosecuting crimes that are the most subjective and arbitrary in nature, using standards it alone has defined.

---

[141] Thomas L. Jipping, And Justice for Nobody, http://www.worldnetdaily.com/news/article.asp?ARTICLE_ID=28185, July 5, 2002.

Those who have raised objections to the formation and structure of this court have usually done so based upon concerns it could be used for political gain. Questions of the court's objectivity began to arise almost as soon as it was convened. During the first month the court was open for business the Palestinian Authority announced it would file a complaint over an Israeli air strike on Gaza City. Nabil Abu Rudeina, Palestinian leader Yasser Arafat's top adviser said, "We will ask the ICC for an urgent trial over the crime against humanity carried out last night by the occupation forces. This will be a real test for this court. We hope the trial will start immediately, to look into Sharon's policies, which have destroyed the peace process and all international efforts to put it back on track."[142] Is this a crime against humanity? Should a nation retaliating against an aggressor be charged, and possibly convicted, of crimes against humanity?

Influential Private Organizations

Through the centuries, influential and powerful private organizations and individuals have attempted to manipulate world affairs to their advantage. It is no different today. Private organizations such as the Council on Foreign Relations, the Trilateral Commission, and the Bilderbergs, meet with the expressed purpose of influencing world affairs. Attendees of these meetings include leading statesmen, executives of multinational corporations, heads of major financial institutions, and representatives of the press from practically every nation of the world. Their agenda is very clear: to control the world economy and centralize power in the hands of a very few.

The Bilderbergs, so called because of their first meeting in 1954 at the Bilderberg Hotel in Holland, meet annually to discuss topics of global importance. These gatherings are not announced to the public, and accounts of what goes on are not published. Approximately one hundred participants attend each meeting, and these individuals represent many

---

[142] Palestinian Authority plans to Accuse Ariel Sharon in Front of International Criminal Court, http://www.drudgereportarchives.com/data/2002/07/24/20020724_165849_flash2.htm, July 23, 2002.

disciplines, including politics, finance, journalism, and education. Admittedly, this is a private organization. Yet, the scope and breadth of those in attendance raises serious concerns as to the power and influence of organizations such as the Bilderbergs.

How could the ten kings or powers establish a one-world government? They could construct it by methodically dismantling the current system of sovereign nations, and in its place, create a new world order of their own choosing. Several years ago the phrase new world order was used constantly in the media; however, some believed the phrase was too Orwellian. Therefore, the current phraseology in vogue is globalization, internationalization, or global governance. No matter what label is given to these efforts to create a one-world government, the goal is for all nations to gather under the umbrella of a unified world power. All nations or peoples would become equals economically, militarily, and politically. There would be a just and equitable distribution of wealth. The ten kings or powers would aid the underdeveloped nations at the expense of the more developed nations. What form the final one-world government of the End Times will take is presently unclear; however, a transformation of the United Nations from its current form into a one-world government consisting of ten kings or powers would appear to be a reasonable possibility.

The United States and One-World Government

The seeds of a one-world government are growing in the United States. Following the crisis of September 11, 2001, legislation was passed that centralized more power in the hands of the federal government. The result of this legislation has been increased control over the lives of US citizens. A pattern has emerged where a crisis develops and legislation is passed to prevent similar incidents. Each new piece of legislation creates new laws that take away the liberties of US citizens, but do little to punish those who committed the acts of violence, and even less to prevent them from occurring again. The rights and freedoms of every United States citizen, guaranteed under the Constitution, are steadily disappearing.

The US Patriot Act, passed by Congress in October of 2001, gives government intelligence agencies sweeping new powers, including the right to perform secret searches, and the authority to install listening devices in private homes without a judge's order. The Homeland Security Act, enacted by Congress in July of 2002, was a massive reorganization of a large portion of the federal government that was enacted with a complete disregard for the US Constitution. This act combines twenty-two different enforcement divisions of various government agencies, consisting of 170,000 employees, into one enormous federal police force. The Secretary of Homeland Security has significant new powers that enable this agency to intrude into the daily lives of citizens, compile massive files of data on individuals and corporations, and to interfere in state and local affairs, all under the guise of protecting the US public from terrorism. The Federal Emergency Management Agency has also been given broad powers in the event of a national crisis. FEMA, whose main role is supposed to be disaster response, is also tasked with handling US domestic unrest. In the events of a crisis, FEMA is authorized to enact executive orders providing for suspension of the constitution, the imposition of martial law, the establishment of internment camps, and the yielding of all governmental control to the president and to FEMA.

The American public was outraged by the attacks on September 11, 2001. US citizens applauded the President when he directed the military to strike back at the terrorists in Afghanistan. When the federal government took over airport security, citizens were willing to endure the considerable inconveniences that followed. The American people were told they must be prepared to sacrifice some of their freedom if the country was to be free from terrorism. It was later discovered the US military had secretly detained American citizens suspected of terrorism. Consider the case of accused terrorist Jose Padilla. The federal government seized this US citizen, held him without bringing charges, without an attorney, without a trial, or plans for a trial. He may or may not be a terrorist, but he is a US citizen. As a citizen, he is guaranteed certain protections under the Constitution, including protection from cruel and unusual punishment, the right to choose counsel, and the right to a trial by a jury. However, he had his citizenship revoked by Executive Order, and was placed in military custody.

How long will American citizens, suspected of terrorism, be detained? It has been said some may be held until the war on terrorism ends. It has become quite clear the war on terrorism may never end. Therefore, these suspects could be held indefinitely. If the war on terrorism lasts for decades, many of the freedoms Americans have come to count on will have vanished. What should the American public be more concerned with – terrorists, or a federal government that is slowly eroding US citizen's constitutional rights?

In January of 2002, the Pentagon recommended the US military be allowed the option of deploying troops on American streets. The Director of Homeland Security suggested the federal government consider using the military for law enforcement duties because of the threat of terrorism. The Posse Comitatus Act of 1878 prohibits the Army, Navy, Air Force, and Marines from participating in domestic law enforcement. If the federal government is successful in finding a way to use armed forces to police citizens, the US will be taking one more step toward governmental control of every facet of life, and will have edged ever closer to functioning as a police state.

The War on Terrorism has put American citizens at the mercy of a federal government that is violating the Constitution in the name of national security. The American people have been told that constitutional rights do not apply because the country is at war. They have been told they must put up with violations of civil liberties that normally accompany war. Since the foreign power the government is waging war on is not located in any specific part of the world, and a formal declaration of war has not been made, the government can do whatever it wants, for as long as it wants. We have been told the war on terror may never end. We have also been told the war on terrorism may last our entire lives, and that we must prepare to sacrifice freedom for security. Therefore, constitutional freedoms could be revoked indefinitely.

A future one-world government will emerge on the global stage. Many of the steps necessary to bring this final world government into existence have already taken place. Nations appear to be more than willing to give up their sovereignty, and to yield the will of their people to a greater power. This one-world government will be a tool in the hands of Satan to subdue the world, and to accomplish his purposes.

Printed in the United States
by Baker & Taylor Publisher Services